SOLARO

STUDY GUIDE

Biology 11 University Prep (SBI3U)

SOLARO Study Guide is designed to help students achieve success in school. The content in each study guide is 100% curriculum aligned and serves as an excellent source of material for review and practice. To create this book, teachers, curriculum specialists, and assessment experts have worked closely to develop the instructional pieces that explain each of the key concepts for the course. The practice questions and sample tests have detailed solutions that show problem-solving methods, highlight concepts that are likely to be tested, and point out potential sources of errors. ***SOLARO Study Guide*** is a complete guide to be used by students throughout the school year for reviewing and understanding course content, and to prepare for assessments.

Rao, Gautam, 1961 –.
SOLARO Study Guide:
Biology 11 – University Preparation (SBI3U) Ontario
ISBN: 978-1-77044-474-4

1. Science – Juvenile Literature. I. Title

Published by
Castle Rock Research Corp.
2000 First & Jasper
10065 Jasper Avenue
Edmonton, AB T5J 3B1

10 9 8 7 6 5 4 3

Publisher
Gautam Rao

Contributors
Pardip Chopra
Ruby Grewal
Sandy Grewal
Helen Grijo
Crystal Homeniuk
Selma Losic
Simone Labi-Han
Lori Spurway

Dedicated to the memory of Dr. V.S. Rao

SOLARO STUDY GUIDE

Each ***SOLARO STUDY GUIDE*** consists of the following sections:

Key Tips for Being Successful at School gives examples of study and review strategies. It includes information about learning styles, study schedules, and note taking for test preparation.

Class Focus includes a unit on each area of the curriculum. Units are divided into sections, each focusing on one of the specific expectations, or main ideas, that students must learn about in that unit. Examples, definitions, and visuals help to explain each main idea. Practice questions on the main ideas are also included. At the end of each unit is a test on the important ideas covered. The practice questions and unit tests help students identify areas they know and those they need to study more. They can also be used as preparation for tests and quizzes. Most questions are of average difficulty, though some are easy and some are hard—the harder questions are called *Challenger Questions*. Each unit is prefaced by a ***Table of Correlations,*** which correlates questions in the unit (and in the practice tests at the end of the book) to the specific curriculum expectations. Answers and solutions are found at the end of each unit.

Key Strategies for Success on Tests helps students get ready for tests. It shows students different types of questions they might see, word clues to look for when reading them, and hints for answering them.

Practice Tests includes one to three tests based on the entire course. They are very similar to the format and level of difficulty that students may encounter on final tests. In some regions, these tests may be reprinted versions of official tests, or reflect the same difficulty levels and formats as official versions. This gives students the chance to practice using real-world examples. Answers and complete solutions are provided at the end of the section.

For the complete curriculum document (including specific expectations along with examples and sample problems), visit http://www.edu.gov.on.ca/eng/curriculum/

SOLARO STUDY GUIDE *Study Guides* are available for many courses. Check www.castlerockresearch.com for a complete listing of books available for your area.

For information about any of our resources or services, please call Castle Rock Research at 1.800.840.6224 or visit our website at http://www.castlerockresearch.com.

At Castle Rock Research, we strive to produce an error-free resource. If you should find an error, please contact us so that future editions can be corrected.

CONTENTS

Key Tips for being Successful at School

KEY TIPS FOR BEING SUCCESSFUL AT SCHOOL

KEY FACTORS CONTRIBUTING TO SCHOOL SUCCESS

In addition to learning the content of your courses, there are some other things that you can do to help you do your best at school. You can try some of the following strategies:

- **Keep a positive attitude:** Always reflect on what you can already do and what you already know.
- **Be prepared to learn:** Have the necessary pencils, pens, notebooks, and other required materials for participating in class ready.
- **Complete all of your assignments:** Do your best to finish all of your assignments. Even if you know the material well, practice will reinforce your knowledge. If an assignment or question is difficult for you, work through it as far as you can so that your teacher can see exactly where you are having difficulty.
- **Set small goals for yourself when you are learning new material:** For example, when learning the parts of speech, do not try to learn everything in one night. Work on only one part or section each study session. When you have memorized one particular part of speech and understand it, move on to another one. Continue this process until you have memorized and learned all the parts of speech.
- **Review your classroom work regularly at home:** Review to make sure you understand the material you learned in class.
- **Ask your teacher for help:** Your teacher will help you if you do not understand something or if you are having a difficult time completing your assignments.
- **Get plenty of rest and exercise:** Concentrating in class is hard work. It is important to be well-rested and have time to relax and socialize with your friends. This helps you keep a positive attitude about your schoolwork.
- **Eat healthy meals:** A balanced diet keeps you healthy and gives you the energy you need for studying at school and at home.

How to Find Your Learning Style

Every student learns differently. The manner in which you learn best is called your learning style. By knowing your learning style, you can increase your success at school. Most students use a combination of learning styles. Do you know what type of learner you are? Read the following descriptions. Which of these common learning styles do you use most often?

- **Linguistic Learner:** You may learn best by saying, hearing, and seeing words. You are probably really good at memorizing things such as dates, places, names, and facts. You may need to write down the steps in a process, a formula, or the actions that lead up to a significant event, and then say them out loud.
- **Spatial Learner:** You may learn best by looking at and working with pictures. You are probably really good at puzzles, imagining things, and reading maps and charts. You may need to use strategies like mind mapping and webbing to organize your information and study notes.
- **Kinesthetic Learner:** You may learn best by touching, moving, and figuring things out using manipulatives. You are probably really good at physical activities and learning through movement. You may need to draw your finger over a diagram to remember it, tap out the steps needed to solve a problem, or feel yourself writing or typing a formula.

SCHEDULING STUDY TIME

You should review your class notes regularly to ensure that you have a clear understanding of all the new material you learned. Reviewing your lessons on a regular basis helps you to learn and remember ideas and concepts. It also reduces the quantity of material that you need to study prior to a test. Establishing a study schedule will help you to make the best use of your time.

Regardless of the type of study schedule you use, you may want to consider the following suggestions to maximize your study time and effort:

- Organize your work so that you begin with the most challenging material first.
- Divide the subject's content into small, manageable chunks.
- Alternate regularly between your different subjects and types of study activities in order to maintain your interest and motivation.
- Make a daily list with headings like "Must Do," "Should Do," and "Could Do."
- Begin each study session by quickly reviewing what you studied the day before.
- Maintain your usual routine of eating, sleeping, and exercising to help you concentrate better for extended periods of time.

Creating Study Notes

Mind-Mapping or Webbing

Use the key words, ideas, or concepts from your reading or class notes to create a mind map or web (a diagram or visual representation of the given information). A mind map or web is sometimes referred to as a knowledge map. Use the following steps to create a mind map or web:

1. Write the key word, concept, theory, or formula in the centre of your page.
2. Write down related facts, ideas, events, and information, and link them to the central concept with lines.
3. Use coloured markers, underlining, or symbols to emphasize things such as relationships, timelines, and important information.

The following examples of a Frayer Model illustrate how this technique can be used to study vocabulary.

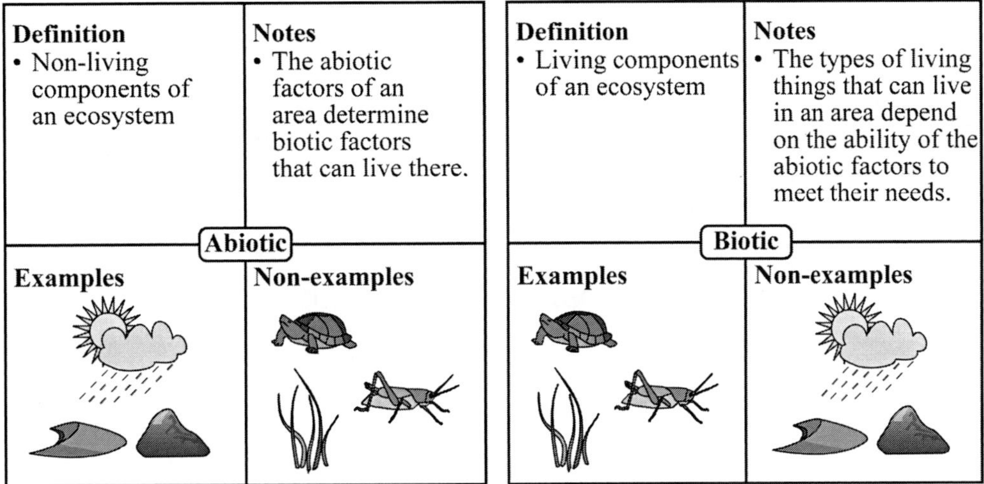

Index Cards

To use index cards while studying, follow these steps:

1. Write a key word or question on one side of an index card.
2. On the reverse side, write the definition of the word, answer to the question, or any other important information that you want to remember.

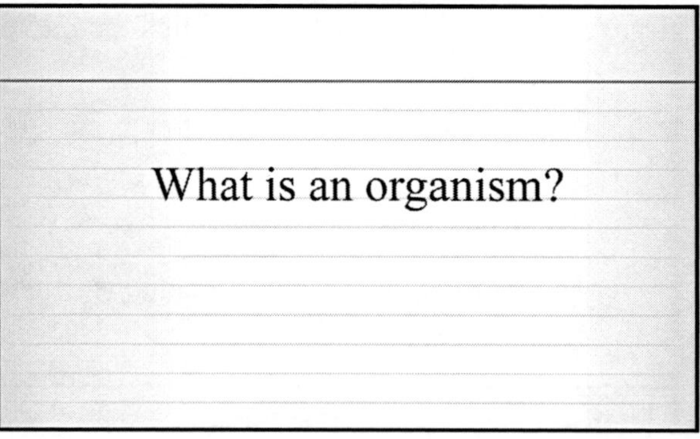

What is an organism?

An organism is a living thing.
For example, a plant or animal.

Symbols and Sticky Notes—Identifying Important Information

Use symbols to mark your class notes. The following are some examples:

- An exclamation mark (!) might be used to point out something that must be learned well because it is a very important idea.
- A question mark (?) may highlight something you are not certain about
- A diamond (◊) or asterisk (*) could highlight interesting information that you want to remember.

Sticky notes are useful in the following situations:

- Use sticky notes when you are not allowed to put marks in books.
- Use sticky notes to mark a page in a book that contains an important diagram, formula, explanation, or other information.
- Use sticky notes to mark important facts in research books.

MEMORIZATION TECHNIQUES

- **Association** relates new learning to something you already know. For example, to remember the spelling difference between dessert and desert, recall that the word *sand* has only one *s*. So, because there is sand in a desert, the word *desert* has only one *s*.
- **Mnemonic** devices are sentences that you create to remember a list or group of items. For example, the first letter of each word in the phrase "Every Good Boy Deserves Fudge" helps you to remember the names of the lines on the treble-clef staff (E, G, B, D, and F) in music.

- **Acronyms** are words that are formed from the first letters or parts of the words in a group. For example, RADAR is actually an acronym for Radio Detecting and Ranging, and MASH is an acronym for Mobile Army Surgical Hospital. HOMES helps you to remember the names of the five Great Lakes (Huron, Ontario, Michigan, Erie, and Superior).
- **Visualizing** requires you to use your mind's eye to "see" a chart, list, map, diagram, or sentence as it is in your textbook or notes, on the chalkboard or computer screen, or in a display.

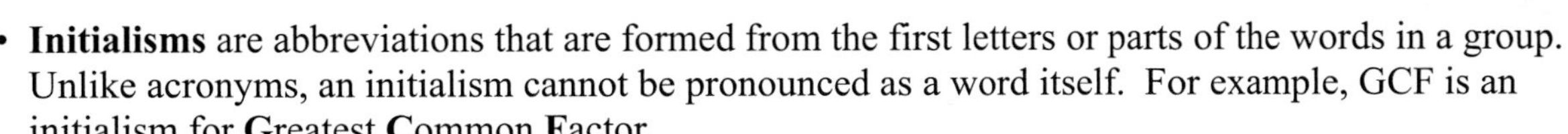

- **Initialisms** are abbreviations that are formed from the first letters or parts of the words in a group. Unlike acronyms, an initialism cannot be pronounced as a word itself. For example, GCF is an initialism for **G**reatest **C**ommon **F**actor.

KEY STRATEGIES FOR REVIEWING

Reviewing textbook material, class notes, and handouts should be an ongoing activity. Spending time reviewing becomes more critical when you are preparing for a test. You may find some of the following review strategies useful when studying during your scheduled study time:

- Before reading a selection, preview it by noting the headings, charts, graphs, and chapter questions.
- Before reviewing a unit, note the headings, charts, graphs, and chapter questions.
- Highlight key concepts, vocabulary, definitions, and formulas.
- Skim the paragraph, and note the key words, phrases, and information.
- Carefully read over each step in a procedure.
- Draw a picture or diagram to help make the concept clearer.

KEY STRATEGIES FOR SUCCESS: A CHECKLIST

Reviewing is a huge part of doing well at school and preparing for tests. Here is a checklist for you to keep track of how many suggested strategies for success you are using. Read each question, and put a check mark (✓) in the correct column. Look at the questions where you have checked the "No" column. Think about how you might try using some of these strategies to help you do your best at school.

Key Strategies for Success	Yes	No
Do you attend school regularly?		
Do you know your personal learning style—how you learn best?		
Do you spend 15 to 30 minutes a day reviewing your notes?		
Do you study in a quiet place at home?		
Do you clearly mark the most important ideas in your study notes?		
Do you use sticky notes to mark texts and research books?		
Do you practise answering multiple-choice and written-response questions?		
Do you ask your teacher for help when you need it?		
Are you maintaining a healthy diet and sleep routine?		
Are you participating in regular physical activity?		

Diversity of Living Things

DIVERSITY OF LIVING THINGS

Table of Correlations

	Specific Expectation	Practice Questions	Unit Test Questions	Practice Test 1	Practice Test 2
11.2.B1	analyse the effects of various human activities on the diversity of living things				
11.2.B1.1	*analyse some of the risks and benefits of human intervention to the biodiversity of aquatic or terrestrial ecosystems*	17	1, 2	10	9
11.2.B1.2	*analyse the impact that climate change might have on the diversity of living things*	1, 2	3	11	10
11.2.B2	investigate, through laboratory and/or field activities or through simulations, the principles of scientific classification, using appropriate sampling and classification techniques				
11.2.B2.1	*use appropriate terminology related to biodiversity, including, but not limited to: genetic diversity, species diversity, structural diversity, protists, bacteria, fungi, binomial nomenclature, and morphology*	3, 4, 5	4, 5	12, 13	11, 12
11.2.B2.2	*classify, and draw biological diagrams of, representative organisms from each of the kingdoms according to their unifying and distinguishing anatomical and physiological characteristics*	13	6	14	13, 14
11.2.B2.3	*use proper sampling techniques to collect various organisms from a marsh, pond, field, or other ecosystem, and classify the organisms according to the principles of taxonomy*	6	7		15
11.2.B2.4	*create and apply a dichotomous key to identify and classify organisms from each of the kingdoms*	14	8	15	
11.2.B3	demonstrate an understanding of the diversity of living organisms in terms of the principles of taxonomy and phylogeny				
11.2.B3.1	*explain the fundamental principles of taxonomy and phylogeny by defining concepts of taxonomic rank and relationship, such as genus, species, and taxon*	7a, 7b, 8	9	16	16
11.2.B3.2	*compare and contrast the structure and function of different types of prokaryotes, eukaryotes, and viruses*	9, 10	10	17, 18	17, 18
11.2.B3.3	*describe unifying and distinguishing anatomical and physiological characteristics of representative organisms from each of the kingdoms*	11, 12	11	19, 20	19, 20
11.2.B3.4	*explain key structural and functional changes in organisms as they have evolved over time*	15	12	21	21, 22
11.2.B3.5	*explain why biodiversity is important to maintaining viable ecosystems*	16	13	22	23

11.2.B1.2 analyse the impact that climate change might have on the diversity of living things

The Effects of a Changing Climate on Biodiversity

Global climate change can potentially influence natural systems in a variety of complex interconnected ways. It is predicted that if the climate continues to change at its current pace, there will be dramatic transformations in global precipitation patterns, ecosystem processes, species diversity and distribution, global sea levels and ice cover, and the occurrence of extreme weather events, just to name a few.

In general, the rising average temperatures associated with climate change are altering many of the natural habitats that Earth's organisms rely upon. More specifically, rises in atmospheric temperatures have contributed to glacial ice decline on a large scale, which will inevitably cause an increase in the volume of water entering streams, rivers, lakes, and oceans. Loss of glacial ice is currently being witnessed with declines in polar sea ice, which results in a loss of polar bear habitat.

Polar bears rely on sea ice for hunting. During the winter when ice cover is thickest, polar bears traverse large distances in search of their favourite prey species, the ringed seal. It is during these winter months that polar bears accumulate the fat reserves they require to sustain them through the summer. As the average sea-ice cover shrinks, the amount of time the polar bears can spend hunting also decreases. Shorter hunting periods during the winter mean the bears are unable to store the required fat reserves to comfortably sustain them throughout the summer. This is demonstrated through scientific research indicating lower polar bear survival and reproduction rates, which suggests the survival of the species as a whole is at risk.

Additionally, changes in the volume of meltwater entering freshwater systems can directly impact ecosystems in a variety of ways. Changes in meltwater distribution and levels can cause changes in soil nutrient content and rates of erosion and, as a result, can alter many habitats. As larger volumes of meltwater reach the ocean, there is the potential not only for rises in sea level, but also a disruption of oceanic currents. Consequently, this alters atmospheric wind and precipitation patterns, which could result in droughts, floods, and extreme weather in many regions. Within natural ecosystems, such events would lead to changes in food availability, the completion of life cycles, and migration and hibernation patterns. Even an increase of a single degree in average global temperatures can greatly impact physiological processes, such as photosynthetic rates in plants or the symbiotic relationship between algae and coral.

Ultimately, if organisms do not possess the phenotypic traits needed to survive these habitat changes, they will be at risk of extirpation or even extinction. Biodiversity is being challenged by both climate change and human activities that cause habitat destruction. The combination of these effects will impact biodiversity in extensive and complex ways that are difficult to understand and even more difficult to predict.

1. Which of the following statements **best** describes the impact of rapid climate change on the polar bear species?

A. Polar bears would be severely impacted by rapid climate change because they are adapted to a cold-weather habitat.

B. Polar bears would be minimally impacted by rapid climate change because they are suited to a wide range of habitats.

C. Polar bears would be severely impacted by rapid climate change because more people would start hunting them for food.

D. Polar bears would be minimally impacted by rapid climate change because melting sea ice would increase their available habitat.

Open Response

2. Name at least **three** potential consequences of climate change that result in the heating of the Earth. At least one consequence should deal with terrestrial ecosystems and one with aquatic ecosystems.

____
____
____
____
____
____
____

11.2.B2.1 use appropriate terminology related to biodiversity, including, but not limited to: genetic diversity, species diversity, structural diversity, protists, bacteria, fungi, binomial nomenclature, and morphology

Terminology Associated with Biodiversity and Binomial Nomenclature

Biodiversity refers to the variation of all living organisms in a given local, regional, or global area considered at multiple levels of organization and from a range of different perspectives.

There are several categories of diversity:

- **Species diversity** refers to the number of different species within a given area, their relative distribution, and their relative proportions.
- **Genetic diversity** refers to the variation among the characteristics of individuals within the species as determined by their genetic makeup.
- **Ecosystem diversity** refers to the combination of different species and the ensuing population and community dynamics that occur within an area.
- **Compositional diversity** considers biodiversity based on the different number of elements within the given system, such as total number of genes within species, species within communities, and communities within ecosystems.
- **Structural diversity** considers biodiversity based on the variation in patterns and organization of species genetics and morphology, specific habitats, populations, and communities within the system.
- **Functional diversity** considers biodiversity based on the number and variation of ecological processes, such as predator-prey interactions, decomposition, parasitism, and nutrient cycling that occur within a given system.

Binomial Nomenclature

In order to organize and keep track of Earth's biodiversity, living organisms are categorized and named according to the Linnaean system of classification. This system uses two Latin name categories, genus and species, to designate each type of organism. This is known as **binomial nomenclature**. For example, the scientific name, or binomial name, for humans is *Homo sapiens*. The genus is *Homo*, and the species is *sapiens*. When using binomial nomenclature, genus and species are always italicized.

This system provides a consistent method by which all organisms can be classified into the hierarchical structure. Using this standardized approach, scientists anywhere in the world can evaluate the characteristics of an organism and logically determine, through comparison with other groups of organisms, what the organism is (if it is a known species) or how to name it (if it is an unknown species). The process allows for organisms to be identified globally using only two labels; this scientific name stays the same in any language. The system inherently favours stability because it eliminates the confusion associated with common names and reduces the probability of species misnomers.

The highest category of the Linnaean system is kingdom. The biodiversity of organisms in kingdoms is distinguished based on cellular organization and methods of nutrition. These organisms can be single-celled or multicelled and can either absorb, ingest, or produce food. Based on these distinctions, there are five main kingdoms of living organisms:

1. Monera—bacteria, blue-green algae (cyanobacteria)
2. Protista—protozoans, other algae
3. Fungi—mushrooms, yeast, mould, mildew
4. Plantae (plants)—mosses, ferns, woody and non-woody flowering plants
5. Animalia (animals)—mammals, birds, fish, sponges, worms, insects, amphibians, reptiles

3. Which of the following characteristics is **not** always the same between members of a single species?

A. Number of chromosomes

B. Morphological features

C. Evolutionary origin

D. Anatomical design

4. The system of binomial nomenclature for living organisms was created by Carolus Linnaeus. In this system, the scientific name of an organism includes its

A. genus and species

B. phylum and genus

C. phylum and order

D. order and species

Use the following information to answer the next question.

> The **most common** classification scheme for the diversity of living things places all living organisms within one of _________ kingdoms?

5. Which of the following numbers accurately completes the given statement?

A. Three **B.** Five

C. Six **D.** Eight

11.2.B2.3 use proper sampling techniques to collect various organisms from a marsh, pond, field, or other ecosystem, and classify the organisms according to the principles of taxonomy

Ecosystem Sampling and Organism Classification

In order to get an accurate measure of an ecosystem's diversity and to classify the organisms within the ecosystem, a representative sample of the organisms present must be taken. There are a number of sampling techniques and classification tools used by ecologists to determine these ecosystem characteristics.

Using a Dichotomous Key to Classify Pond Organisms

A pond ecosystem contains a large diversity of organisms. In addition to the immediately visible organisms such as waterfowl and fish, a sample of water taken from a pond contains many more organisms. Using techniques such as a dip net, plankton net, or grab bottom sampler, a single cup of water would reveal a collection of common microorganisms such as algae, plankton, and a number of small invertebrates.

These organisms can be accurately classified to their most specific taxonomic rank (typically genus and species) by using a dichotomous key.

A dichotomous key is a map of characteristics used by researchers to identify the organism by slowly narrowing down the options using a series of paired statements. After selecting an appropriate key, the researcher will consider the first set of paired statements, which are based on the broader characteristics of organisms. When the researcher selects the statement that best describes the organism, this statement will lead to another set of paired statements, which are slightly more specific. Each selected statement will slowly narrow down the classification until a genus or species is identified.

Example

Small invertebrates in a pond sample would more than likely include the larvae of many flying insects such as damselflies, dragonflies, and caddisflies. Using reference material, the researcher could determine the broader classification of the flying insect larvae as follows:

Kingdom	Animalia
Phylum	Arthropoda
Class	Insecta
Order	Odonata

Once the broader classifications are identified, the specific classification of each of the larvae could be achieved by using a detailed dichotomous key that would aid in determining the more specific taxonomic ranks of family, genus, and species for each of the different larva collected.

Even smaller inhabitants can be examined and classified using a dichotomous key with the aid of a dissecting or compound microscope.

6. What is the name of a common reference tool that uses pairs of descriptive statements representing mutually exclusive choices to classify an unknown organism into its genus and species?

A. Cladogram

B. Field guide

C. Dichotomous key

D. Phylogenetic tree

11.2.B3.1 explain the fundamental principles of taxonomy and phylogeny by defining concepts of taxonomic rank and relationship, such as genus, species, and taxon

The Principles of Taxonomy

Taxonomy is a way of grouping organisms. It is also known as the "science of classification," and it assigns taxa or taxonomic units to organisms or groups of organisms. Taxa are further assigned taxonomic ranks and are arranged into a hierarchical structure that reflects evolutionary relationships. There are seven main taxonomic ranks: kingdom, phylum, class, order, family, genus, and species. An organism's morphological characteristics as well as its phylogeny (evolutionary history) are used to determine the likely evolutionary relationships required for designation into the respective taxa.

A genus is a taxonomic category that consists of a group of different species that share common characteristics and qualities. In contrast, a species can be defined as a group of organisms of a specific genus that share common characteristics or qualities and are capable of reproducing within their own species to produce fertile offspring.

Example

The following chart gives the genus and species names for two different species of fox:

Common Name	Genus	Species
Arctic fox	*Vulpes*	*lagopus*
Red fox	*Vulpes*	*vulpes*

These two species of fox are very similar in their characteristics and qualities, and as such, they are designated into the same genus: *Vulpes*. Since they cannot successfully reproduce with one another, they are designated into separate species.

Arctic fox

Red fox

Use the following information to answer the next multipart question.

7. Taxonomy is the area of biological sciences that is devoted to the identification, naming, and classification of living things.

a) Which of the following levels of classification is **not** a taxonomic category?

A. Family **B.** Order

C. Class **D.** Clan

Open Response

b) List the seven taxonomic categories in order from the lowest to the highest level.

Open Response

8. Define the following four branches of biology: phylogenetics, systematics, taxonomy, and cladistics.

11.2.B3.2 compare and contrast the structure and function of different types of prokaryotes, eukaryotes, and viruses

Prokaryotes, Eukaryotes, and Viruses

According to the cell theory, all living things are made up of cells. They are the smallest functional units of an organism and are often referred to as the building blocks of life. There are two types of cells: prokaryotic and eukaryotic. By default, viruses are not considered to be living organisms because they are not composed of either type of cell.

Prokaryotic and Eukaryotic Cells

Prokaryotic cells lack membrane-bound organelles and are unicellular, meaning that the whole organism consists of only one cell. Bacteria and cyanobacteria (blue-green algae) are examples of prokaryotic cells.

Eukaryotic cells have a membrane-bound nucleus and contain membrane-bound structures called organelles. Organelles such as mitochondria and chloroplasts serve to perform metabolic functions and energy conversion. Others provide motility and structural support. One example of a eukaryotic cell is a plant cell.

Prokaryotic cells are different from eukaryotic cells in that their genetic information is in a circular loop instead of in the form of chromosomal DNA like a eukaryote. Prokaryotic cells can be distinguished by their shape, which is typically either rod-shaped, spherical, or helical. Prokaryotic cells also divide by binary fission (asexual reproduction) unlike eukaryotic cells that can reproduce through meiosis (sexual reproduction) or mitosis (cell division that produces identical daughter cells). Eukaryotes are about 10 times the size and can be 1 000 times greater in volume than a prokaryotic cell.

VIRUSES

Viruses are not classified into a kingdom because their status as living organisms is currently being debated. They are much smaller and less complex than either prokaryotic or eukaryotic cells. They are macromolecular units composed of DNA or RNA that are surrounded by an outer protein shell. Viruses do not have a cytoplasm, membrane-bound organelles, ribosomes, or a source of energy production. They do not perform cellular respiration or gas exchange and cannot metabolize. Despite the structures they lack, viruses can reproduce, but only with the help of a host cell.

Assuming they are an organism, viruses are the smallest known, and their life cycle requires that they infect the cells of other living organisms in order to reproduce. In a generalized life cycle of a virus, upon recognition of a host cell, the virus either enters or injects its genetic material into the host. This genetic material takes charge and begins replicating and constructing new viruses by using the host cell's nucleotides, enzymes, and proteins. The newly created components then reassemble themselves into new viruses and proceed to exit the host cell, often causing the host cell's death. They then disperse and infect new host cells.

Use the following information to answer the next question.

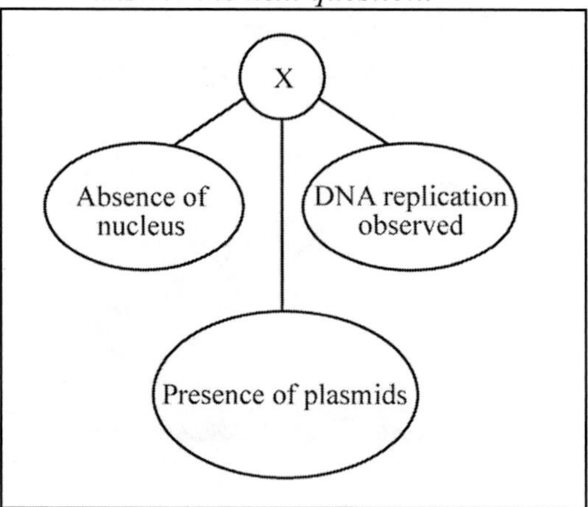

9. Which of the following organisms is **most appropriately** represented by X in the given figure?

A. Bacterium **B.** Animal

C. Plant **D.** Virus

Use the following information to answer the next question.

Despite their apparent differences, prokaryotic and eukaryotic cells have common structural components and perform similar functions:

1. The cytoplasm of both prokaryotic and eukaryotic cells is enclosed by plasma membranes.
2. Prokaryotic and eukaryotic cells both contain ribosomes.
3. Prokaryotic and eukaryotic cells both contain DNA.

10. Which of the following structures is similarly constructed in eukaryotic and prokaryotic cells?

A. Nucleus

B. Cell wall

C. Flagellum

D. Plasma membrane

11.2.B3.3 describe unifying and distinguishing anatomical and physiological characteristics of representative organisms from each of the kingdoms

11.2.B2.2 classify, and draw biological diagrams of, representative organisms from each of the kingdoms according to their unifying and distinguishing anatomical and physiological characteristics

11.2.B2.4 create and apply a dichotomous key to identify and classify organisms from each of the kingdoms

Classification of Organisms according to Kingdoms

Living organisms can be classified into five kingdoms of organization based on their life cycles, nutritional patterns, habitats, and morphology. The kingdoms are Monera, Protista, Fungi, Plantae, and Animalia.

Monera

The kingdom Monera consists of prokaryotic cellular organisms in the domains Eubacteria (also called Bacteria, including Gram-positive, Gram-negative, and cyanobacteria) and Archaebacteria (also called Archaea, including methanogens, extreme halophiles, extreme thermophiles, and acidophiles). Prokaryotic cells are distinguished by their shape and are usually rod (bacillus), spherical (coccus), or spiral (spirochaete), although other less common shapes also exist.

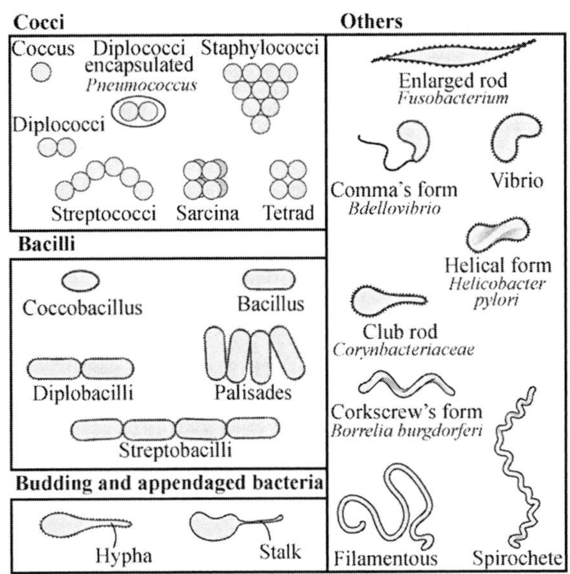

Prokaryotes inhabit every environment and obtain nutrients using a variety of methods. The bacterial life cycle involves asexual reproduction by binary fission. These organisms can be free-living but will often closely associate with other prokaryotes to form colonies or exist symbiotically with eukaryotes at some point during their life cycle. They acquire nutrition through means of photosynthesis, chemosynthesis, or absorption. Metabolically, depending on the species, oxygen may be toxic, tolerated, or required.
During unfavourable environmental conditions, some species of bacteria will alter their life cycle to form endospores.

Protista

Protists are a variable group of primarily aquatic eukaryotes that require oxygen for metabolism. Depending on the species, their nutrient intake can be through photosynthesis, absorption, or ingestion. Most are unicellular, although some are multicellular. Some are free-living and planktonic, while others form symbiotic relationships. They are classified as either plant-like because they are photosynthetic (algae), fungus-like because they are absorptive, or animal-like because they are ingestive (protozoans). All reproduce asexually, and some can also reproduce sexually.

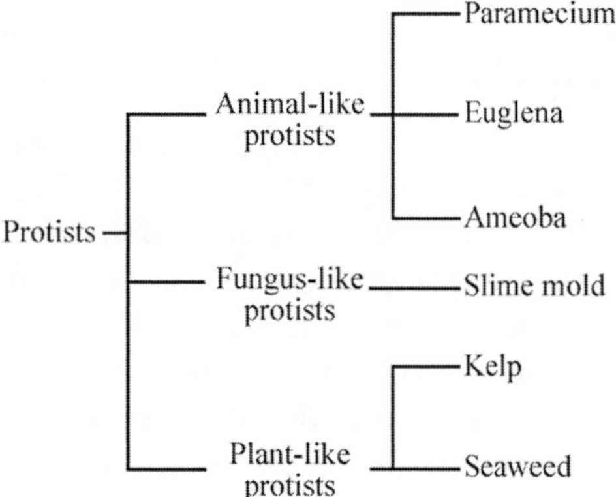

Flow chart of representative protists

Many of the protozoans are parasitic, undergoing a complicated life cycle of both sexual and asexual reproduction during which they transfer between two or more hosts in order to survive.

The fungus-like protists also have complicated life cycles. Of the multicellular algae, many alternate between stages, existing at one time or another as either a multicellular gametophyte or a multicellular sporophyte. This alternation of generations is also characteristic of the kingdom Plantae. Examples of organisms in the kingdom Protista are amoebas, green and blue algae, euglena, diatoms, and slime molds.

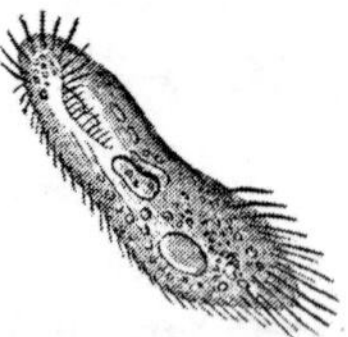

Paramecium, Unicellular protozoan with cilia

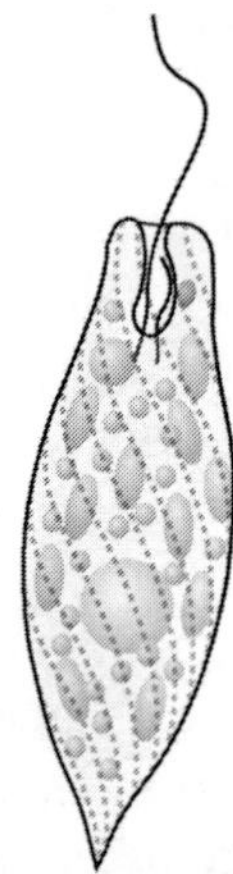

Euglena, unicellular protozoan with flagellum

Fungi

Fungi, including mushrooms, yeasts, and moulds, are non-vascular organisms. This group of multicellular, heterotrophic, eukaryotic organisms acquires nutrition through absorption. They most commonly inhabit terrestrial habitats, although some are aquatic, and they often exist in close association with other organisms (in parasitic or mutualistic relationships) or with non-living organic material (in a saprobic relationship). They require oxygen for metabolism and to absorb their nutrients. Fungi can reproduce through either asexual or sexual reproduction. During asexual reproduction, an individual organism can create a duplicate through fission, budding, or the production of asexual spores called mitospores that are produced by mitosis. During sexual reproduction, male and female gametes fuse to produce a diploid zygote. In most fungi, this stage is then followed by meiosis to produce haploid spores called meiospores, which then germinate to produce the adult organism.

Different forms of fungi

Plantae

The Plantae kingdom consists of multicellular, photosynthetic eukaryotes. They are mostly terrestrial, although some species have adapted to aquatic habitats. They require oxygen for metabolism and acquire their nutrients through photosynthesis. This kingdom is often divided into four groups, based on modes of reproduction and physical structures, such as presence or absence of vascular tissues. These four groups are mosses, ferns, gymnosperms, and angiosperms.

A gymnosperm

An angiosperm

Fern

Moss

Almost all plants reproduce sexually, although many are also capable of asexual propagation. An alternation of generations takes place in the life cycle of all plants, where a haploid gametophyte generation alternates with a diploid sporophyte generation, with one always giving rise to the other. The most noticeable difference between the plants' alternation of generations and that observed in the multicellular algae of the kingdom Protista is that the two plant generations always differ in morphological appearance, whereas this is not always true for algae.

Animalia

Mammals, birds, reptiles, amphibians, fish, molluscs, sponges, cnidarians (jellyfish), arthropods (insects), and worms all comprise the kingdom Animalia. This group of multicellular, heterotrophic eukaryotes acquires nutrition through the ingestion of organic materials.

This diverse group inhabits nearly all environments, but it is found at its highest diversity in marine habitats. Most animals reproduce sexually and exist predominantly in the diploid stage of their life cycle. In most species, reproduction occurs through the fertilization of an egg by a flagellated sperm and produces a diploid zygote, which undergoes a number of cellular divisions in order to develop into an organism.

A number of different life cycles are exhibited by the diverse range of animals. Some animals undergo embryonic development during which they start life as an embryo in their parent's body and are born looking similar to how they will look in their mature form, only smaller.

Other animals will start life morphologically distinct from their mature forms, often eating different food and occupying different habitats than their adult counterparts. These organisms will pass through different stages, changing morphologically at each stage until they reach their adult form. This process is called metamorphosis.

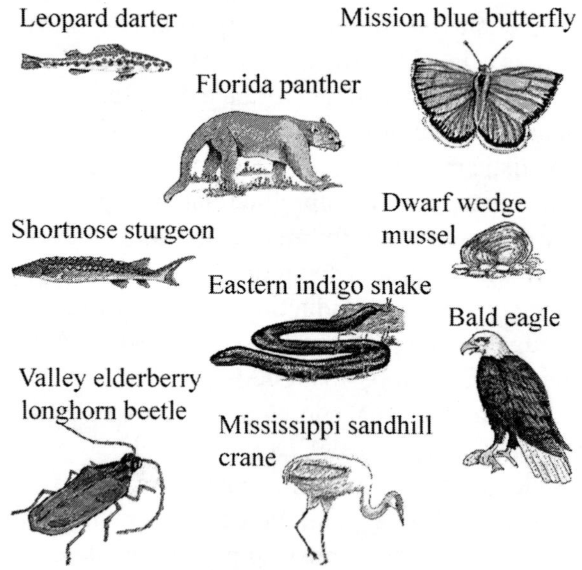

Some common animals

Dichotomous Keys

A dichotomous key is a helpful tool for classifying the widely diverse organisms encompassed by the five kingdoms of life. The following is an example of how a dichotomous key could be used to classify eight different groups of animals.

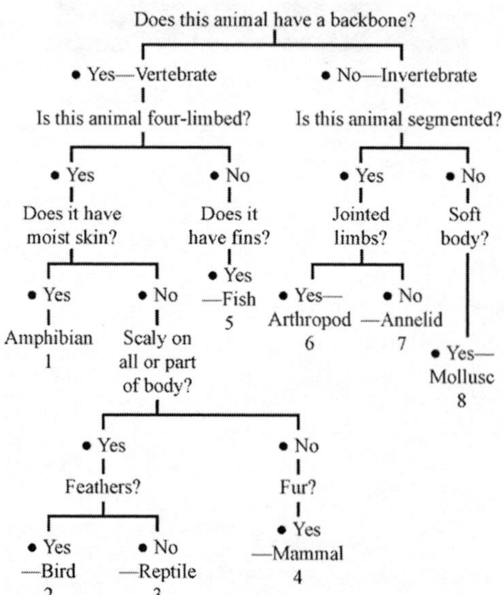

Dichotomous key for the kingdom Animalia

Use the following information to answer the next question.

11. Which of the following kingdoms do the organisms growing on the tree in the given picture belong to?

A. Fungi **B.** Plantae
C. Monera **D.** Protista

12. Which of the following kingdoms is composed of multicellular eukaryotes that **cannot** photosynthesize?

A. Monera **B.** Plantae
C. Protista **D.** Animalia

13. Gymnosperms are plants that are characterized by the presence of

A. fruit and flowers

B. monocot seeds

C. motile ovules

D. naked seeds

Use the following information to answer the next question.

A biology lab instructor asks her class to create a dichotomous key for classifying organisms within the kingdom Animalia into their respective phyla. As an example, she states that a dichotomous key for the classification of plants into their phyla might include a descriptive pair that asks about the presence or absence of vascular tissues.

Open Response

14. List four key characteristics that would be included in the mutually exclusive descriptive pairs of a dichotomous key for classifying organisms within the kingdom Animalia into their respective phyla.

____
____
____
____
____
____
____

11.2.B3.4 explain key structural and functional changes in organisms as they have evolved over time

Key Changes in Organisms through Evolution

Scientists can only make predictions about the evolution of species over time by examining fossils for clues and, more recently, by using molecular evidence. It appears that species evolved both in structure and function as the climatic conditions of Earth changed. A current idea suggests that the progression is from a unicellular prokaryotic ancestor to a unicellular eukaryote that eventually evolved into a multicellular eukaryotic organism. This idea is supported by the sequential appearance of these groups of organisms in the fossil record and their relative genetic relationships.

Appearance of Prokaryotes

The oldest fossil records indicate that simple unicellular organisms, or prokaryotes, were present as early as 3.4 billion years ago. The structure of a prokaryote is different from all other types of cells. They are much smaller and lack many of the internal structures, such as the membrane-bound organelles that are present in eukaryotic cells. As time passed and the climatic conditions of Earth changed, the number of prokaryotic species increased as did the complexity of their structures, which was demonstrated by the appearance of colonial and aggregate forms.

Appearance of Eukaryotes

It has been suggested that the close living associations that had developed among some of the prokaryotes eventually led to the appearance of the first eukaryotic cells as one or more prokaryotes merged together during an endosymbiotic event. This led to the creation of membrane-bound organelles as smaller prokaryotes, each with unique metabolic function, took up residence inside larger prokaryotes. Based on this hypothesis, the first eukaryotes to evolve were likely unicellular and would be considered protists. Modern protists are typically unicellular (all the processes of life are carried out within one cell), but sometimes they can be found in colonial or simple multicellular forms. They have a membrane-bound nucleus and organelles. Protists are typically aquatic, and they display a wide diversity of structural, locomotive, and nutritional patterns.

Appearance of Multicellular Organisms

It is widely believed that protists are the ancestral organisms for all multicellular life (plants, animals, fungi) that has ever existed. The extreme diversity and complexity of the Protista provided the necessary ancestral building blocks for the wide range of multicellular organisms that came into existence following the appearance of the first eukaryotes. Multicellular organisms have multiple systems made up of many cells. In all multicellular organisms, cells are specialized to perform specific tasks. Although the basic structure of all cells is the same, the presence of specialized cells in multicellular organisms allows for the performance of a variety of functions.

Based on current molecular evidence, as well as physiological and structural similarities, it is hypothesized that plants diverged from a common protistan ancestor similar to the green algae around 450 million years ago (mya), whereas modern phyla of fungi and animals likely diverged from a common colonial protistan ancestor similar to flagellated eukaryotes during the Cambrian explosion around 545 mya. Simple invertebrates, such as sponges and cnidarians (jellyfish and corals), were the first to appear. This was followed by the appearance of complex invertebrates, such as worms, mollusks, and arthropods. Fish were the first vertebrates to appear, followed by amphibians, reptiles, birds, and mammals.

Use the following information to answer the next question.

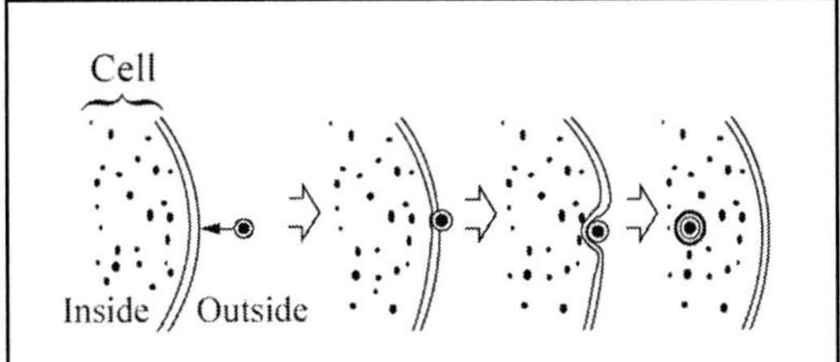

Open Response

15. Identify the term used to describe the process depicted in the diagram, and explain how this process might have led to the evolution of eukaryotes from a prokaryotic ancestor.

____

____

____

____

____

____

____

11.2.B3.5 explain why biodiversity is important to maintaining viable ecosystems

11.2.B1.1 analyse some of the risks and benefits of human intervention to the biodiversity of aquatic or terrestrial ecosystems

Human Activities and Ecosystem Diversity

Humans rely heavily on the great diversity of species on Earth, but this intervention in natural ecosystems can have lasting consequences. Natural lands are cleared so that agricultural crops and tree plantations can be grown for food as well as for fibre that is used to make clothing, paper, and other products. Forests of trees are cut down to make lumber and other building products. Livestock are raised for food and clothing. Plants, fungi, and other organisms are harvested directly from their natural environments for food and to make medicines. The biological impact of these human interventions on the planet's natural ecosystems is extensive, complicated, and diverse, and it is only now that people have finally begun to understand the effect that limitless consumption is having on the planet's irreplaceable and invaluable biodiversity.

Tree Plantations

Tree plantations can lead to the destruction of habitat and a reduction in biodiversity when the location of the new plantation requires clearing or modification of a natural land area. These losses are amplified when the tree species that is planted is non-native and the existing fauna is unable to adapt to the new tree species. However, tree plantations that are established in an area that was previously altered by human activity may function to increase biodiversity by providing a more suitable habitat than was being provided by the earlier modified landscape. Also, even when the tree species is non-native, plantations are often still used by wildlife as movement corridors and they can function to reduce the impact of human disturbance in natural areas by acting as a buffer zone between a disturbed region and any adjacent natural regions.

Monocultures and Pesticide Use

Monocultures inherently lack biodiversity because they are composed of a single species with a limited genetic makeup. Monocultures are especially susceptible to pests and disease because these crops are not equipped with the genetic variability required to adapt to changing environmental conditions. Specifically, a few diseased plants in one field could kill the entire crop if it lacks the genetic variability to resist infection.

Banana plantations provide one example of how monocultures are more susceptible to disease. The bananas that many people enjoy are seedless genetic clones that are cultivated on monogenetic plantations and reproduced asexually through vegetative propagation. The threat to this commercially important variety comes from a fungus called the Black Sigatoka, which is known to reduce crop yields by 30 to 40%.

Pests pose a threat to plants because a pest that favours a certain crop will eat and multiply quickly if the plant is both abundant and grown year after year. A farmer may use a pesticide to get rid of the pest, but pesticides present their own problems. They pollute the air, water, and plants they are meant to protect. Additionally, pesticides sometimes kill non-targeted or helpful species and can promote pesticide resistance in targeted species.
Repeated use of pesticides to control pests can cause undesirable changes in the gene pool by leading to a form of artificial selection known as pesticide resistance. When a pesticide is first used, a small portion of the targeted population may survive because of variability in their genetic makeup that allows them to resist the effects of the pesticide. The genes that code for this resistance then get passed on to the next generation. Through this process of selection, the population gradually develops an immunity or resistance to the pesticide.

Overharvesting of Wild Plants for Medicinal Purposes

Phytochemicals describe a group of chemical compounds that may have potential human health-promoting properties, which are derived from a plant. Recent advancements in the use of phytochemicals for the development of treatments for human illness and disease has led to a trend toward overharvesting these chemicals' respective source plants. This exploitation of natural plant resources for their medicinal properties is compounded by the fact that many of these plants are native to tropical regions, where developing countries are still practicing destructive land clearing and deforestation techniques for agriculture. The combination of these impacts poses a serious threat to the biodiversity of these medically important species of flora as they are in increasing danger of extinction.

Suppression of Wildfires

Fire management also has an effect on biodiversity. Fires are typically suppressed in forests as they threaten both communities and the logging industry. However, fires naturally occur every 50 to 75 years. These natural fires produce new grasslands that eventually grow into primary forests. Forest fires allow the area to rotate from grasslands to primary forests. Suppressing forest fires keeps old-growth forests longer and prevents natural shifts in community composition. In the long run, this limits the biodiversity in an area by reducing the total variability of the community's gene pool.

Fundamentally, in order for an ecosystem to remain viable, the organisms in the ecosystem must be able to adapt to changing environmental conditions so that they may continue to participate in the many different ecological processes and interactions that contribute to the ecosystem's functionality. This ability to survive or adapt to changes in the environment is referred to as the organism's resiliency, which is typically imparted to it through its genetic makeup. Genetic variability both within a species and between species provides the phenotypic variability, otherwise known as biodiversity, necessary for the adaptation of an organism to environmental change. Specifically, biodiversity equips the organism with a variety of different characteristics of which a particular phenotypic trait or quality may be present that better suits it to deal with the conditions created by the environmental change or better arms it to deal with the impacts of disease or invading species.

Use the following information to answer the next question.

A small and isolated population of lions live in the Olduvai Gorge of East Africa. Despite the favourable climate and ample food supply in the gorge, the lions are not healthy. The lions have a low fertility rate and are susceptible to disease.

16. Based on the given information, the **most likely** reason for the poor health of the Olduvai lion population is their

A. degraded habitat

B. low genetic variability

C. inadequately varied diet

D. over-competitive environment

Use the following information to answer the next question.

When farmers in some areas of the world require new land for agriculture, they will cut down sections of rainforest and burn the plants and trees to create bare land on which to grow new crops. This process is referred to as slashing and burning. The farmers find that the soil in these newly created agricultural areas becomes unproductive after only a short time, so they abandon the field and relocate to a new forested area, where they must slash and burn again to create another new patch of agricultural land.

17. What causes the soil to become unproductive in the described agricultural practice?

A. Fire used to burn the plants and trees chemically alters the soil.

B. Crop roots are not as well developed as tree roots, and do not provide the soil with the required aeration to be productive.

C. An increase in ultraviolet penetration at the forest floor caused by the removal of the forest canopy has resulted in nutrient degradation in the soil.

D. The naturally nutrient-poor soil of this rainforest ecosystem becomes depleted of nutrients because of an increase in surface run-off and soil erosion.

ANSWERS AND SOLUTIONS
DIVERSITY OF LIVING THINGS

1. A	6. C	10. D	15. OR
2. OR	7. a) D	11. A	16. B
3. B	b) OR	12. D	17. D
4. A	8. OR	13. D	
5. B	9. A	14. OR	

1. A

The polar bear is very well adapted to a cold-weather habitat. When the Arctic regions become warmer, it will become harder for the polar bear to hide from prey, and the sea ice that forms an important part of the polar bear's hunting habitat will melt.

2. OR

Many potential consequences are possible.

1. Aquatic ecosystems will be severely impacted as the heating of Earth causes the melting of mountain glaciers, icecaps, and icebergs.
2. All of these factors will increase sea levels and threaten low-lying coastal areas.
3. Floods will also increase, which will have devastating effects on nations around the world.
4. Increases in water temperatures would be detrimental to a variety of aquatic species, leading to the extinction of some.
5. In terrestrial ecosystems, there will be an increase in desertification and a loss of vital cropland. Likewise, increased summer dryness would lead to crop failure which, in turn, would result in food shortages.
6. The melting of permafrost in such biomes as the tundra would alter the distribution and function of these ecosystems.
7. More extreme weather conditions would also be observed, increasing the incidence of fires, hurricanes, tornadoes, and drought—all of which alter the function and structure of an ecosystem. Consequently, while some species would be able to tolerate, adapt, or flourish with the changes brought about by the global warming, others would be unable to cope and would become extinct.

3. B

Members of the same species can have morphological differences. These differences can arise as a result of changes in geography, topography, and environment. They are acknowledged in categories such as subspecies, variety, and race.

Chromosome number remains constant for all members of a species. All members of a species descend from a common ancestor. Therefore, their evolutionary origin is the same. Anatomical traits are the same for members of the same species unless a member has undergone a genetic mutation or deformity.

4. A

In binomial nomenclature, the scientific name of every species includes two parts. The first part of the name is the genus, while the second part of the name is the species.

5. B

The most common classification scheme for the diversity of living things places all living organisms within one of **five** kingdoms: Monera, Protista, Fungi, Plantae, and Animalia.

6. C

A dichotomous key is a helpful tool that uses pairs of statements representing mutually exclusive choices to lead a researcher to the correct taxonomic name or to another pair of descriptive statements. This tool, often presented in the form of a flow chart, helps the researcher identify an unknown organism.

A field guide provides a researcher with valuable information on general characteristics and may aid identification, but it does not typically provide paired descriptive statements that lead to the correct organism. Cladograms and phylogenetic trees are tools employed in the field of systematics to demonstrate the evolutionary relatedness of groups of organisms, but they do not provide descriptive statements useful in the identification of unknown organisms.

7. a) D

Clan is not a taxonomic category; it is sometimes mistaken as a formal unit of animal classification.

Taxonomic categories classify living organisms into different groups. The taxonomic hierarchy includes species, genus, family, order, class, phylum, and kingdom.

b) OR

Taxonomic categories classify living organisms into different groups. The taxonomic hierarchy from the lowest to the highest level is species, genus, family, order, class, phylum, and kingdom.

8. OR

Phylogenetics is a branch of evolutionary biology that studies the evolutionary history of various organisms to determine their relatedness.

Systematics is the field of science that deals with the diversity of organisms in relation to their classification.

Taxonomy is the branch of biology that deals with identifying, naming, and classifying organisms based on their shared characteristics.

Cladistics is the science of classifying organisms based on their relatedness on the evolutionary tree rather than their morphological characteristics.

9. A

Bacteria are prokaryotes. They do not contain a nucleus but possess structures such as a nucleoid and plasmids. These organelles carry out the process of DNA replication in prokaryotes. In contrast, eukaryotic organisms contain a nucleus, and they lack plasmids. Animal cells are eukaryotic and possess an organized nucleus. Plant cells are eukaryotic and possess an organized nucleus. DNA replication in a virus requires a host cell and although they lack a nucleus, they also lack plasmids.

10. D

The plasma membrane has a similar phospholipids-bilayer structure in eukaryotic and prokaryotic cells. The membranes in both cell types contain glycoproteins and lipids.

11. A

The organisms growing on the side of the tree belong to kingdom Fungi. Commonly known as conks, they are a sign that the tree is infected with fungus. The fruiting bodies of the fungus, shown here, spread spores.

12. D

The kingdoms Monera (prokaryotes) and Protista (single-celled eukaryotes) are composed mainly of unicellular organisms. Members of the kingdom Plantae are eukaryotic but they are also able to photosynthesize. Members of the kingdoms Animalia and Fungi are eukaryotic and cannot photosynthesis so they both fit the description given, but only Animalia is listed.

13. D

Gymnosperms are typically characterized by the presence of naked seeds. The seeds are formed without the production of fruits and flowers.

Fruit and flowers are produced by angiosperms. Monocot and dicot seeds are produced by angiosperms. Gymnosperms have sessile ovules, not motile ovules.

14. OR

1. Presence or absence of true tissues—to distinguish the parazoa (sponges) from the eumetozoa (all other organisms)
2. Radial or bilateral body symmetry—to distinguish the radiata (jellyfish, corals, and anemones) from the bilateria (all other organisms)
3. Type of body cavity and blood vascular system —to determine whether acoelomate (flatworms), pseudocoelomate (rotifers and round worms), or coelomate (all other organisms)
4. First body opening the mouth or the anus (fate of the blastopore)—to distinguish the protostomes (molluscs, annelids, arthropods, etc.) from the deuterostomes (sea stars, urchins, vertebrates)

15. OR

The diagram depicts the process of **endocytosis**, or **endophagocytosis**, in which one cell joins with or engulfs another cell. One hypothesis suggests that the colonial living arrangements that had developed among some of the earliest prokaryotes eventually led to the appearance of the first eukaryotic cells as one or more prokaryotes merged together during an endocytic event. This led to an **endosymbiotic** living relationship and the creation of membrane-bound organelles as smaller prokaryotes, each with unique metabolic functionality, took up residence inside larger prokaryotes. Based on this hypothesis, the first eukaryotes to evolve were likely unicellular and would be considered protists.

16. B

The information indicates that the Olduvai lions have a low fertility rate, which indicates that the small population size and the isolation of this group limits their breeding opportunities. This likely leads to increased incidences of inbreeding. Inbreeding results in a decrease in the genetic variability within a population. The lack of genetic variation in the population increases the lions susceptibility to changing environmental conditions, such as the introduction of disease.

Lions are carnivorous, so an inadequately varied diet is an unlikely cause of their poor health.

Competition in a small isolated group of lions is not likely to be great enough to affect the fertility rates of the group or to increase their susceptibility to disease.

Habitat degradation could potentially impact the fertility rates and disease susceptibility of a group of lions, but there is no indication of habitat degradation in the given information, so it is not the most likely cause of the poor health of the Olduvai population.

17. D

In a rainforest ecosystem, more than 90% of the available nutrients are locked in the biomass of the plants and trees themselves. When the plants and trees are removed, the remaining soil is nutrient-poor. Although burning the trees will have returned some of the nutrients stored in the forest biomass to the soil, the now relatively unprotected soil is continuously washed by rains that leech out any of the nutrients that remain. This is in contrast to a forested region, where the plant biomass would capture most of the rainwater and dissolved nutrients through their root systems. In the absence of the original forest biomass, most of the rainwater has nowhere to go, so it drains away. The agricultural crops do not have the same biomass as the original forest and cannot capture enough rainwater to prevent water run-off. In this way, nutrients are lost to the watershed and river system. Another concern is the erosion of soil that accompanies this problem.

UNIT TEST — DIVERSITY OF LIVING THINGS

1. After a forest is clear cut for timber, the area is often replanted with only one species of tree—a desirable species for logging. What is the effect on biodiversity when an area is replanted and maintained with only one species?
   A. Biodiversity increases
   B. Biodiversity decreases
   C. Biodiversity is not affected
   D. Biodiversity first decreases but then increases

Open Response

2. Describe some major causes of biodiversity loss in Canada.

____
____
____
____
____
____
____

Use the following information to answer the next question.

The polar bear is well adapted for life in the Arctic. Polar bears have white fur to blend into the snowy background when they are hunting for food. They have a thick layer of blubber (fat) and two layers of fur to help them keep warm. They have black skin underneath their fur to help absorb heat from the sun. Seals are the polar bear's main food source. Polar bears hunt seals by travelling out onto sea ice.

Open Response

3. Explain how a warmer climate in the polar bear's ecosystem could affect the polar bear.

____
____
____
____
____
____
____

Use the following information to answer the next question.

Macroevolution can be defined as the formation of new species. Microevolution can be defined as the evolution of a species as the environment changes.

4. Which of the following statements expresses the **best** support for the existence of macroevolution?
   A. Every organism is made up of many unique characteristics.
   B. Species today are more complex than in prehistoric times.
   C. Many insects have become resistant to pesticides.
   D. A large and diverse number of organisms exist.

5. The rate of extinction of species around the world has been very high during the past few centuries. For ecologists, the high rate of extinction is
   A. a cause for concern because cloning endangered animals has become very expensive
   B. a cause for concern because the loss of species due to extinction reduces biodiversity
   C. not a cause for concern because natural selection only allows the fittest to survive
   D. not a cause for concern because massive extinctions have occurred in the past

Use the following information to answer the next question.

Characteristics Displayed by Organisms

1. Unicellular
2. Membrane-bound organelles
3. Autotrophic
4. Peptidoglycan
5. Asexual reproduction
6. Sexual reproduction
7. Prokaryotic
8. Eukaryotic
9. Bacillus

Numerical Response

6. Three characteristics belonging exclusively to organisms in the kingdom Monera are __________, __________, and __________. (Record your answer as a three-digit number in lowest-to-highest numerical order.)

Use the following information to answer the next question.

This pond creature is a Predacious Diving Beetle.

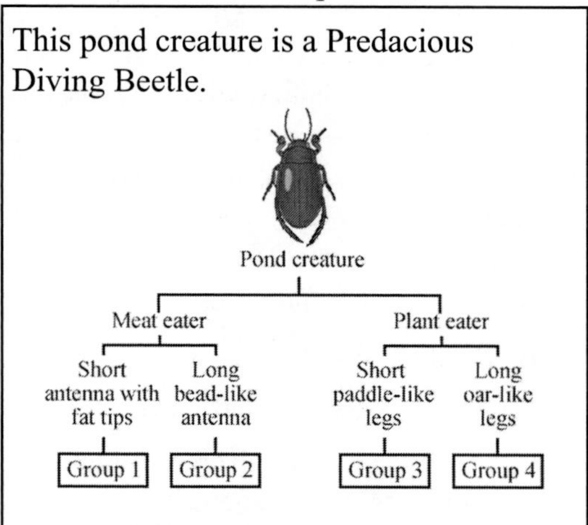

Numerical Response

7. To which group in the chart does the Predacious Diving Beetle belong? ______

Use the following information to answer the next question.

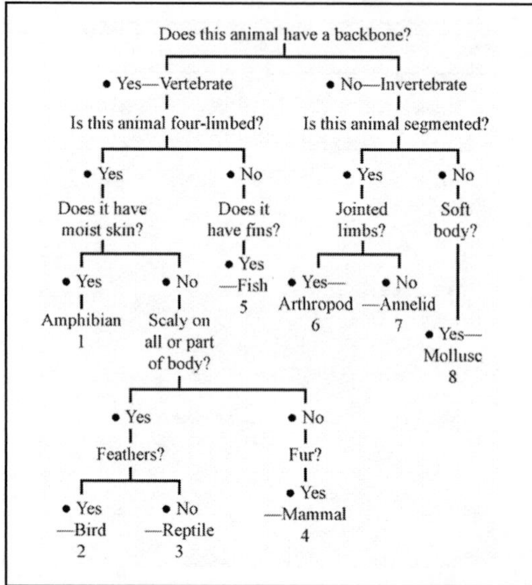

8. Use the dichotomous key to determine which of the following organisms has no backbone, a segmented body and legs that are not jointed?
   A. Amphibian
   B. Annelid
   C. Arthropod
   D. Mollusc

Use the following information to answer the next question.

The levels of taxonomic classification are as follows:

1. Species
2. Class
3. Phylum
4. Order
5. Genus
6. Family
7. Kingdom

Numerical Response

9. Place the levels of taxonomic classification in correct order from greatest number of organisms included to least number of organisms included.

____

Use the following information to answer the next question.

Cellular respiration is the most efficient way for cells to harvest the energy stored in food. The mitochondrion is a eukaryotic cell's power producer, supplying the energy required to carry out all of the cell's jobs. The energy supplied by the mitochondrion is generated through cellular respiration.

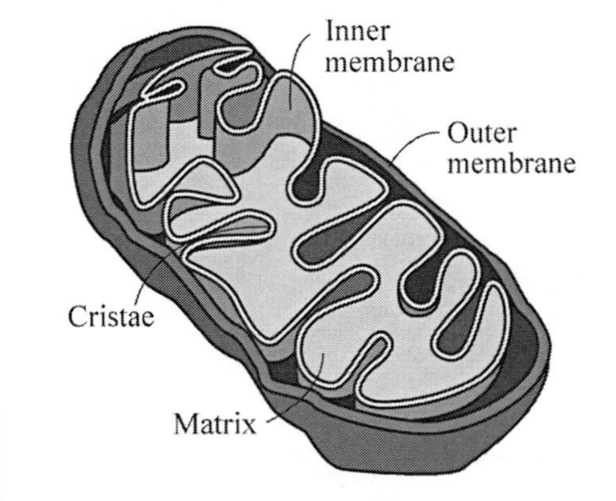

10. Unlike eukaryotic cells, the enzymes required for cellular respiration in prokaryotic cells are located in the

A. cell membrane **B.** gas vacuoles

C. plasmids **D.** nucleoid

11. Which of the following kingdoms is being reclassified by scientists into several kingdoms because there are few unifying characteristics within this diverse group of organisms?

A. Fungi **B.** Plantae

C. Protista **D.** Animalia

12. Which of the following characteristics **most strongly** links green algae evolutionarily to plants?

A. The presence of chloroplasts

B. The role as a producer in ecosystems

C. The use of both sexual and asexual reproduction

D. The capacity to provide shelter for microorganisms

Open Response

13. How does variation within a species occur? Explain why this is important.

ANSWERS AND SOLUTIONS — UNIT TEST

1. B	5. B	9. 7324651	13. OR
2. OR	6. 479	10. A	
3. OR	7. 2	11. C	
4. D	8. B	12. A	

1. B

Biodiversity is a measure of the variety of organisms in an area. When only a single species of tree is replanted, the biodiversity of plant species decreases, as does the available types of habitats for animals in the forest. Animal biodiversity is also likely to decrease as a result of the decreased variety in habitat. As long as the monoculture tree plantation is maintained with a single species of tree, biodiversity will not increase. Only if the area is abandoned will biodiversity begin to increase again as the area starts to return to its natural state.

2. OR

Habitat destruction and degradation resulting from expanding agricultural production are the greatest threats to biodiversity, not only in Canada, but around the world. Farmers are clearing more land and filling in existing wetland areas for more crop production to sustain Canada's growing population.

The use of pesticides and fertilizers to improve crop yields compounds the impact of habitat loss by adding pollution to those habitats that still exist around agricultural land areas.

Other major human-induced threats to biodiversity in Canada include, but are not limited to, overharvesting, wildfire suppression, waste disposal, and the introduction of exotic species.

3. OR

Because the polar bear is adapted to the cold climate it would not do well in a warmer climate. It would overheat because of all its insulation. It would be more difficult for the polar bear to hunt if the snow melted and the polar bear was no longer able to camouflage itself as it hunted its prey. As the sea ice melted because of warmer temperatures, there would be no way for the polar bear to get to the seals it must hunt to survive. Climate change would have drastic consequences for the polar bear.

4. D

It has been suggested that the fossil record shows a very low biodiversity throughout the approximately 600 million years it represents. Conservative estimates put the number of species represented in the fossil record at around 250 000. Considering that the number of species living on Earth at the present time is at least 3.5 million, and could be as high as 30 million, it seems likely that there are more species now than at any one other time period in Earth's history. This indicates that there has been a gradual increase in the number of species over time.

Only macroevolution, evolution involving the formation of new species, could explain this. There is no reason to suggest that species today are more complex than during prehistoric times. Regardless, there is evidence for evolution from one species to another. The fact that organisms are made of unique characteristics indicates that species have genetic variability but does not necessarily indicate macroevolution. Becoming resistant to pesticides represents change within a species, or microevolution.

5. B

The high rate of extinction is a concern for ecologists because biodiversity is important for the healthy functioning of Earth's ecosystems and natural cycles. Although massive extinctions have occurred in the past and natural selection allows only the fittest to survive, the rate of extinction is higher now than it has ever been before, making it a definite concern for ecologists.

6. 479

Organisms in the kingdom Monera are bacteria. The characteristics that are exclusive to bacteria are 4, 7, and 9. Characteristic 4 is correct because some bacteria have peptidoglycan as a component of their cell wall and Monera is the only kingdom where this particular component is present. Characteristic 7 is correct because only bacteria are prokaryotic. Characteristic 9 is correct because the term bacillus is used specifically to describe the rod-like shape commonly displayed by bacteria.

Characteristic 1 is incorrect because although organisms within the kingdom Monera are unicellular, there are also many unicellular protists in the kingdom Protista. Characteristic 2 is incorrect because bacteria do not have membrane-bound organelles. Characteristic 3 is incorrect because although bacteria are autotrophic, there are also many autotrophic protists and plants. Characteristic 5 is incorrect because although bacteria do reproduce asexually, there are many examples of asexual reproduction in the other kingdoms. Characteristic 6 is incorrect because sexual reproduction occurs in eukaryotes. Characteristic 8 is incorrect because bacteria are prokaryotic.

7. 2

Because the beetle is predacious, it can be considered to be a meat eater. The next step gives a choice between the type of antennae, and inspection of the diagram reveals that the antenna are long and bead-like. As such the beetle can be classified in to group 2.

8. B

Use the dichotomous guide to classify the organism. Beginning at the top, each question that is posed by the guide must be answered to decide which branch to follow to the next question in the guide. In this example, the animal has no backbone, so you must select the right branch and move on to "Is this animal segmented?" The answer is yes, so the correct branch forks to the left. The next question is "Does the animal have jointed limbs?" According to the information given about the animal the answer is "No," so the right branch reveals that the animal would be classified as an Annelid.

9. 7324651

Kingdom (7) is the highest level of classification (has the greatest number of organisms) followed by phylum (3), class (2), order (4), family (6), genus (5), and species (1), which is at the lowest level of classification and includes the least number of organisms.

10. A

The enzymes required for cellular respiration are located in the cell membrane of prokaryotic cells. The entire prokaryotic cell functions like a mitochondrial unit.

11. C

The protists are eukaryotic organisms. The group has few other unifying characteristics that do not have exceptions. This, in combination with new genetic and molecular evidence, has led scientists to reassess the kingdom.

12. A

Green algae contain chloroplasts nearly identical in structure and pigment composition to those found in plants. Although both green algae and plants can act as producers and provide shelter in ecosystems, this is not evidence for an evolutionary link, nor is the use of both sexual and asexual reproduction.

13. OR

Variation within a species occurs because of sexual reproduction. Both the male and female equally donate genetic information to the offspring. Half of the genetic information comes from the male and half from the female. In this way, a new individual is produced that is genetically different from the mother and the father.

Variation is important because it results in not every single organism of a species being exactly alike. These differences in phenotypic representation allow for adaptation of a population in the face of environmental change by the process of natural selection, which in turn promotes species survival and can potentially lead to speciation.

NOTES

Evolution

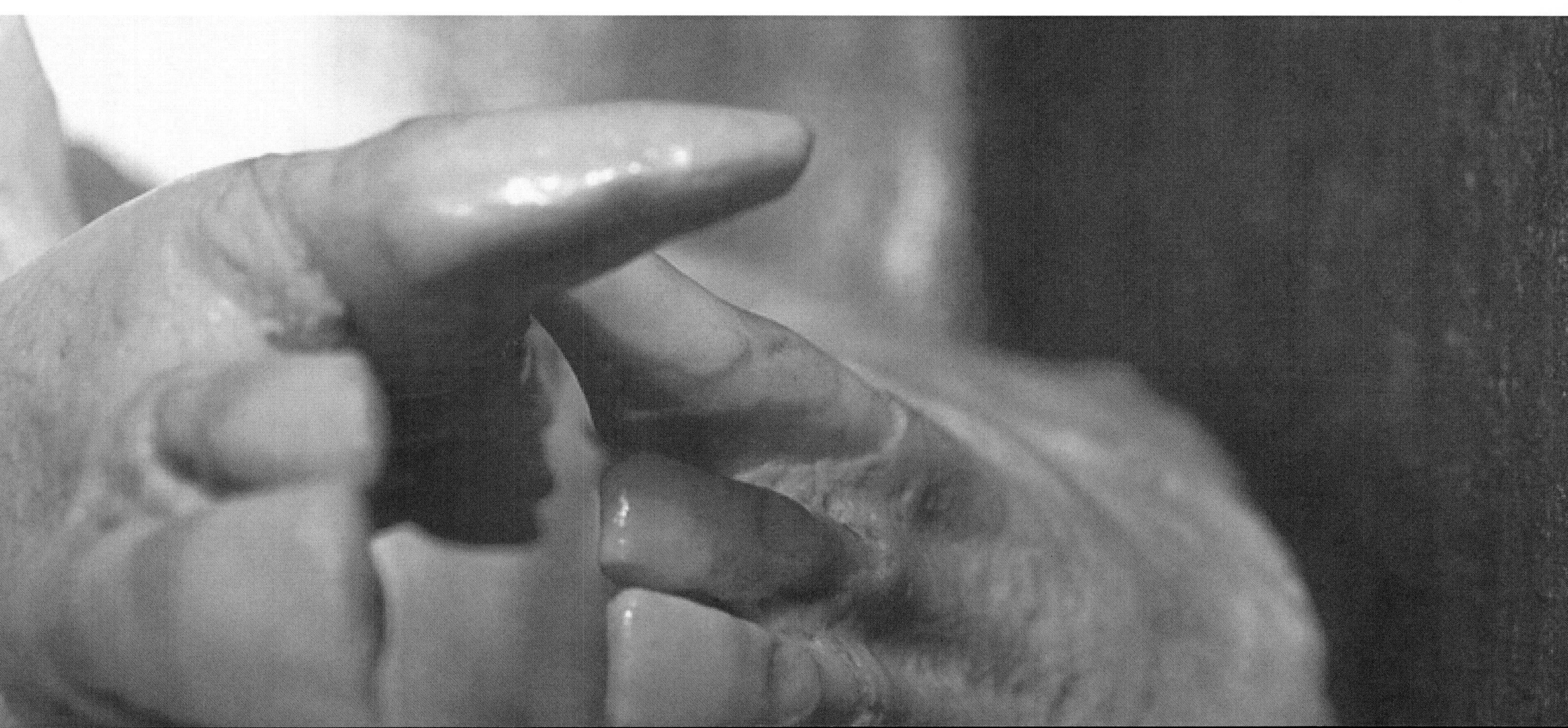

EVOLUTION

Table of Correlations

Specific Expectation		Practice Questions	Unit Test Questions	Practice Test 1	Practice Test 2
11.3.C1	analyse the economic and environmental advantages and disadvantages of an artificial selection technology, and evaluate the impact of environmental changes on natural selection and endangered species				
11.3.C1.1	*analyse, on the basis of research, the economic and environmental advantages and disadvantages of an artificial selection technology*	16	1	23	24
11.3.C1.2	*evaluate the possible impact of an environmental change on natural selection and on the vulnerability of species*	4	2	24	25
11.3.C2	investigate evolutionary processes, and analyse scientific evidence that supports the theory of evolution				
11.3.C2.1	*use appropriate terminology related to evolution, including, but not limited to: extinction, natural selection, phylogeny, speciation, niche, mutation, mimicry, adaptation, and survival of the fittest*	5, 6, 7	3, 4, 5a, 5b, 5c	25, 26, 27	26, 27, 28
11.3.C2.2	*use a research process to investigate some of the key factors that affect the evolutionary process*	14	6	28	29
11.3.C2.3	*analyse, on the basis of research, and report on the contributions of various scientists to modern theories of evolution*	2, 3	7, 8	29	30
11.3.C2.4	*investigate, through a case study or computer simulation, the processes of natural selection and artificial selection*	15		30	31
11.3.C3	demonstrate an understanding of the theory of evolution, the evidence that supports it, and some of the mechanisms by which it occurs				
11.3.C3.1	*explain the fundamental theory of evolution, using the evolutionary mechanism of natural selection to illustrate the process of biological change over time*	1	9	31, 32a, 32b, 32c	32, 33
11.3.C3.2	*explain the process of adaptation of individual organisms to their environment*	8	10		34
11.3.C3.3	*define the concept of speciation, and explain the process by which new species are formed*	9, 10	11	33	35
11.3.C3.4	*describe some evolutionary mechanisms, and explain how they affect the evolutionary development and extinction of various species*	11, 12, 13	12, 13	34, 35, 36	36, 37, 38

11.3.C3.1 explain the fundamental theory of evolution, using the evolutionary mechanism of natural selection to illustrate the process of biological change over time

11.3.C2.3 analyse, on the basis of research, and report on the contributions of various scientists to modern theories of evolution

Evolutionary Ideologies throughout History

The late 18th and 19th centuries were times of profound shifts in ideas about the existence of life on Earth. Prevailing views dominated by creationism and natural theology were challenged by the emergence of evolutionary concepts.

Historical Developments in Evolutionary Theory

In 1809, Jean Baptiste Lamarck (1744-1829) published an early theory that identified evolution as the process responsible for the diversity of life on Earth. Lamarck theorized that an organism could intentionally change its use of various traits (e.g., organs) depending on whether they were required. He suggested that subsequent generations would inherit these changes, and populations would become increasingly adapted to their environments. Although research eventually showed that acquired characteristics are not heritable, Lamarckian theory is recognized for its valuable contributions to evolutionary concepts, including these ideas:

- Earth had to be much older than was being suggested by biblical authority.
- Evolution was the best explanation for Earth's biological diversity.
- Evolution was a result of adaptation.

Charles Lyell's (1797-1875) *Principles of Geology*, published in three volumes from 1830 to 1833, provided evidence for a much older geological Earth. This strengthened the argument for uniformitarianism and gradualism. Lyell theorized that since geological processes that shape Earth's surface are slow and continuous, Earth must be very old to display the geology it does today. This idea was in contrast to the existing belief in catastrophism that suggested Earth's present conditions could be explained by great changes that occurred as the result of a few sudden catastrophic events.

Thomas Malthus' (1766-1834) theories, published in *An Essay on the Principle of Population* in 1798, were not concerned with evolution, but they played a part in shaping the concept of evolution as an explanation for the entirety of biological diversity on Earth. Darwin derived the principle of natural selection as the mechanism by which evolution occurs by recognizing that populations are inherently variable in their phenotypic characteristics. Based on this observation, Darwin theorized that only those individuals with traits best suited to obtaining the scarce resources of the environment will successfully compete, survive, and reproduce. This concept, termed "survival of the fittest," was thought to promote adaptation in a population through the gradual accumulation in succeeding generations of favourable traits inherited by the offspring. Gradual accumulation of favourable traits over vast expanses of time was thought to eventually lead to the biological change responsible for speciation. Darwin published his findings in *On the Origin of Species* in 1859.

Charles Darwin

Although a variety of transitional fossil forms have been found, as suggested by Darwin's idea of gradualism, the sudden appearance and disappearance of a number of species in the fossil record without any type of transitional form at all is much more common. Stephen Jay Gould (1941-2002) and Niles Eldredge (born 1943) introduced the idea of punctuated equilibrium in 1972 to account for the inconsistency. This theory is a modification of gradualism, and suggests that although change occurs slowly from one generation to the next, speciation occurs relatively quickly as isolated populations quickly adapt to new environmental conditions. Therefore, evolution is characterized by long periods of stability interrupted by relatively quick periods of change. Gould and Eldredge's contributions to evolutionary concepts have stimulated valuable research into the rate of speciation.

1. Which of the following ideas is **not** in agreement with Darwin's theory of the evolution of organisms?
   A. Species change over time in response to their environment.
   B. Populations have variability in the characteristics of their individual organisms.
   C. Individual organisms acquire characteristics that they subsequently pass on to their offspring.
   D. Evolution is a process by which organisms become better adapted to their particular environment.

2. Thomas Malthus was an English economist known for his theories on population growth. In *An Essay on the Principle of Population*, Malthus suggested that
   A. food supply will always be sufficient to support an increasing population
   B. food supply does not affect population growth in any way
   C. population increases at a slower rate than food supply
   D. population increases at a faster rate than food supply

3. The theory of natural selection was proposed by
   A. Lyell **B.** Darwin
   C. Eldredge **D.** Lamarck

11.3.C3.3 define the concept of speciation, and explain the process by which new species are formed

11.3.C1.2 evaluate the possible impact of an environmental change on natural selection and on the vulnerability of species

11.3.C2.1 use appropriate terminology related to evolution, including, but not limited to: extinction, natural selection, phylogeny, speciation, niche, mutation, mimicry, adaptation, and survival of the fittest

11.3.C3.2 explain the process of adaptation of individual organisms to their environment

Natural Selection as a Mechanism for Adaptation and Speciation

The term **speciation** can be defined as the evolution of a new species over time, also known as **macroevolution**. It takes place through the mechanism of **natural selection**. Described by Charles Darwin, natural selection is the process by which favourable characteristics in a population of a species become more common as they are passed from one generation to the next, while less favourable characteristics become less common. Speciation occurs when individuals within a population, who vary in their genetic composition and phenotypic traits, have different levels of reproductive success. Genetic variation arises due to spontaneous mutation and genetic recombination of an organism's DNA. Those individuals with phenotypic traits best suited (favourable) to their particular environmental conditions or a particular niche are more likely to survive and reproduce. The phrase that is used to describe this process is **survival of the fittest**. Note that the term "fittest" does not necessarily mean that it is always the strongest members of a species that survive.
In biological terms, the definition of fitness is the individuals in a population that are best able to survive long enough to produce offspring.

Therefore, the individuals with the most favourable traits are able to pass these on to the next generation, resulting in the gradual change and adaptation of an organism to its environment, also known as **microevolution**. For example, an environmental change is triggered by the introduction of a new species of fast-running predator to a particular region. The likely result is that the slowest animals in that area would be eaten first. The faster animals would now be considered more fit because they would be more likely to survive, reproduce, and pass their fast genes on to their offspring. However, if none of the prey species have the genetic variability required to adapt to being preyed upon by the new speedy predator (as is often witnessed in small populations of endangered species), then they become more vulnerable to extinction as their reproductive success declines to a level that will not sustain the population in the face of this environmental change.

Natural selection acting on a population of bacteria with a short life span and fast rate of proliferation allows for rapid adaptation to changing environmental conditions, such as antibiotic treatment. Individuals that have the favourable trait of antibiotic resistance will survive the initial treatment, reproduce, and pass the resistance to the next generation. In this manner, the bacterial population adapts to its new environmental conditions and creates an entirely resistant population in a very short time.

In some cases, a favourable trait that increases the reproductive fitness of a certain species will also be selected for in another species, which will evolve to exhibit a similar trait. This trait similarity, called **mimicry**, can sometimes be superficial, such as a palatable butterfly that has similar wing patterns to a butterfly that is poisonous.

If changing environmental conditions were to result in natural selection acting on an entire species, the whole species would gradually evolve into a new form, but there would still only be one species. This is referred to as **phyletic speciation**. In order for an additional species to evolve, populations must become separated by a physical barrier, such as the Grand Canyon, that would prevent them from interbreeding. As natural selection operates on the isolated groups independently from each other, the two groups evolve separately and eventually become different enough that they could not breed with each other even if the opportunity presented itself. At this point, it can be said that the two populations have become separate species. This is referred to as **allopatric speciation**.

Examining the phylogeny, or evolutionary history, of a particular organism is useful in determining the evolutionary relatedness of different species. Through these two forms of speciation, natural selection promotes biodiversity if a new species arises and the parent species continues to thrive. If, however, an entire species gradually evolves into a new species so that the parent species no longer exists, then natural selection can lead to extinction.

Use the following information to answer the next question.

The Karner Blue butterfly completely depends on wild lupines for its life cycle. Wild lupine plants are especially vulnerable to pesticides.

4. Widespread use of pesticides ultimately affects the Karner Blue butterfly by

A. increasing its available habitat

B. decreasing its population

C. increasing its food supply

D. decreasing its predation

Use the following information to answer the next question.

On the Galapagos Islands off the coast of Ecuador, there are two types of iguanas that are uniquely adapted to eat the different types of island food sources. The land iguana primarily eats cactus leaves, and the marine iguana primarily eats seaweed. Both iguanas are believed to share one land iguana ancestor.

5. The description of the two different types of Galapagos iguanas that share a common ancestor is an example of

A. abiotic factors

B. adaptive radiation

C. convergent evolution

D. ecological succession

6. Which of the following population characteristics is **most likely** to lead to rapid evolutionary change?

A. Trophic level

B. Reproductive rate

C. Population density

D. Variable morphology

Use the following information to answer the next question.

Some animals and plants are better equipped to survive under changing environmental conditions than others because they have the genetic variability necessary for __________. The process responsible for acting on this genetic variability and promoting differential reproductive success among individuals is referred to as __________. The common phrase associated with this theory is __________.

Open Response

7. Accurately complete the given statement by selecting the **best** choice for each blank from the following terminology:

- adaptation
- mutation
- natural selection
- evolution
- survival of the fittest

A term or phrase may be used only once, or not at all.

____

____

8. Which of the following characteristics of a population of bacteria does **not** facilitate its rapid adaptability under changing environmental conditions?

A. Asexual reproduction

B. Short generation span

C. Rapid rate of proliferation

D. Ability to recombine genes

Use the following information to answer the next question.

Three Types of Speciation	
1	Sympatric
2	Allopatric
3	Phyletic

Numerical Response

9. Match each of these types of speciation with the descriptor below that applies to it.

Description	Number
Random genetic divergence leading to reproductive isolation of a small subpopulation	________
Speciation of an entire species population due to changing environmental conditions	________
Geographic isolation of two or more different populations of the same species so that they can no longer meet to interbreed.	________

Open Response

10. What is the definition of speciation? What is another term used to describe speciation? What is the underlying mechanism by which speciation takes place?

____

____

____

____

____

11.3.C3.4 describe some evolutionary mechanisms, and explain how they affect the evolutionary development and extinction of various species

Evolutionary Mechanisms

Genetic variation stems from the spontaneous mutation and genetic recombination of an organism's DNA and is responsible for the variation of observed phenotypic traits in a population. Natural selection promotes the adaptation of an organism to its environment by acting on these variations and selecting for the traits that better enable the organism to compete, survive, and reproduce.

For example, in any given giraffe population, some individuals will have slightly longer necks, while others will have slightly shorter necks. The giraffes with longer necks were naturally selected over successive generations, which gradually led to the long necks found in giraffes today. This likely occurred because the individuals with longer necks were more successful at reaching the leaves on the higher branches, which increased their chances of survival.

If the cumulative changes within a species are large enough, speciation may result over time. In this manner, natural selection promotes biodiversity if a new species arises while the original parent species continues to thrive. If, however, an entire species gradually evolves into a new species without preserving the parent species, then natural selection can lead to extinction.

Artificial selection refers to the attempt to direct changes in the characteristics of a population in an effort to exhibit traits that humans find desirable. This early form of biotechnology saw the intentional selection of agricultural breeding stock from those plants or animals that had either beneficial or favourable characteristics to humans. It leads to a weaker form of biodiversity as new varieties of plants and breeds of animals are created for human benefit without regard for their environmental suitability. As a result, they would likely be lost to extinction within a few generations without human intervention. More recent biotechnologies, such as genetic engineering, use recombinant DNA methods to alter the genetic makeup of a variety of different organisms so that they display genetic modifications useful to humans that would not have evolved naturally. These genetically modified organisms (GMOs) could interbreed with their non-genetically modified (wild) counterparts, potentially altering the genetic makeup of natural populations. The potential ramifications that this artificial shift in genetic variation could have on evolutionary development and biodiversity are unpredictable.

11. The phenomenon of genetic drift is more common when there

A. is a decrease in a population

B. is an increase in a population

C. are mutations in a population

D. are variations in a population

Use the following information to answer the next question.

Insecticides have been used to control mosquito populations in order to prevent the spread of malaria, but mosquitoes in malaria-infested areas are developing resistance to these insecticides.
In addition, anti-malarial drugs that were once very effective in protecting individuals against *Plasmodium* (the causative agent of malaria) have become increasingly ineffective. Scientists have identified a gene in *Plasmodium* that allows the *Plasmodium* to mount resistance to these anti-malarial drugs. This research could be used by scientists to develop new versions of the anti-malarial drugs that will sidestep the parasite's resistance and, therefore, effectively protect people against malaria.

12. The mounting resistance to anti-malarial drugs by *Plasmodium* is **most likely** a result of

A. all the Hardy-Weinberg conditions being met

B. being naturally selected for as a beneficial gene

C. the non-random mating of resistant *Plasmodium*

D. the growing resistance the mosquito carrier has developed

Use the following information to answer the next question.

Famous for being the world's fastest land mammal, the cheetah can reach speeds of up to 112 km/hr. The South African cheetah population has extremely low genetic diversity, likely as a result of population decline following the last ice age. This already low genetic diversity was lowered again when South African cheetahs were nearly hunted to extinction at the beginning of the twentieth century.

13. Which of the following processes is responsible for the cheetah's lowered genetic diversity?

A. Population bottleneck

B. Non-random mating

C. Founder effect

D. Genetic drift

11.3.C2.2 use a research process to investigate some of the key factors that affect the evolutionary process

Examining Evolution in a Laboratory Setting

The role of genetic mutation in evolutionary processes is often investigated through several sequential hybrid crosses of small, genetically variable, and rapidly proliferating organisms with simple genomes, such as fruit flies.

Male (left) and female (right) Drosophila melanogaster

The hybrid crosses are performed so that the inheritance patterns of specific traits can be observed and documented through multiple generations. This research process provides important information regarding genetic and phenotypic characteristics and how they relate to the evolutionary mechanism of natural selection.

The impact of environmental stress on evolutionary processes can be witnessed first-hand with tests designed to evaluate antibiotic resistance in microorganisms. This research process is designed to determine, for clinical and treatment purposes, the relative sensitivity of different pathogenic organisms to different types of antibiotics. Typically, the research method involves growth of the microorganism of interest on an agar plate that houses small absorbent discs soaked with variable concentrations of antibiotics. As the target bacteria grow, the antibiotic will diffuse out of each of the discs into the surrounding agar medium.

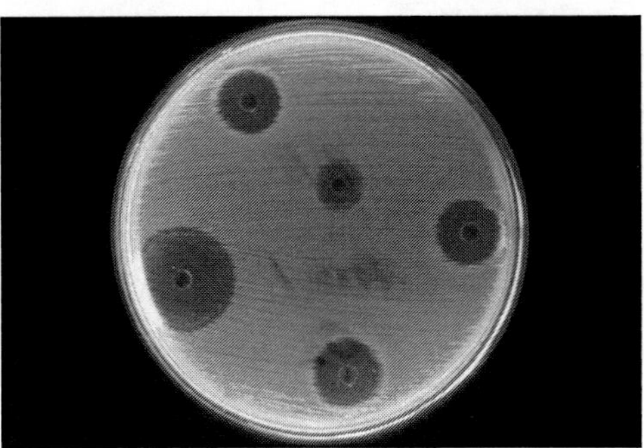

Antibiotic resistance testing in bacteria

The diameter of the inhibition ring can be compared with a known antibiotic resistance standard to determine whether or not the bacteria have developed a resistance. This controlled laboratory research process demonstrates, in a relatively short time period, the adaptability of a genetically variable population of organisms to environmental stress.

The influence of selective pressures on evolutionary processes is made evident by the human practices of artificial selection, selective breeding, and domestication. In each of these human-influenced activities, changes in the phenotypic characteristics of an organism occur as a result of the direct selection for particular desirable traits.
These changes can be observed by comparing extreme types of an organism. For example, some dog breeds such as the Chihuahua and the Great Dane show large phenotypic variation.

Additional examples of the impact of human selection pressures can be observed in the historical development of corn (maize) from the wild teosinte grass and the domestication of wild cattle into the many different livestock breeds used for the production of food and other valuable commodities. These relatively small-scale human practices demonstrate the influence that selective pressures can have on the evolutionary process. They also illustrate the potential effect that natural selection and environmental selective pressures could have on global biodiversity when viewed over millions of years.

Use the following information to answer the next question.

A human arm, a cat leg, a bat wing, and a whale flipper vary greatly in size and shape, but because these four structures all have the same number of bones, they are considered to be homologous. The fact that humans, cats, bats, and whales share these homologous structures indicates that they have a common ancestor.

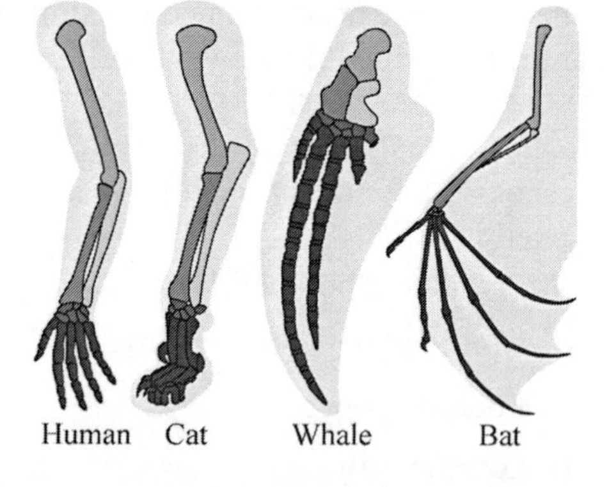

14. The homologous structures described above were produced through the process of

A. divergent evolution caused by similar environmental selective pressures

B. divergent evolution caused by different environmental selective pressures

C. convergent evolution caused by similar environmental selective pressures

D. convergent evolution caused by different environmental selective pressures

11.3.C2.4 investigate, through a case study or computer simulation, the processes of natural selection and artificial selection

The Processes of Natural and Artificial Selection

While natural selection results in the adaptation and evolutionary development of a population, artificial selection promotes changes in a population to exhibit traits that humans find desirable.
Although there is no real difference in the underlying genetic processes driving artificial selection and natural selection since they both act on the genetic variability present within a given population, the use of their new traits in adapting to the environment is profoundly different.
While natural selection increases the suitability of an organism to its respective environment and promotes biodiversity, artificial selection creates new varieties and breeds of plants and animals that are created for human benefit and also typically reduces diversity. However, given that each new variety is created without regard for its environmental suitability, it is likely these organisms would be lost to extinction within a few generations if left to exist in the natural environment without human intervention.

Natural Selection

Galápagos Island finches represent one of the most well-known examples of natural selection promoting adaptation. The Galápagos islands are located off the western coast of Ecuador, South America, and are volcanic in origin with no past connection to mainland South America. Consequently, the diverse flora and fauna found on the islands are a direct result of incidental colonization by mainland species. Of particular interest is that these islands are colonized by an extremely diverse range of 13 different finch species. The primary difference observed among the different finch species is variation in beak shape. Each species has a beak shape that is uniquely adapted to the particular food resource present in its respective island habitat. It is theorized that a common ancestral species arrived on the islands from the mainland some time in the past, and that natural selection promoted adaptation and subsequent speciation of the initial finch population as the ancestral species began to inhabit a wide variety of unoccupied ecological niches.

Variation in beak shape of Galápagos finches

Artificial Selection

The first domestication of wild wheat species occurred as a result of humans selecting wild wheat types that had larger grains, tough ears that were able to withstand harvesting, and spikelets that remained on the stalk until harvested.
These characteristics, although beneficial to the farmer, resulted in these wheat species losing their ability to disperse their seeds. As a result, domesticated wheat has a limited ability to reproduce on its own, and it is now heavily reliant on humans to continue propagation.

Domesticated wheat field

Open Response

15. **Explain** why adaptations that arise through natural selection are more resilient than adaptations that arise through selective breeding techniques.

____
____
____
____
____
____
____

11.3.C1.1 analyse, on the basis of research, the economic and environmental advantages and disadvantages of an artificial selection technology

Aritifical Selection Technology: Social Implications

Artificial selection promotes changes in the characteristics of an organism to exhibit traits that humans find desirable. Essentially, it results in the modification of many wild plants and animals to serve some human purpose. Typically, these animals and plants are altered for these reasons:

- Production of food or some other valuable commodity (e.g., livestock and crops)
- Use in various types of work (e.g., transportation or protection)
- Human enjoyment (e.g., pets and ornamental plants)
- Scientific purposes (e.g., medicinal and treatment properties)

Advantages of Artificial Selection

As artificial selection technologies, such as selective breeding and genetic engineering, continue to aim for increasingly superior plant varieties and animal breeds, the human benefits and economic advantages are demonstrated through improved crop yields, livestock productivity, retail profit (pharmaceutical, pet, and ornamental plant sales), medicinal advances, and overall quality of life. This is because these organisms are producing at levels, and demonstrating development of characteristics, well beyond that which existed in nature. This is a direct result of human selection pressures that aim for certain desirable characteristics.

The following characteristics are typically selected in plants:

- Higher germination rates
- Greater germination predictability
- Changes in biomass of desired structures
- Disease resistance
- Increased shelf life
- Higher nutritional value

The following characteristics are typically selected in animals:

- Predictability in temperament, disposition, and behaviour
- Increased biomass (e.g., larger beef cattle)
- Improved production of a desired commodity (e.g., woollier sheep)

Disadvantages of Artificial Selection

One major disadvantage of artificial selection is the loss in genetic variability that often accompanies the changes in the genotypic structure of the artificially altered organisms in response to human selection pressures. As these organisms are continually interbred to produce plants and animals with the most superior characteristics of the species, other characteristics in the population are inadvertently lost in the process. Economically, this poses a problem since it often leads to major crop failure and livestock decline because the decreased genetic variability of these populations results in a limited ability to respond to changing environmental conditions such as exotic species invasion or disease.

Environmentally, animals and plants developed for human purposes pose a genetic threat to wild populations by functioning as a potential source of unnatural gene flow in naturally evolved gene pools. This environmental disadvantage is often reflected in a decline or extinction of the native species as its genetic makeup shifts in an unnatural direction that is not necessarily suited to its respective environmental conditions.
This phenomenon, which is often referred to as genetic pollution, is of special concern when considering more recent biotechnologies, such as genetic engineering. Hybridization of these genetically modified organisms (GMOs) with their wild counterparts could irreversibly alter the genetic makeup of natural populations. The potential ramifications that this unnatural shift in genetic variation may have on biodiversity are unpredictable.

Open Response

16. List **three** economic advantages of artificial selection technology, and **explain** how those economic advantages might relate to some environmental advantages.

____
____
____
____
____
____
____

ANSWERS AND SOLUTIONS
EVOLUTION

1. C	5. B	9. 132	13. A
2. D	6. B	10. OR	14. B
3. B	7. OR	11. A	15. OR
4. B	8. A	12. B	16. OR

1. C

Darwin did not believe that an organism could acquire particular characteristics throughout its lifetime and then pass the acquired characteristic on to its offspring. Instead, he believed that nature would determine which characteristics would be passed on by selecting for those characteristics that made an individual organism more suited to its particular environment, and therefore more likely to survive and reproduce. The principle of the inheritance of acquired characteristics is an idea attributed to Jean-Baptiste Lamarck. Both men accepted that species change over time in response to their environment. Both saw evolution as a process in which organisms became better adapted to their environment.

2. D

In *An Essay on the Principle of Population*, Malthus suggested that population grows at a much faster rate than food supply, eventually leading to a decrease in the amount of food per person.

3. B

The theory of the natural selection was proposed by Charles Darwin. He published his ideas on natural selection and evolution in *On the Origin of Species* in 1859.

4. B

The widespread use of pesticides would greatly reduce the number of wild lupines. Because the Karner Blue butterfly is completely dependent on wild lupines for its survival, a decrease in the number of wild lupines would lead to a decrease in the population size of Karner Blue butterflies.

The Karner Blue's food supply and available habitat (wild lupines) would decrease with widespread use of pesticides. The widespread use of pesticides would not have an effect on the predation of the Karner Blue.

5. B

Adaptive radiation is the development of different species from a single common ancestor, where the new species are adapted to occupy different niches. Abiotic factors are non-living, so the iguanas would be biotic factors. Convergent evolution is the development of similar characteristics in unrelated lineages due to similar environmental pressures. Ecological succession is the subsequent progression of an ecosystem.

6. B

As the rate of reproduction of a population increases, so too does the opportunity for more genetic variation and mutation. Many geneticists study population diversity and evolution using tiny flies called *Drosophila melanogaster* for this reason. The rapid production of new generations demonstrates natural selection as successful new characteristics are adopted and reproduced. Population density is a measurement of population per unit area; it does not cause rapid evolutionary change. The trophic level of a population merely indicates where the organisms that constitute the population fit into the food chain or food webs of their ecosystem. Variable morphology may be a factor that influences the mechanics of natural selection, but does not suggest any sort of condition that would lead the population toward rapid evolutionary change by itself.

7. OR

In order, the blanks are best completed by these terms or phrases: adaptation, natural selection, survival of the fittest.

8. A

Asexual reproduction functions to produce genetically identical offspring, but it fails to produce genetic variability in the population, which does not facilitate the rapid adaptability of a population of bacteria. The short generation span and rapid rate of proliferation of a population of bacteria permit natural selection to act on genetic variations, such as antibiotic resistance, created by spontaneous mutation and genetic recombination.

9. 132

Sympatric speciation occurs when populations are reproductively isolated due to a random genetic divergence (1). Phyletic speciation occurs when an entire species is affected by changing environmental conditions (3). Allopatric speciation occurs when populations are geographically isolated (2).
The correct numerical response is 1, 3, 2.

10. OR

The term speciation can be defined as the **evolution of a new species** over time. Another term used to describe speciation is **macroevolution**. Speciation takes place through the underlying mechanism of **natural selection** acting on genetic variability within a population.

11. A

Genetic drift is more common when there is a decrease in a population.

12. B

Plasmodium, which bear the anti-malarial drug resistance gene, are most likely to survive exposure to anti-malarial drugs and continue reproducing because they are naturally selected for when these drugs are employed for treatment of malaria.

13. A

When a population's size is decreased because of natural disasters or human interference, the genetic diversity of the population is also decreased. Unless genetic diversity is reintroduced to the population through large amounts of immigration (not the case for cheetahs), the gene pool will remain much smaller than the original population for many years. The process of lowered genetic diversity resulting from dramatic decreases in population size is referred to as a population bottleneck.

14. B

The term *homology* refers to the evolutionary process in which a specific structure found in different organisms evolved from one common ancestor. It is believed that the ancestor was exposed to various environmental selective pressures and over time, as new species were formed, the common structure took on different forms. This form of evolution is referred to as divergent evolution.

15. OR

Although there is no real difference in the underlying genetic processes behind selective breeding and natural selection (they both act on inherent genetic variability), the relative adaptability and resiliency of the resultant characteristics is profoundly different. This is because adaptations that arise through natural selection increase the suitability of an organism to its respective environment and will remain present as long as the environmental conditions do not change, whereas adaptations that arise through selective breeding are created for human benefit, often without regard for environmental suitability. As a result, these adaptations are typically lost within a few generations when left to exist without human intervention.

16. OR

Economic Advantages

1. Improved crop yields
2. Medicinal advancements
3. Increased livestock productivity

Some Possible Environmental Advantages Related to the Economic Advantages

- Improved crop yields and livestock productivity equates to less land area required for the same amount of food production, resulting in less habitat destruction for new agricultural development
- Improved crop yields equates to less fertilizer required for growth and therefore less environmental pollution from fertilizer run-off
- Pest-resistant crops theoretically decrease the amount of pesticides required, thereby decreasing environmental pollution from pesticides
- Medicinal advancements resulting from artificial selection alleviate pressure on natural plant resources and decrease over-harvest of medicinal plants

UNIT TEST — EVOLUTION

Open Response

1. Give two **environmental disadvantages** of artificial selection technologies.

Use the following information to answer the next question.

The most serious drawback of using chemicals to control pests is that most pest populations, especially insects, develop a resistance to the chemicals.

Open Response

2. How do insect populations develop this resistance, and how does this adaptation to changing environmental conditions affect the population's reproductive success?

3. The resemblance between unrelated groups of organisms as a result of a common adaptation is called
   A. parallel evolution
   B. phyletic evolution
   C. divergent evolution
   D. convergent evolution

4. Darwin's finches are examples of all the following types of evolution **except**
   A. microevolution
   B. macroevolution
   C. divergent evolution
   D. convergent evolution

Use the following information to answer the next multipart question.

5. The monarch butterfly is found throughout the world. Each year, monarchs fly as far as from Ontario to California, Mexico, and Florida to lay their eggs on the underside of milkweed leaves. Once the caterpillar emerges from the eggs, it feeds on the milkweed and accumulates the alkaloids of the plant in its body. The alkaloids of the milkweed contain poisonous compounds that produce a strong pungent taste in the mouth of a predator if the caterpillar is consumed.
The viceroy butterfly is also common to North America. As an adult, it very much resembles the monarch. The two species are referred to as Mullerian mimics.

Open Response

a) In terms of Darwinian evolution, explain how natural selection has favoured the monarch butterfly's association with the milkweed. Include a description of what natural selection is and a possible hypothesis of how it applies to the monarch butterfly.

b) Suggest two benefits and two costs of the trip made by the monarch butterfly. Explain whether you believe the benefits outweigh the costs.

____

____

____

____

____

____

____

c) Discuss why the viceroy butterfly may benefit from mimicking the monarch as well as how it also may be harmed.

____

____

____

____

____

____

____

Use the following information to answer the next question.

In the given figure, populations A and B of a given species grow in size one generation after another. This leads to the migration of organisms to a larger territory, and populations A and B settle in opposite ends of this territory.

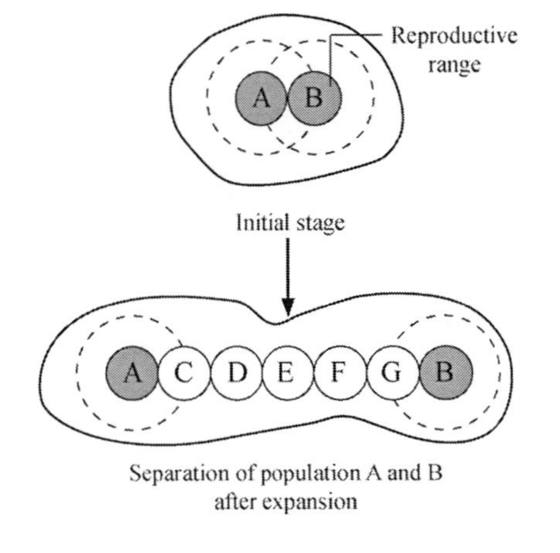

6. Which of the following predictions about populations A and B after the isolation is **false**?

A. Natural selection will act differently on populations A and B.

B. Direct gene flow will not occur between populations A and B.

C. Populations A and B will become subspecies that can interbreed if given the opportunity.

D. Populations A and B will never become reproductively isolated even if they accumulate a large number of variations.

7. Which of the following features does **not** support the use and disuse of organs hypothesis?

A. Long neck in giraffes

B. Constant size of the heart

C. Absence of flight in flightless birds

D. Large muscular biceps in blacksmiths

Use the following information to answer the next question.

Six Scientists

1. Stephen Gould and Niles Eldredge
2. Charles Darwin
3. Jean-Baptiste Lamarck
4. Thomas Malthus
5. Charles Lyell

Numerical Response

8. Match each of the given scientists with the theories or ideologies to which they contributed. (Record your answer as a five-digit number.)

Theory or Ideology	Number
The principle of use and disuse	________
Uniformitarianism and gradualism	________
Natural selection	________
Principles of population and the struggle for existence	________
Punctuated equilibrium	________

Use the following information to answer the next question.

Factors related to theories of evolution:

1. Natural selection
2. Phenotypic variability
3. Survival of the fittest
4. Genotypic equilibrium
5. Struggle for existence
6. Punctuated equilibrium
7. Inheritance of acquired characteristics

Numerical Response

9. According to Charles Darwin's theory of evolution, there are four key factors leading to the origin of a new species. When these factors are arranged in order from the lowest to the highest number from the given list, the order is ________, ________, ________, and ________. (Record your answer as a four-digit number.)

Open Response

10. **Describe** how natural selection functioned to promote a shift towards the dark-coloured morph of the peppered moth during the Industrial Revolution.

Open Response

11. Name **three** types of speciation, and **explain** the main differences between them.

Use the following information to answer the next question.

The northern elephant seal is one of two species of elephant seal, which is characterized by its great elephant-like snout. In the 1700s, these seals were hunted for their blubber, and their population was reduced to approximately 30 individuals by the 1890s. Since gaining protection by the Mexican government in the late 20th century, the population has grown, with current estimates of over 100 000 individuals.

12. In the northern elephant seal population, genetic variation has **most likely**

A. increased due to the founder effect

B. decreased due to random breeding

C. decreased due to the bottleneck effect

D. not changed due to Hardy–Weinberg equilibrium

Use the following information to answer the next question.

Scientists working in laboratories identify characteristics that may be manipulated. If cows with a high milk yield are desired, the animal breeders select those cows that produce a large quantity of milk.
The calves of the high milk-yielding cows are then interbred. After repeating the process for a number of generations, a breed of high milk-yielding cows is produced.

13. This process used in this case to produce high milk-yielding cows is known as

A. recombinant DNA technology

B. artificial selection

C. natural selection

D. genetic drift

ANSWERS AND SOLUTIONS — UNIT TEST

1. OR	5. a) OR	7. B	11. OR
2. OR	b) OR	8. 35241	12. C
3. D	c) OR	9. 1235	13. B
4. D	6. D	10. OR	

1. OR

1. Genetic Pollution—unnatural gene flow into wild populations can occur if interbreeding occurs between artificially selected for organisms and their wild counterparts i.e., hybridization between artificial organisms and their wild counterparts.
2. Pesticide Pollution—many artificially selected crops lack the genetic variability to resist new pests and, as a result, pesticide use has increased in some cases. Therefore, while artificial selection attempts to increase pest resistance in some crops against certain known pests, it cannot protect all crops against threats from potential unknown pests.
3. Loss of Genetic Variability - when organisms from wild populations are used to create artificially selected organisms, genetic variation is inadvertently lost from the wild parent population forever.

2. OR

Insect populations develop resistance to insecticides through the process of natural selection. Some individuals within the population have random genetic mutations that confer insecticide resistance. The mutated individuals have an advantage because they are able to adapt to the changing environmental conditions imposed by the insecticide application. Only those individuals within the population that have the mutation will survive and successfully reproduce. In this manner, changing environmental conditions influence the reproductive success of the organisms by ensuring that only individuals that are able to adapt will reproduce. Eventually, gene frequencies within the population will change until most of the insects in the population carry the mutation and are resistant to the insecticide. This is because those insects that did not have the mutation died before having the chance to reproduce and therefore did not contribute their genes to the population's gene pool. If no individuals within the population carried a mutation conferring insecticide resistance, the entire population would be vulnerable to extinction.

3. D

Convergent evolution is the evolution and development of similar traits by unrelated groups of organisms because of a common adaptation.
An example is the similar body shape shared by sharks and dolphins. Both groups of organisms have adapted to an aquatic lifestyle and so they display similar features such as streamlined bodies and fins for motion. However, these two groups of organisms are highly unrelated given that sharks belong to a group of cartilagenous fish in the class Chondrichthyes, whereas dolphins belong to a group of aquatic mammals called cetaceans in the class Mammalia.

4. D

The Galapagos Islands are home to 13 species of Darwin's finches. These birds originated on the mainland. They resemble the mainland finches in general body pattern, but their food habits and a number of physical features are different from mainland finches.

The different islands of the Galapagos provided different environmental conditions and food sources. As such, Darwin's finches serve as an example of divergent evolution, because they diversified under different environmental selection pressures. They serve as an example of microevolution because they demonstrate phenotypic variability as a result of adaptation to different food resources. They are also an example of macroevolution because they demonstrate speciation from a single mainland ancestor.

Darwin's finches do not serve as an example of convergent evolution because their similarities are the result of a high degree of relatedness, not an adaptation to a common environmental pressure.

5. a) OR

Darwin observed that species produce more offspring than can survive, live to maturity, and reproduce. Therefore, there is a competition for existence in which only the fittest survive. He also observed that there were variations in physical traits within species. He concluded that an organism that has physical traits that give it an advantage in a particular environment over other similar organisms would help that organism survive and reproduce. This will also give a similar advantage to its offspring born with the same traits. Conversely, as organisms with this advantage become more numerous, it becomes less likely that organisms without this advantage will survive and reproduce.

For example, monarch butterflies lay their eggs on a variety of plants. By chance, one plant happens to be the milkweed. The caterpillars that consume the milkweed leaves obtain the alkaloids and, in turn, are found to be distasteful to the predators.
These predators learn to recognize the monarch and avoid it in future encounters. The caterpillars that do not obtain the alkaloids are mostly likely eaten by the predators.

b) OR

Benefits:

- Constant milkweed availability ensures breeding can occur.
- Monarchs can utilize a food source that other animals cannot.
- Accumulating the alkaloids can deter attacks by predators.

Costs:

- The trip is long, and many butterflies will die before completing it.
- Sudden cold spells could kill off milkweed before eggs hatch.
- An absence of milkweed would require farther migration and more risk.

c) OR

Because of its similar markings and appearance to the monarch butterfly, viceroy butterflies are not preyed upon by predators that believe they are monarchs. Once a predator has had an experience with the monarch butterfly, it learns to recognize its appearance and to avoid it during future encounters. The viceroy is then also avoided because of its close resemblance to the monarch even though it is safe to eat. Thus, it is spared from predators.

If viceroy caterpillars emerge from their cocoons prior to the monarch, the results could be harmful to the viceroy. The best time for a viceroy adult to emerge from a cocoon is after the emergence of the adult monarch butterfly. This gives time for predators to be exposed to the monarch butterfly and experience its effects and be able to make a correlation between the butterfly and what occurs when it is eaten. Thus, predators that avoid monarchs will also avoid viceroys.

Any other appropriate advantage or disadvantage may also be accepted.

6. D

Two populations of a species will become reproductively isolated if separated by geographical barriers. This results from differences in selection pressures in their new habitats and the accumulation of variations in their gene pool.

7. B

In Lamarck's hypothesis of use and disuse of organs, the heart should increase in size because of its constant beating. However, this has not occurred in any organism; therefore, this example does not favour the given hypothesis.

8. 35241

The principle of use and disuse is attributed to Jean-Baptiste Lamarck (3), who proposed that through the use and disuse of specific body parts, organisms would acquire characteristics that specifically suited them to their particular environments and that those acquired characteristics would subsequently be passed on to their offspring. Charles Lyell (5) was a geologist whose work provided evidence for a much older geological Earth and lent support to the ideas of uniformitarianism and gradualism. Charles Darwin (2) is credited with proposing the theory of natural selection, the idea that those organisms possessing traits that give them an adaptive advantage in their environments are better able to adapt, survive, and successfully reproduce. Thomas Malthus (4) devoted his research to human population growth and the struggle for existence, which occurs when the population growth rate outpaces food production. Punctuated equilibrium is a theory on evolution proposed by Gould and Eldredge (1) that suggests that speciation occurs in relatively quick bursts of change that disrupt long periods of evolutionary stability.

The correct response is 3, 5, 2, 4, 1.

9. 1235

Darwin's theory of evolution states that in the struggle for existence, phenotypic variability plays a role in differential reproductive success, and leads to survival of the fittest, which ultimately results in natural selection. Therefore the factors that are related to Darwin's theory of evolution are 1, 2, 3, and 5.

Genotypic equilibrium is associated with Hardy-Weinberg. Punctuated equilibrium is associated with Eldredge-Gould. Inheritance of acquired characteristics is associated with Lamarck.

10. OR

The peppered moth exists as two different morphs: a light-coloured morph with dark flecks and a dark-coloured morph. Historically, the light-coloured morph was more common because it was better camouflaged as it rested on the trunks of light-coloured trees and lichens, and was therefore more likely to avoid predation than its dark-coloured counterpart. During the industrial revolution the increase in pollution resulted in the death of many lichens and the darkening of tree trunks by soot. As a result, the dark-coloured morph gained the camouflage advantage by becoming selected-for as it was now more likely to avoid predation. A shift in number occurred as more dark-coloured moths successfully survived, reproduced and passed more of the dark-coloured trait to the next generation relative to the light-coloured trait which was now more susceptible to predation and therefore less likely to survive and reproduce.

11. OR

1. Allopatric
2. Sympatric
3. Phyletic

Allopatric speciation requires geographic isolation of two or more populations from each other so that they can no longer interbreed. This can lead to the development of one or more new species and may or may not lead to the extinction of the parent species.

Sympatric speciation does not require geographic isolation and in fact results from reproductive isolation of a small group of individuals within the same geographic region as the parent species. It usually leads to the development of a new species alongside the parent species.

Phyletic speciation results from the speciation of the entire species due to changing environmental conditions acting on the entire group. Phyletic speciation results in the extinction of the parent species.

12. C

When the northern elephant seal was hunted to near extinction in the 19th century, the population was reduced to a small number of individuals, significantly decreasing the gene pool. This sudden population decrease, which results in lower genetic variation, is called the bottleneck effect. The founder effect refers to a small group of individuals leaving one population to start another. Random breeding would not decrease genetic variation, and the conditions of Hardy–Weinberg equilibrium are not being met.

13. B

Scientists take advantage of natural genetic variations to improve the quality of domesticated plants and animals. They select the individuals with desired characteristics and separate them from those that do not have such characteristics. The selected individuals are then interbred. This process is called artificial selection. If the process is repeated for many generations, a new breed with the desired characters is produced.

When members of the same species or different species struggle and compete for common resources, the organisms that possess the most favourable variations survive. This is called natural selection. Recombinant DNA technology is the process by which the genetic makeup of an organism is modified with genes that it would not contain naturally. Genetic drift is the mechanism of evolutionary change that occurs when gene frequencies shift in a population randomly, without influence by human or environmental selection pressures.

Genetic Processes

GENETIC PROCESSES

Table of Correlations

	Specific Expectation	Practice Questions	Unit Test Questions	Practice Test 1	Practice Test 2
11.4.D1	evaluate the importance of some recent contributions to our knowledge of genetic processes, and analyse social and ethical implications of genetic and genomic research				
11.4.D1.1	*analyse, on the basis of research, some of the social and ethical implications of research in genetics and genomics*	19	1		
11.4.D1.2	*evaluate, on the basis of research, the importance of some recent contributions to knowledge, techniques, and technologies related to genetic processes*	18	2		
11.4.D2	investigate genetic processes, including those that occur during meiosis, and analyse data to solve basic genetics problems involving monohybrid and dihybrid crosses				
11.4.D2.1	*use appropriate terminology related to genetic processes, including, but not limited to: haploid, diploid, spindle, synapsis, gamete, zygote, heterozygous, homozygous, allele, plasmid, trisomy, non-disjunction, and somatic cell*	11, 12	3, 4	37, 38	39, 40
11.4.D2.2	*investigate the process of meiosis, using a microscope or similar instrument, or a computer simulation, and draw biological diagrams to help explain the main phases in the process*	10	5		
11.4.D2.3	*use the Punnett square method to solve basic genetics problems involving monohybrid crosses, incomplete dominance, codominance, dihybrid crosses, and sex-linked genes*	14, 15	6, 7	39, 40	41, 42
11.4.D2.4	*investigate, through laboratory inquiry or computer simulation, monohybrid and dihybrid crosses, and use the Punnett square method and probability rules to analyse the qualitative and quantitative data and determine the parent genotype*	13a, 13b	8	41, 42	43, 44
11.4.D3	demonstrate an understanding of concepts, processes, and technologies related to the transmission of hereditary characteristics				
11.4.D3.1	*explain the phases in the process of meiosis in terms of cell division, the movement of chromosomes, and crossing over of genetic material*	7, 8, 9	9	43, 44	45
11.4.D3.2	*explain the concepts of DNA, genes, chromosomes, alleles, mitosis, and meiosis, and how they account for the transmission of hereditary characteristics according to Mendelian laws of inheritance*	4, 5	10, 11	45, 46	46, 47, 48
11.4.D3.3	*explain the concepts of genotype, phenotype, dominance, incomplete dominance, codominance, recessiveness, and sex linkage according to Mendelian laws of inheritance*	1, 2, 3	12, 13	47, 48	49, 50
11.4.D3.4	*describe some genetic disorders caused by chromosomal abnormalities or other genetic mutations in terms of chromosomes affected, physical effects, and treatments*	6	14	49	51
11.4.D3.5	*describe some reproductive technologies, and explain how their use can increase the genetic diversity of a species*	16, 17	15, 16	50	52

11.4.D3.3 explain the concepts of genotype, phenotype, dominance, incomplete dominance, codominance, recessiveness, and sex linkage according to Mendelian laws of inheritance

11.4.D3.2 explain the concepts of DNA, genes, chromosomes, alleles, mitosis, and meiosis, and how they account for the transmission of hereditary characteristics according to Mendelian laws of inheritance

Mendel's Laws of Heredity

Often referred to as the "father of genetics," Gregor Mendel was an Austrian monk who studied pea plants to examine how traits are passed from generation to generation. By conducting breeding experiments that focused on one or two clearly identifiable traits, Mendel discovered that traits were always passed from parent to offspring in a certain manner. Specifically, he determined that there are alternate forms of a trait, or different **alleles** for each gene, that can be passed from parent to offspring. These observations led him to the conclusion that during sexual reproduction, an individual organism inherits two alleles: one allele from each parent. Although both alleles code for the same trait, heterozygous individuals receive an allele from one parent that is different from the allele inherited from the other parent, while homozygous individuals inherit the same allele from each parent. The particular combination of alleles that an organism inherits is referred to as its **genotype**.

During Mendel's experiments with pea plants, he noted occurrences of dominance and recessiveness when he observed that one characteristic, such as round seeds often dominated another characteristic, such as wrinkled seeds. He examined this by crossing a homozygous dominant round seed plant (*RR*) with a homozygous recessive wrinkled seed plant (*rr*). All offspring exhibited heterozygous round seeds (*Rr*), which allowed him to determine that the influence of the recessive allele (wrinkles) on an organism's **phenotype**, or observable characteristics, were masked by the dominant allele (roundness).

Since Mendel's time, different modes of inheritance have been identified that follow simple Mendelian genetics.

Codominance

Codominance occurs when one trait is equally dominant to another trait. For example, a red-haired bull (H^RH^R) that breeds with a white-haired cow (H^WH^W) will produce a calf that is roan-haired, that is it has both red and white hair (H^RH^W).

Incomplete Dominance

Incomplete dominance occurs when there is a blending of traits. For example, a red snapdragon (C^RC^R) crossed with a white snapdragon (C^WC^W) will produce offspring that are all pink (C^RC^W).

Sex Linkage

Sex linkage is characterized by the expression of a trait in one sex more than the other. For example, colorblindness is a trait that is much more common in males than it is in females. That is because a mother who carries the allele for this recessive sex-linked trait (X^CX^c) will pass on either an X^C or an X^c to her son. The son will receive a Y chromosome from his father that will not mask the effect of this gene. He may end up having normal vision (X^CY) or being colorblind (X^cY). If the father has normal vision (X^CY), all his daughters will have normal vision because they will inherit the allele X^C. If their mother is heterozygous for this allele (X^CX^c), the daughters will end up being either homozygous for normal vision (X^CX^C) or a carrier of the colorblind allele (X^CX^c).

Transmission of Hereditary Characteristics

The underlying biological mechanisms that explain Mendel's laws of inheritance were not understood until many years later. However, it is now known that every living organism on this planet is made up of one or more cells. Each cell contains a control centre called the nucleus (with a few exceptions including bacteria, which only contain a nucleoid and enucleated red blood cells). The chromosomes are found within the nucleus. Each **chromosome** contains hundreds or even thousands of segments called **genes**. The genes are made up of DNA (deoxyribonucleic acid) and contain all the genetic information necessary to build an organism. Hereditary characteristics are determined by an organism's genes, which are transmitted from parent to offspring and generation to generation.

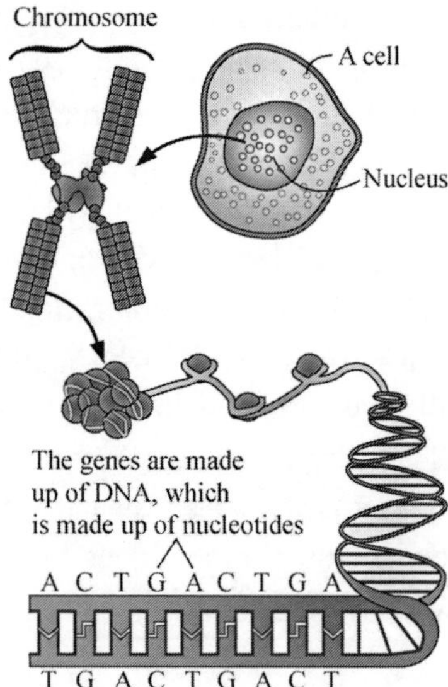

Genetic building blocks

The Mitotic Cell Cycle

Mitosis is the process of cellular division responsible for the growth and development of living things. It is also the process by which new cells are formed to replace cells lost during the many activities that occur every day. For example, skin cells and hair cells undergo rapid cell division. An embryo developing in the womb can easily achieve over 100 million cell divisions per second. Therefore, organisms depend upon mitotic cell division to ensure that life processes, such as growth, development, repair, and reproduction, continue throughout their life.

The cell cycle consists of two stages: interphase and mitosis. Only 10% of the cell cycle is spent dividing and undergoing mitosis. Ninety percent of the time, during interphase, a cell is growing, metabolizing nutrients to produce energy, replicating DNA, and performing various other cellular functions. This diagram depicts a cell cycle.

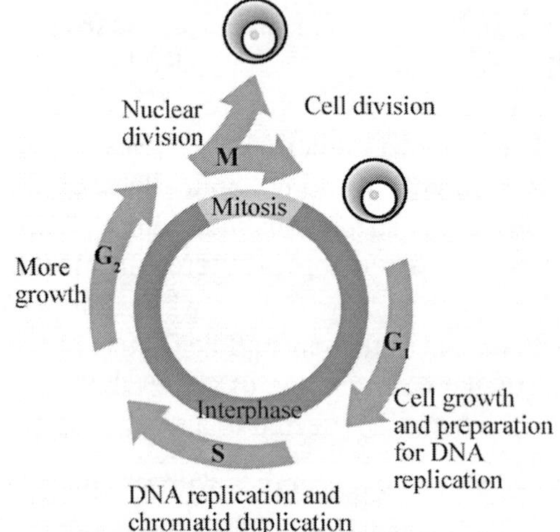

Interphase

Interphase is divided into three distinct phases. The cell enters the first stage of interphase, known as the Gap 1 (G_1) phase, once the cell has completed mitosis. The cell begins to grow and prepare itself for DNA replication. The cell produces proteins and enzymes that are necessary to replicate DNA.

The next phase is the synthesis (S) phase of interphase. Proteins and enzymes replicate DNA found in one chromatid to produce a duplicate chromatid. This ensures that mitosis begins with paired chromosomes, each consisting of two identical chromatids (called sister chromatids) attached together at the centromere. The cell continues growing in this phase.

During Gap 2 (G_2), the cell begins its preparations for mitosis. Chemical switches determine if the DNA has been properly replicated and if the cell is ready to divide. Depending upon the condition checks performed by these chemical switches, the cell either enters the M (mitosis) stage or a cell death stage called apoptosis.

If DNA has been properly replicated, mitosis (M) occurs.

Mitosis

Mitosis is the mechanism that allows the nuclei of cells to split and provide each daughter cell with a complete set of chromosomes during cellular division.

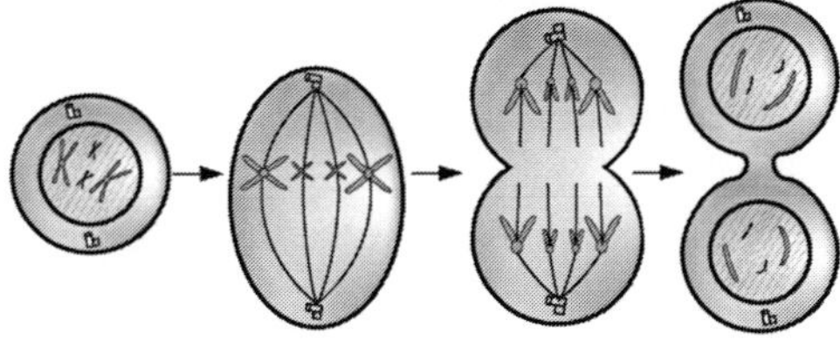

Prophase Metaphase Anaphase Telophase

The first phase of mitosis is known as **prophase**. During prophase, chromosomes thicken and condense, the nuclear membrane disappears, and spindle fibres begin to radiate from the **centrioles**. One centriole begins moving toward one pole of the cell, and the other centriole moves to the opposite pole.

The next phase is called **metaphase**. Paired chromosomes line up at the **equatorial plate** (midline of the cell), and spindle fibres radiating from the centrioles attach to the **centromere** of each paired chromosome.

During **anaphase**, the spindle fibres shorten, and the paired chromosomes separate to become individual chromosomes. Each paired chromosome is made up of two identical **sister chromatids**. When the chromatids split from each other, they become individual chromosomes. Each individual chromosome contains the same genetic information as the sister it split from.

During the late phase of mitosis, called **telophase**, an important event called **cytokinesis** occurs. The cytoplasm divides, and two daughter cells are produced. The nuclear membrane reforms, and the chromosomes decondense. After telophase is completed, the cell cycle continues, and each daughter cell is ready to enter the G_1 phase of interphase.

Use the following information to answer the next question.

> Phenylketonuria is a disorder of the liver enzyme phenylalanine hydroxylase. The offspring belonging to a female with the disorder and a male without the disorder are all **unaffected**.

1. Phenylketonuria is a disorder that is caused by

A. an X-linked gene

B. a co-dominant gene

C. an autosomal dominant gene

D. an autosomal recessive gene

Use the following information to answer the next question.

> *T* represents the tall characteristics, and *t* represents the dwarf characteristics of a pea plant. A tall pea plant can possess either the heterozygous genotype *Tt* or the homozygous genotype *TT*.

2. The allele that *T* represents is

A. codominant **B.** sex-linked

C. dominant **D.** recessive

Use the following information to answer the next question.

In humans, blood type is determined by a combination of alleles that can be either co-dominant or that demonstrate a dominant-recessive relationship.

Numerical Response

3. What is the number of alleles used to determine the four human blood group phenotypes? 3

4. Cytokinesis is the process in which the cytoplasm divides to form two individual daughter cells. Cytokinesis begins during

A. prophase **B.** anaphase

C. telophase **D.** metaphase

5. Genes are composed of a molecule that is transmitted from each generation to the next and is responsible for the inheritance of characteristics. This molecule is called

A. RNA **B.** DNA

C. tRNA **D.** mRNA

11.4.D3.4 describe some genetic disorders caused by chromosomal abnormalities or other genetic mutations in terms of chromosomes affected, physical effects, and treatments

11.4.D2.1 use appropriate terminology related to genetic processes, including, but not limited to: haploid, diploid, spindle, synapsis, gamete, zygote, heterozygous, homozygous, allele, plasmid, trisomy, non-disjunction, and somatic cell

11.4.D2.2 investigate the process of meiosis, using a microscope or similar instrument, or a computer simulation, and draw biological diagrams to help explain the main phases in the process

11.4.D3.1 explain the phases in the process of meiosis in terms of cell division, the movement of chromosomes, and crossing over of genetic material

Meiosis and Genetic Disorders

Meiosis is the cell division process responsible for dividing the cell chromosome number in half and producing gametes. It occurs in a number of steps that involve the replication and separation of chromosomes. Genetic disorders can result if an error occurs during replication of the genetic material or while chromosomes are separating and migrating into their respective new cells.

Meiosis

Meiotic cell division takes place within the **germ cells** of diploid organisms. Depending on the type of organism, it results in the formation of either **gametes** (sperm and ova) or spores. It is different from mitotic cell division, which takes place in the **somatic cells** of an organism and results in the formation of all other cell types.

Meiotic cell division occurs in two main steps:

1. Interphase
2. Meiosis

Interphase

During interphase, the cell prepares for the first stage of meiosis (meiosis I) as the DNA of individual chromosomes replicates and the chromosomes begin migrating to join with their homologous partner.

Each homologous pair consists of two replicated chromosomes: one paired chromosome from the father and one paired chromosome from the mother.

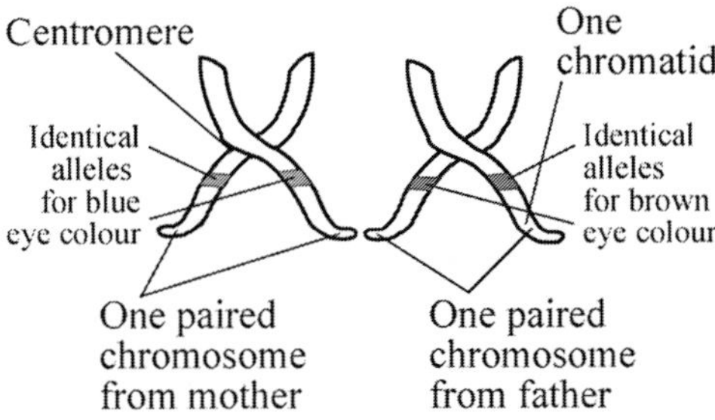

A homologous pair of replicated chromosomes

Each of the paired chromosomes in turn consist of two **chromatids**. Each homologous pair, therefore, consists of four chromatids and is referred to as a **tetrad**. Each chromatid of the paired chromosomes consists of the same genes. Additionally, the paired chromosomes from the mother and father are the same shape and size, and the sequence of their gene loci are perfectly aligned. However, the allele on the paired chromosome from the mother may be different than the allele for that same gene loci on the father's chromosomes. If the two corresponding alleles are the same, then the individual is said to be **homozygous** at that gene loci. If the alleles are different, then the individual is said to be **heterozygous**. It is the different combinations of alleles present on the chromosomes that determine an organism's unique genotype. When a paired chromosome splits during meiosis II, its chromatids become separated. It is at this point that they are once again referred to as individual chromosomes.

After interphase, the cell is **diploid** (2n) because it contains 46 paired chromosomes.

Meiosis I

There are four phases of meiosis I:

- Prophase I
- Metaphase I
- Anaphase I
- Telophase I

During prophase I, homologous pairs synapse (one paired chromosome from the mother and one paired chromosome from the father), forming a tetrad that undergoes **crossing over**. Crossing over occurs when sections of DNA (alleles) are exchanged between adjacent non-sister chromatids. This is referred to as **recombination**. It is the combined effects of recombination and sexual reproduction that are primarily responsible for the wide genetic variability observed in eukaryotes.

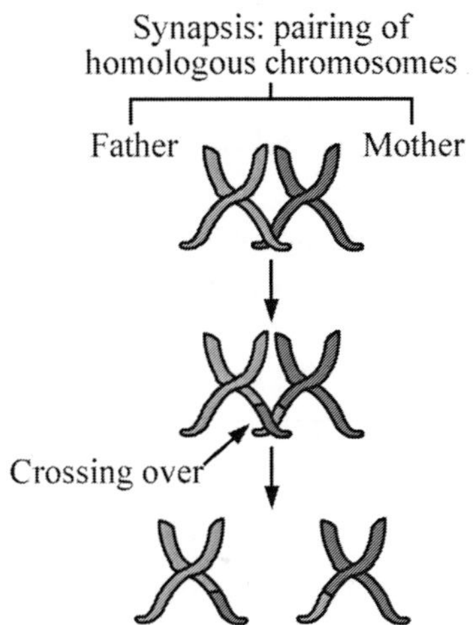

Synapsis, crossing over and recombination

In metaphase I, the homologous pairs line themselves up at the equatorial plate, and spindle fibres radiating from centrioles at opposite poles of the cell attach to the centromere. During anaphase I, the spindle fibres contract and shorten, causing the homologous pairs to separate. This pulling apart ensures that the two cells resulting from meiosis I will each have a total of 23 paired chromosomes. During telophase I, cytokinesis is completed, and two separate **haploid** (half of its original diploid number, or 1n) cells are produced.

Meiosis I

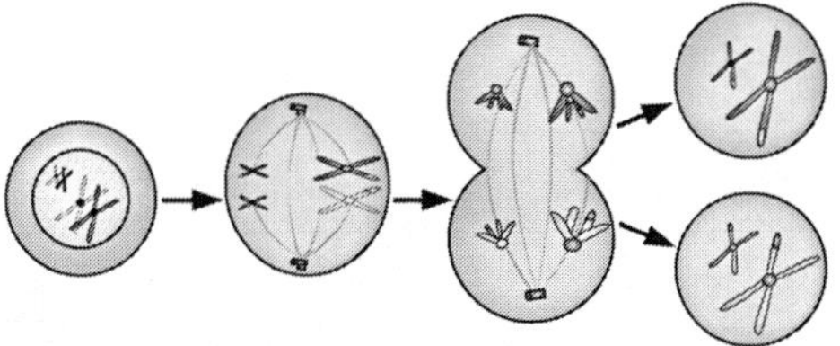

Meiosis II

There are four phases of meiosis II:

- Prophase II
- Metaphase II
- Anaphase II
- Telophase II

During prophase II, the 23 paired chromosomes condense and become distinct. In metaphase II, these paired chromosomes line up at the equatorial plate, and their centromeres attach to spindle fibres radiating from centrioles. During anaphase II, the spindle fibres contract and shorten, and the two chromatids of the paired chromosomes separate and become individual chromosomes. Finally, during telophase II, cytokinesis is completed, and four daughter cells are produced, each with 23 individual chromosomes. Each cell still contains only 23 chromosomes, so the cell remains haploid (1n).

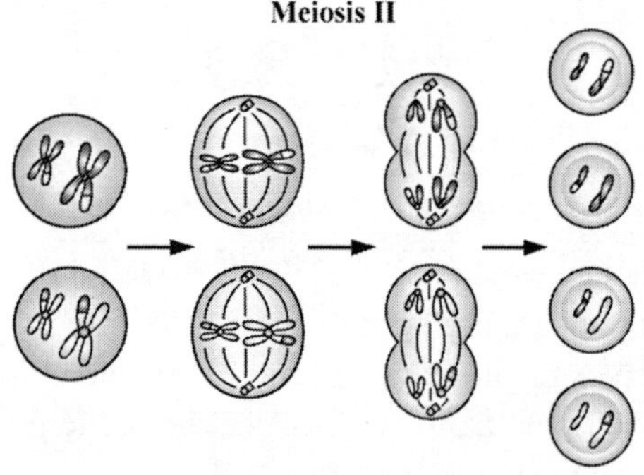

Mitosis

1 daughter cell has 46 chromosomes

Meiosis

1 daughter cell will have 23 chromosomes (4 daughter cells in total)

The entire process of meiotic cell division is summarized in this diagram.

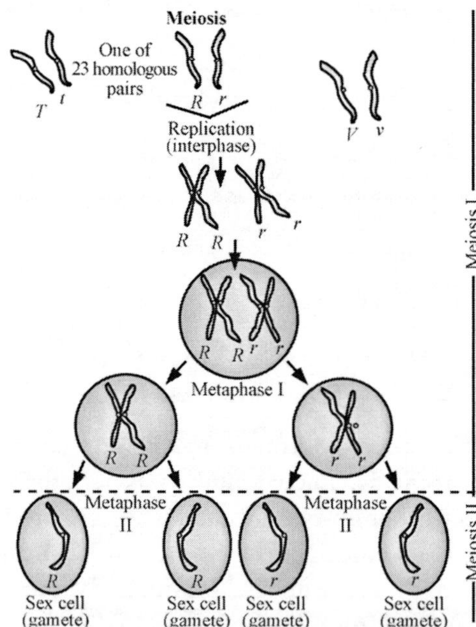

Homologous pairs separate during meiosis I, and sister chromatids separate during meiosis II.

During sexual reproduction, the haploid (1n) cells or gametes from two parents fuse during fertilization in order to create a diploid (2n) **zygote**. If during either meiosis I or II the homologous chromosomes or sister chromatids fail to separate properly, it is referred to as **nondisjunction**.
A nondisjunction event can result in the formation of a zygote with an odd number of chromosomes, which can lead to a number of different genetic disorders. Genetic disorders may also be in response to a defective gene resulting from a mutation that occurred during replication.

Genetic Disorders

Down syndrome and cystic fibrosis provide two different examples of genetic disorders.

Down syndrome is a genetic disorder caused by an extra chromosome 21 (trisomy 21). Instead of having 46 paired chromosomes, a child with Down syndrome will have 46 paired chromosomes plus one extra unpaired chromosomes, resulting in 47 chromosomes total. This is a result of nondisjunction (failure to separate properly) of paired chromosomes during meiosis I or sister chromatids during meiosis II.

Karotype: Down Syndrome (Trisomy 21)

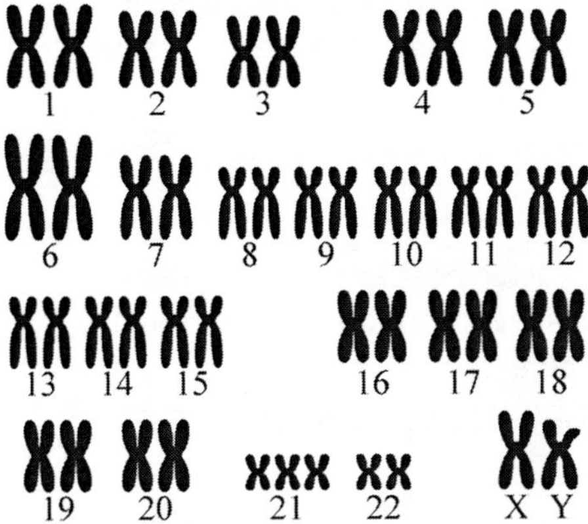

The physical effects include decreased cognitive ability, impaired physical growth, and distinct facial characteristics, such as slanted, almond-shaped eyes. Although there is no treatment for Down syndrome, there are many educational programs that help develop cognitive skills and numerous medications that can help counter health problems they may have.

Cystic fibrosis (CF) is a genetic disorder that affects the lungs and digestive system. It is caused by a defective gene (called the CFTR gene) found on chromosome 7. This gene causes the body to produce sticky, thick mucus that can obstruct the lungs and cause life-threatening lung infections. This thick mucus also causes obstructions in the pancreas. This prevents the passage of enzymes, which are essential to the breakdown of food, and as a result, the body becomes deprived of nutrients. Although there is no complete cure for CF, there are drugs that help clear the mucus from the airways, allowing individuals to breathe normally and lead more active lives.

Use the following information to answer the next question.

Turner syndrome is a genetic disorder that affects females. The characteristic features present in affected individuals include short stature, webbed neck, shield-like chest, and sterility.

6. Which abnormality of the X chromosome results in Turner syndrome?

A. Trisomy

B. Monosomy

C. Deletion of long arm

D. Deletion of short arm

7. During meiosis, four cells with non-identical chromosomes are produced. The recombination of genetic material occurs in

A. metaphase II **B.** metaphase I

C. prophase II **D.** prophase I

8. Which of the following statements about linked genes is **true**?

A. Linked genes do not undergo crossing over.

B. Linked genes do not segregate independently.

C. Linked genes give a phenotypic ratio of 9:3:3:1 in a dihybrid cross.

D. Linked genes undergo crossing over more frequently than unlinked genes.

Use the following information to answer the next question.

Three Stages of Meiosis

1. Metaphase II
2. Anaphase I
3. Anaphase II

Numerical Response

9. Match each of the given descriptors with the numbered stage of meiosis to which it applies. (Record your answer as a three-digit number.)

Descriptor	Numbered Stage of Meiosis
Separation of sister chromatids	______
Separation of homologous chromosomes	______
Attachment of spindle fibres to the chromosomes	______

Use the following information to answer the next question.

Some vocabulary words of meiosis are shown.

1. centromere
2. sister chromatids
3. chromatin
4. homologous chromosomes

Numerical Response

10. A student is examining the phases of meiosis using a microscope. He uses the following descriptions to explain what he sees for each slide. Match each descriptor with the numbered term that it **best** describes.

Tangled uncoiled strands of DNA	______
A duplicated chromosome	______
Structure that attaches chromatids together is attached to spindle fibers	______
Paired chromosomes lined up at equatorial plate	______

11. Alternate forms of the same gene are known as

A. alleles **B.** gametes
C. genotypes **D.** heterozygotes

12. The pairing of homologous chromosomes that occurs during meiosis is also known as

A. non-disjunction
B. monosomy
C. synapsis
D. trisomy

11.4.D2.4 investigate, through laboratory inquiry or computer simulation, monohybrid and dihybrid crosses, and use the Punnett square method and probability rules to analyse the qualitative and quantitative data and determine the parent genotype

11.4.D2.3 use the Punnett square method to solve basic genetics problems involving monohybrid crosses, incomplete dominance, codominance, dihybrid crosses, and sex-linked genes

Genetic Crosses Using the Punnett Method

In order to predict the outcome of various genetic crosses, it is useful to use the Punnett method. The Punnett method uses the Punnett square to find the outcome of a particular genetic cross. The gametes of each parent are found across the top row and far left column of the table. The parent's gametes are used to find the genotype of the offspring. The following examples of genetic crosses use a Punnett square to help predict the genotype of the offspring.

Codominance

Codominance occurs when both alleles in a heterozygous individual are expressed equally.

In humans, blood type is determined by alleles that are codominant $(I^A$ and $I^B)$ and the allele *i*, which is recessive to I^A and I^B.

Example

If a mother with type AB blood (genotype I^AI^B) marries a man with type B blood (genotype I^Bi), the percentage of their offspring that will have type O (*ii*) blood can be determined.

The parental (P) generation cross is $I^AI^B \times I^Bi$. The mother can contribute the allele I^A or the allele I^B to her offspring. The father can contribute the allele I^B or the allele *i* to his offspring.

Parental Gametes	I^A	I^B
I^B	I^AI^B	I^BI^B
i	I^Ai	I^Bi

The Punnett square indicates that 25% of the offspring have the genotype I^AI^B, so they have type AB blood. Another 25% of the offspring have the genotype I^Ai, so they have type A blood (recall that I^A is dominant to *i*). The remaining 50% of the offspring will have type B blood because genotypes I^BI^B and I^Bi both represent type B blood (recall that I^B is dominant to *i*). None of the offspring have the genotype *ii*, which means that 0% of the offspring will have type O blood.

Sex-Linked Genes

Sex-linked traits occur due to morphological differences between the sex chromosomes resulting in the alleles located on the X and Y chromosomes not always being equally paired. As such, an allele for a particular trait may be located on one sex chromosome (typically the X) but not the other. Since these sex-linked genes do not always have paired alleles, their expression is slightly different than autosomal genes and will be dependent on an individual's phenotypic sex.

A common example of a sex-linked trait is eye colour in fruit flies.

Example

In fruit flies, the wild type or red-eyed allele (X^R) is dominant to the recessive white-eyed allele (X^r).

If a red-eyed female (X^RX^R) is crossed with a white-eyed male (X^rY), the percentage of their offspring that will be red-eyed males can be determined.

The parental generation cross is $X^RX^R \times X^rY$. The female fruit fly can only contribute one allele to all of her offspring, which is X^R. The male fruit fly can contribute the allele X^r or the chromosome Y to his offspring.

Parental Gametes	X^R
X^r	X^RX^r
Y	X^RY

The Punnett square shows that 50% of the offspring are red-eyed males $(X^R Y)$. The other 50% of the offspring are heterozygous red-eyed females $(X^R X^r)$. Every female carries the white-eyed allele. None of the males are carriers for the white-eyed allele.

Incomplete Dominance

Incomplete dominance is a phenotypic expression that occurs when neither of the alleles is dominant, and the heterozygous individuals express a third phenotypic trait that is intermediate between the two homozygous parental varieties. A common example is petal colour in carnations.

Example

A red flower parent (*RR*) crossed with a white flower parent (*WW*) produces an F_1 generation that is completely heterozygous (*RW*), all of which express a pink flower.
parental generation: $RR \times WW$

Parental Gametes	*W*	*W*
R	*RW*	*RW*
R	*RW*	*RW*

A second cross between the F_1 hybrids reveals that the alleles for red and white still exist independently within the heterozygous individuals as the reappearance of all three phenotypes occurs in the F_2 generation.
F_1 hybrid cross: $RW \times RW$

F_1 Gametes	*R*	*W*
R	*RR*	*RW*
W	*RW*	*WW*

The F_2 generation results in both a phenotypic and genotypic ratio of 1 RR:2 RW:1 WW. This can also be expressed as 25% of the offspring have red flowers, 50% have pink flowers, and 25% have white flowers.

Using the rules of probability, it is also possible to work in reverse, determining the parent genotype from the phenotypic ratios observed in the first and second generations of a given cross.

Monohybrid Cross

A monohybrid cross can be used to follow the inheritance of a single trait from parents to offspring.

Example

A pea plant that displays dominant purple flowers (parent 1 genotype: either *PP* or *Pp*) is crossed with a pea plant that displays recessive white flowers (parent 2 genotype: *pp*). The exact genotype of parent 1 can be determined from the offspring's characteristics.

The observed phenotypic ratios of the offspring are as follows:

- F_1 generation: 100% of the plants have purple flowers.
- F_2 generation: 75% of the plants have purple flowers, and 25% have white flowers (3:1 dominant to recessive ratio).

Since 100% of the F_1 generation display the dominant trait of purple flowers, and it is known that parent 2 displayed the recessive trait (*pp*), then it follows that parent 1 must be homozygous dominant (*PP*). This is because if parent 1 were heterozygous (*Pp*), some of the plants in the F_1 generation would have displayed the recessive white flowers (*pp*).

This can be illustrated by comparing the two alternative monohybrid crosses
Cross 1: $Pp \times pp$

Parental Gametes	*P*	*p*
p	*Pp*	*pp*
p	*Pp*	*pp*

In the F_1 generation, 50% of the offspring have purple flowers (*Pp*) and 50% have white flowers (*pp*).

Cross 2: $PP \times pp$

Parental Gametes	*P*	*P*
p	*Pp*	*Pp*
p	*Pp*	*Pp*

In the F_1 generation, 100% of the offspring have purple flowers (*Pp*). To confirm this finding, the monohybrid cross can be applied to the F_2 generation. Since 100% of the F_1 generation were determined to have the genotype *Pp*, the cross would be as follows:
Pp × *Pp*

F_1 Gametes	*P*	*p*
P	*PP*	*Pp*
p	*Pp*	*pp*

In this cross, 75% of the plants will have purple flowers (*PP* and *Pp*) and 25% will have white flowers (*pp*), giving a 3:1 ratio. The F_2 generation produces the expected phenotypic ratio of 3:1 dominant to recessive traits and a corresponding genotypic ratio of 1:2:1 (*PP*:*Pp*:*pp*).

Dihybrid Cross

A dihybrid cross can be used to follow the inheritance of two traits from parents to offspring.

Example
A pea plant that displays dominant yellow and round seeds (parent 1 genotype: either *YYRR*, *YYRr*, *YyRr*, or *YyRR*) is crossed with a pea plant that displays recessive green and wrinkled seeds (parent 2 genotype: *yyrr*). The exact genotype of parent 1 can be determined from the offspring's characteristics.

The observed phenotypic ratios of the offspring are as follows:

- F_1 generation: 100% of the plants have yellow and round seeds.
- F_2 generation: 56.25% of the plants have yellow rounded seeds, 18.75% of the plants have yellow wrinkled seeds, 18.75% of the plants have green rounded seeds, and 6.25% of the plants have green wrinkled seeds (9:3:3:1).

Since 100% of the F_1 generation display the dominant yellow and round seed traits and it is known that parent 2 displayed the recessive traits (*yyrr*), then it follows that parent 1 must be homozygous dominant (*YYRR*). This is because if parent 1 were heterozygous for either seed shape, colour, or both (*Yy*, *Rr*), then some of the plants in the F_1 generation would have displayed the recessive wrinkled seed shape, or green colour, or both (*Yyrr*,*yyRr*, or *yyrr*).

This can be illustrated by comparing the alternative dihybrid crosses:
Cross 1: *YYRr* × *yyrr*

Parental Gametes	*YR*	*Yr*
yr	*YyRr*	*Yyrr*

In the F_1 generation, 50% of the offspring have yellow and round seeds (*YyRr*) and 50% have yellow and wrinkled seeds (*Yyrr*).

Cross 2: *YyRR* × *yyrr*

Parental Gametes	*YR*	*yR*
yr	*YyRr*	*yyRr*

In the F_1 generation, 50% of the offspring have yellow and round seeds (*YyRr*) and 50% have green and round seeds (*yyRr*).

Cross 3: *YyRr* × *yyrr*

Parental Gametes	*YR*	*Yr*	*yR*	*yr*
yr	*YyRr*	*Yyrr*	*yyRr*	*yyrr*

In the F_1 generation, 25% of the offspring have yellow round seeds (*YyRr*), 25% have yellow wrinkled seeds (*Yyrr*), 25% have green round seeds (*yyRr*), and 25% have green wrinkled seeds (*yyrr*).

Cross 4: *YYRR* × *yyrr*

Parental Gametes	*YR*	*YR*
yr	*YyRr*	*YyRr*

In the F_1 generation, 100% of the offspring have yellow and round seeds (*YyRr*).

To confirm this finding, the dihybrid cross can be applied to determine the F_2 generation.
Since 100% of the F_1 generation were determined to have the genotype *YyRr*, the cross would be as follows:
YyRr × *YyRr*

F_1 Gametes	YR	Yr	yR	yr
YR	*YYRR*	*YYRr*	*YyRR*	*YyRr*
Yr	*YYRr*	*YYrr*	*YyRr*	*Yyrr*
yR	*yYRR*	*yYRr*	*yyRR*	*yyRr*
yr	*yYrR*	*yYrr*	*yyRr*	*yyrr*

In the F_2 generation, 56.25% of the offspring have yellow round seeds (*YYRR*, *YYRr*, *YyRR*, *YyRr*), 18.75% have yellow wrinkled seeds (*YYrr*, *Yyrr*), 18.75% have green round seeds (*yyRR*, *yyRr*), and 6.25% have green wrinkled seeds (*yyrr*).

The F_2 generation produces the expected phenotypic ratio of 9:3:3:1.

Use the following information to answer the next multipart question.

13. Congenital hypertrichosis is a rare X-linked dominant trait that results in thick hair growth all over the body. A man affected with congenital hypertrichosis ($X^{CH}Y$) and an unaffected woman ($X^{ch}X^{ch}$) plan to have children.

Numerical Response

a) What percentage of the female children will have congenital hypertrichosis? 100 %

b) What percentage of the offspring will inherit congenital hypertrichosis? 50 %

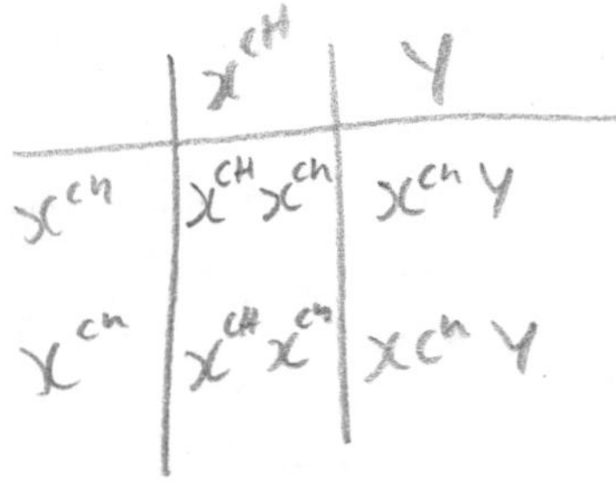

Use the following information to answer the next question.

Hemophilia is a **sex-linked** recessive disorder, carried on the X chromosome.

14. If a hemophilic man marries a woman that is not a carrier of the hemophilia gene, what percentage of the daughters will be carriers of hemophilia?

A. 0% **B.** 25%

C. 50% **D.** 100%

Use the following information to answer the next question.

In humans, the allele for colourblindness is a recessive sex-linked trait located on the X chromosome and is represented by X^c. The dominant gene for normal colour vision is represented by X^C.
The phenotypic expressions for colour vision are as follows:

1. Normal
2. Colourblind
3. Carrier

Marisa is homozygous dominant (X^CX^C) for colour vision. Marisa meets Samson, who has the genotype X^cY. Samson and Marisa marry and decide to have children. Based on their genotypes, they can determine the phenotypic expression for colour vision for any sons or daughters they might have.

Numerical Response

15. Match the individuals with their phenotypic expressions for colour vision. (Record your answer as a four-digit number.)

Individual	Phenotypic Expression Number
Marisa	1
Samson	2
Daughter	3
Son	1

11.4.D3.5 describe some reproductive technologies, and explain how their use can increase the genetic diversity of a species

11.4.D1.1 analyse, on the basis of research, some of the social and ethical implications of research in genetics and genomics

11.4.D1.2 evaluate, on the basis of research, the importance of some recent contributions to knowledge, techniques, and technologies related to genetic processes

Genetic and Reproductive Technologies

Advancements in genetic research have led to developments in gene and reproduction technologies that are aimed at improving people's quality of life. One of the most important accomplishments that has occurred is the mapping of the human genome. Knowing the location of every gene on every chromosome permits for efficient targeting of certain diseases and disorders. Additionally, these new technologies have led to advancements in the areas of genetic screening, genetic engineering, cloning, artificial selection and insemination, and *in vitro* fertilization.

The Human Genome Project

The Human Genome Project was a collaborative international research project that identified all the genes found in human DNA. Consequently, scientists have been able to map the genes responsible for a variety of genetic defects and disorders, such as cystic fibrosis and muscular dystrophy. The knowledge of the precise location of particular genes allows scientists to improve their diagnosis of these and many other genetic disorders. Genetic mapping also aids in the discovery of new technologies to prevent diseases altogether.
For example, gene therapy is the process by which a defective gene is identified and replaced with a normal gene. This type of therapy offers promise as a potential cure for cystic fibrosis, which is an autosomal recessive disease that can be offset with just one normal copy of the implicated gene.

Genetic Screening

Genetic screening can be performed after birth or *in utero* using amniocentesis or chorionic villus sampling. The fluid or tissue sample taken will have chemicals and cells that have come from the fetus. The cells can be used for DNA analysis to conduct genetic screening or to construct a karyotype. Genetic screening provides information about inherited diseases by detecting genetic abnormalities at an early stage of development. The benefit of early detection in many cases allows for preventive treatment measures, improved personal health care management, and informed future reproductive choices.

Genetic Engineering

Genetic engineering is a technology that alters the DNA of an organism. Using recombinant DNA technology, scientists can alter and recombine DNA sequences within organisms to form new DNA sequences that contain genes of interest. This is achieved using restriction enzymes designed to cut specific sequences of DNA. If two different DNA molecules are cut with the same restriction enzymes, they will have complementary ends, which can then be joined by the action of a ligase enzyme. For example, bacteria can be genetically engineered to produce insulin, a compound used to control diabetes. Specifically, bacteria carry an extra-chromosomal DNA molecule called a plasmid that can easily be combined with a gene of interest isolated from another organism. Once reintroduced back into the bacteria, the recombined plasmid will be transcribed and translated as normal, resulting in the expression of the introduced gene, such as insulin production. More recently, recombinant DNA technology has been utilized to create transgenic safflower plants that produce insulin in their seeds. It is predicted that these plants will improve both the quality and quantity of insulin produced for human use while dramatically reducing costs relative to existing insulin-producing technologies.

Genetic engineering technologies are also responsible for the creation of pest-resistant crops. These crops typically have higher yields because they are not as susceptible to pests and help to reduce the use of pesticides, thereby protecting the environment from pollution caused by excessive pesticide use. Recombinant DNA technology increases the genetic diversity of a species by augmenting the organism's natural genetic makeup through the introduction of foreign genes.

Cloning

Cloning is the process of producing an organism that is genetically identical to its parent. It is a natural mode of reproduction in many organisms, such as bacteria and some species of plants and animals. Typically, genetic diversity tends to decrease when organisms are cloned because, unlike sexual reproduction, there is little opportunity for genetic recombination. Occasionally, a mutation can occur in the genome of a clone that better adapts the organism to its particular environment. This type of mutation is passed on to the next generation with increased frequency, and as a result, genetic diversity of the species may increase. One such example is the appearance of antibiotic resistance in some strains of bacteria.

Cloning has become a particularly useful biotechnological technique that can be used to create copies of DNA, cells, and even entire organisms. Some advantages to cloning include the mass production of a particularly effective crop or a particular type of cell used for research, the growth of a specific organ that may help save a life, and the production of new tissue for patients suffering from burn injuries.

Artificial Selection and Insemination

Artificial selection involves intentional breeding to select for the traits that humans find desirable. This early form of biotechnology began with the active selection of plants or animals with characteristics deemed favourable by humans, such as easily harvested wheat or cows that produce more milk. Artificial selection produces genetic diversity, since new varieties of plants and breeds of animals with new genotypes are created for human benefit. However, this diversity is developed without regard for the environmental suitability, and as a result, many of these organisms would quickly die off without human care.

Widely used in the agricultural industry, artificial insemination is a method used to artificially select and reproduce desirable traits. For example, sperm can be collected from a bull with desired characteristics and then inserted into cows with equally desirable traits so that the resulting calves will exhibit a combination of both sets of desirable traits.

In Vitro Fertilization

In vitro fertilization is a method where cells and tissues are cultured and grown in glass petri dishes (the term *in vitro* literally means "in glass"). This gives researchers the opportunity to look more closely at the processes that happen within an organism's body. Additionally, *in vitro* can also be used to facilitate fertilization between a sperm and ovum. A resulting embryo can be implanted into a female's uterus. *In vitro* fertilization promotes the genetic diversity of a species by providing scientists with the ability to create an array of unique genotypes through the union of specific cells with various genetic arrangements in any number of different combinations that may or may not have arisen naturally.

Societal and Ethical Implications Associated with Genetic and Reproductive Technologies

While progress in genetics has resulted in many useful technologies, they are accompanied by much controversy. For example, *in vitro* fertilization and cloning raise social and ethical concerns because they do not represent a natural mode of reproduction in many organisms, including humans.
Some disadvantages to cloning include mass-producing identical organisms without consideration for their resistance to particular diseases or pathogens. As a result, the entire population could potentially be obliterated if subjected to certain stressors. Furthermore, many groups in society are opposed to cloning because they consider it to be against the very nature of how particular organisms should be conceived.
An additional societal concern regarding *in vitro* fertilization is that to ensure pregnancy, multiple embryos are typically implanted in a woman's uterus at one time. This results in a much greater incidence of multiple births, which are considered high risk to the mother and financially difficult for the families involved. Other advancements in gene technologies, such as gene therapy and genetic screening, present a whole suite of ethical and social concerns, including but not limited to procedural costs, potential side effects, religious beliefs, and psychological implications.

Recent biotechnologies, such as recombinant DNA methods, that function to alter the genetic makeup of organisms so that they display genetic modifications that would not have evolved naturally also pose interesting ethical dilemmas.
These genetically modified organisms (GMOs) could interbreed with their non-genetically modified (wild) counterparts, potentially altering the genetic diversity of natural populations.
The potential ramifications that this unnatural shift in genetic variation could have on biodiversity are unforeseeable.

Ethical problems also exist at present in how far researchers should be allowed to venture in developing plant and animal life. Long-term studies have not been performed because these techniques are so new. The applications of genetic engineering are vast. However, the potential for negative consequences exists, so society must behave responsibly when using genetic engineering. Many governments have enacted laws limiting the use of genetic engineering. For example, in Canada, scientists are only allowed to create cloned human cells for medical research purposes.

16. *In vitro* fertilization, cloning, and artificial insemination are methods of reproduction that are grouped into a category called

A. biomagnification

B. biotechnology

C. biogeography

D. biodiversity

Open Response

17. Using examples, describe in terms of **increases** and **decreases** the potential influence that cloning might have on the **genetic diversity** of an organism.

____

____

____

____

____

____

____

Open Response

18. The Human Genome Project has been a massive undertaking that has been responsible for some major steps forward in biological genetics research. Identify the primary purpose of the Human Genome Project and list **two** ways in which the project helps in the battle against genetic disorders.

____

____

____

____

____

____

____

Use the following information to answer the next question.

Charcot-Marie-Tooth disease (CMT) is one of the most common inherited neurological disorders. CMT consists of a group of disorders caused by mutations in genes that affect the normal functions of neurons in the peripheral nervous system. Mutations in one gene can cause demyelination, which is the breakdown of the myelin sheath. Mutations in another gene can cause axonopathy, which is an impairment of axon function. CMT is usually inherited in an autosomal dominant pattern; however, CMT can also be inherited in an autosomal recessive pattern or an X-linked recessive pattern. The different types of CMT are distinguished by inheritance pattern, age of onset, severity of symptoms, and whether the axon or myelin sheath is affected.
Individuals affected with CMT slowly lose motor and sensory function in their feet, legs, hands, and arms as nerves in the extremities degenerate. The muscles in the extremities weaken because of the loss of stimulation by the affected nerves.
The progressive muscular weakening makes fine motor actions of the hands difficult. There is also a loss of sensory nerve function. Most people with CMT have a decreased sensitivity to heat, touch, and pain in the feet and legs.

Diagnosis of CMT involves testing of motor and sensory responses, as well as evaluation of muscle atrophy. Some forms of CMT can now be diagnosed by genetic testing. Although there is no cure for CMT, there are treatments that can manage the symptoms effectively.

Open Response

19. Describe **two** advantages and **two** disadvantages to the individual and/or society of having a genetic test to determine whether a person will have CMT.

ANSWERS AND SOLUTIONS
GENETIC PROCESSES

1. D	**5. B**	**9. 321**	**13. a) 100**	**16. B**
2. C	**6. B**	**10. 3214**	**b) 50**	**17. OR**
3. 3	**7. D**	**11. A**	**14. D**	**18. OR**
4. B	**8. B**	**12. C**	**15. 1231**	**19. OR**

1. D

The disorder phenylketonuria (PKU) is caused by an autosomal recessive gene. This can be determined by evaluating the condition of the parents in the given example. The female (mother) has the disorder and the male (father) does not have the disorder; when they have children, none of the children are affected. Since each child receives one allele from the mother and one from the father, some of the children would also be affected if the disorder were autosomal dominant or X-linked. They would have inherited the dominant allele from their affected mother. The gene is not co-dominant because the disorder presents as either affected or unaffected, not a combination of both.

With this information, the parent genotypes can also be determined. Since the gene is autosomal recessive and the mother is affected, the mother must be homozygous for the recessive allele. Since none of the children are affected, the father must not be a carrier of the recessive allele at all and, therefore, must be homozygous for the dominant allele.

In PKU, the body is unable to convert the amino acid phenylalanine into the amino acid tyrosine. This is because in the homozygous recessive condition, individuals cannot produce the liver enzyme phenylalanine hydroxylase, which is necessary to convert phenylalanine into tyrosine.

2. C

The characteristic of a contrasting pair that is expressed in both the homozygous and heterozygous conditions is known as the dominant allele. This is represented by the *T* allele.

3. 3

Three different alleles of a gene (I^A, I^B, and i) determine the phenotypes of the four human blood groups. The four blood types are type A (I^AI^A or I^Ai), type B (I^BI^B or I^Bi), type AB (I^AI^B), and type O (ii).

4. B

Cytokinesis begins before the end of anaphase and continues until the end of telophase.

5. B

Genes are made from deoxyribonucleic acid (DNA), which is genetic material that is responsible for the inheritance of characteristics. RNA, mRNA, and tRNA are important molecules involved in the transcription and translation of genes (DNA) into proteins.

6. B

Turner syndrome occurs because of the monosomy of an X chromosome that occurs as a result of its nondisjunction during meiosis. As a result, a gamete with no X chromosome is produced. This gives rise to Turner syndrome.

7. D

In prophase I, there is recombination of genetic material from the crossing over of homologous chromosomes and the random arrangement of the homologous pairs, leading to genetic differences in the resulting haploid cells.

8. B

Linked genes do not segregate independently because they are situated on the same chromosome.

Crossing over does occur between linked genes, but it occurs less frequently than in unlinked genes. Therefore, linked genes do not give the expected 9:3:3:1 ratio in the F_2 generation of a dihybrid cross.

9. 321

Descriptor	Numbered Stage of Meiosis
Separation of sister chromatids	3
Separation of homologous chromosomes	2
Attachment of spindle fibers to the chromosomes	1

The sister chromatids separate from each other and move toward the opposite poles of the cell during anaphase II (3).

The homologous chromosomes separate and move toward the opposite poles of the cell during anaphase I (2).

Spindle fibers attach to chromosomes during metaphase II (1).

10. 3214

During interphase, DNA is in the form of chromatin (3) for the majority of the time. At the end of interphase, the chromatin replicates, coils, and thickens into chromosomes. Each stand of a duplicated chromosome is called a chromatid (both together called sister chromatids) (2). The sister chromatids are held together by a centromere (1). In each nucleus, each material chromosome has a matching paternal chromosome based on size and genetic information. During prophase I, these homologous chromosomes (4) match up.

11. A

The term allele is used to describe alternate forms of a gene. Sometimes when people, or even textbooks, are discussing ABO blood types, they will mention the type A gene or the type O gene, but it is actually more correct to say that the gene for ABO blood types has an I^A **allele**, an I^B **allele**, and an *i* **allele**. Another example relates to the gene for height in pea plants: the height gene has a tall **allele** and a short **allele**. It is technically incorrect to say the tall **gene** and the short **gene**.

12. C

The pairing of homologous chromosomes is also known as synapsis. During chromosome pairing, a synaptonemal complex (or tetrad) is formed and crossing-over (genetic recombination) occurs. This occurs during prophase I of meiosis.

Non-disjunction occurs if during either meiosis I or II the homologous chromosomes or sister chromatids fail to separate properly.
A non-disjunction event can result in the formation of a zygote with an odd number of chromosomes, referred to as either a trisomy (one too many chromosomes) or a monosomy (one too few chromosomes).

13. a) 100

Parental Gametes	X^{CH}	Y
X^{ch}	$X^{CH}X^{ch}$	$X^{ch}Y$
X^{ch}	$X^{CH}X^{ch}$	$X^{ch}Y$

Phenotypes of offspring: 50% affected females and 50% normal males

Since hypertrichosis is an X-linked dominant trait and each female child receives an X^{CH} allele from her father, the Punnett square shows that all female children will be affected whereas all male children will be normal.

Therefore, 100% of females will be affected by congenital hypertrichosis because all females have the genotype $X^{CH}X^{ch}$.

b) 50

	X^{CH}	Y
X^{ch}	$X^{CH}X^{ch}$	$X^{ch}Y$
X^{ch}	$X^{CH}X^{ch}$	$X^{ch}Y$

Phenotypes of offspring:

- 50% affected females
- 50% normal males

The Punnett square shows that all female children will be affected and all male children will be normal. Therefore, 50% of the offspring will be affected.

14. D

Make a Punnett square to find the proportion of female offspring that will be carriers of hemophilia.

X^hY	×	XX
Hemophilic man		normal woman
	↓	

Gametes	X^h	Y
X	X^hX	XY
X	X^hX	XY

2 X^hX carrier females : 2 XY normal sons

Thus, 100% of all the daughters born will be carriers of hemophilia because they will always receive the hemophilia allele from their father.

15. 1231

Use a Punnett square to evaluate a cross between a homozygous dominant mother X^CX^C and a father with the genotype X^cY.

Parental Gametes	X^c	y
X^C	X^CX^c	X^CY
X^C	X^CX^c	X^CY

Since Marisa is homozygous dominant for colour vision, she is not colourblind and does not carry the recessive colourblind allele. That means Marisa is normal (1). Samson has a recessive allele X^c. Since males only have one X chromosome, Samson is colourblind (2). Because a female child receives one X chromosome from her mother (X^C) and one X chromosome from her father (X^c), any daughter of Marissa and Samson will be a carrier (3). Because a male child only receives one X chromosome, which is from the mother (X^C), any son of Marissa and Samson will be normal (1).

Individual	Phenotypic Expression Number
Marisa	1. Normal
Samson	2. Colourblind
Daughter	3. Carrier
Son	1. Normal

16. B

Biotechnology refers to a process in science that uses inventive techniques to make changes to living things. In vitro fertilization, cloning, and artificial insemination are all reproductive techniques that involve human control.

17. OR

Typically, genetic diversity tends to **decrease** when organisms are cloned because, unlike sexual reproduction, there is little opportunity for genetic recombination. An example of this is cloning in plants, such as banana trees. The trees on any given plantation are virtually clones of each other and are susceptible to disease and pests because they lack the genetic diversity needed to adapt in the face of environmental change. On the rare occasion a mutation does occur in the genome of a clone that better suits the organism to its particular environment, such that the mutation is passed on to the next generation with increased frequency, genetic diversity of the species may **increase**. One such example is the appearance of antibiotic resistance in some strains of bacteria.

18. OR

The main purpose of the Human Genome project was to identify and sequence all the genes that code for a human. Fundamentally, the project analyzed the human genome (DNA) to identify all of the genes present and to map the genes' relative positions to each other within the genome.

1. The knowledge of the precise location of particular genes allows scientists to improve their diagnosis of genetic disorders such as muscular dystrophy and cystic fibrosis because the genes of concern can be located and examined directly for any defects.
2. Genetic mapping of the human genome has led to gene therapy technologies in which a located defective human gene is replaced with a normal gene. This type of therapy offers promises as a potential cure for genetic disorders such as cystic fibrosis which is an autosomal recessive disease that can be offset with just one normal copy of the implicated gene.
3. Any other reasonable answer related to human genome mapping and detection or treatment of genetic disorders.

19. OR

Advantages:

- An individual can make plans for the future based on the knowledge of the expected development of symptoms of CMT.
- In consultation with their doctor or genetic counsellor, a couple could decide to adopt a child instead of risking the birth of a child with CMT. This could prevent emotional and financial hardship for the couple.
- If a fetus is found to have CMT, a woman/couple could have the choice to terminate the pregnancy. This would reduce the emotional and financial hardship for the couple. The cost to society/the health-care system for the treatment of a CMT child would also be reduced.
- If fewer babies with CMT were born because of prenatal diagnosis of the disorder, the healthcare system would spend less money on treatment of the symptoms of CMT. This would make more money available for treatment of other diseases.
- The more that people are diagnosed with CMT, the more the public will become aware of this disorder, for example, the Muscular Dystrophy Association and other groups publicly campaign for funding to help families affected by CMT. The increased public awareness of CMT could help fundraising for the research and treatment of CMT.
- **or** any other reasonable answer

Disadvantages:

- If an individual learns that his/her health will deteriorate due to the onset of CMT, this knowledge could lead to psychological depression.
- If an employer learns that a potential employee has a genetic mutation for CMT, the person may not be hired because of the expected cost to the employer of health-care and insurance premiums.
- A person who has no symptoms of CMT could be denied health insurance or life insurance because of a positive genetic test for the disorder.
- Certain groups consider the abortion of any fetus to be unethical.
- **or** any other reasonable answer

UNIT TEST — GENETIC PROCESSES

Use the following information to answer the next question.

In the late 1990s a young man participating in a clinical trial was the first admitted death resulting from new gene therapy practices. It is believed that the viral vector used to introduce the replacement gene into the young man's body triggered an immune response that led to multiple system failure and ultimately brain death.

Open Response

1. Investigate and briefly discuss 3 potential social and/or ethical implications of gene therapy.

____
____
____
____
____
____
____

Open Response

2. Describe the fundamental process of **transgenics** and give an example of how this technology is being used in human insulin production.

____
____
____
____
____
____
____

3. The function of centrioles is to aid in
   A. cellular division
   B. DNA translation
   C. protein synthesis
   D. synaptic transmission

4. In an individual that exhibits Down's syndrome, the chromosomes are in a state of
   A. trisomy **B.** nullisomy
   C. tetrasomy **D.** monosomy

Use the following information to answer the next question.

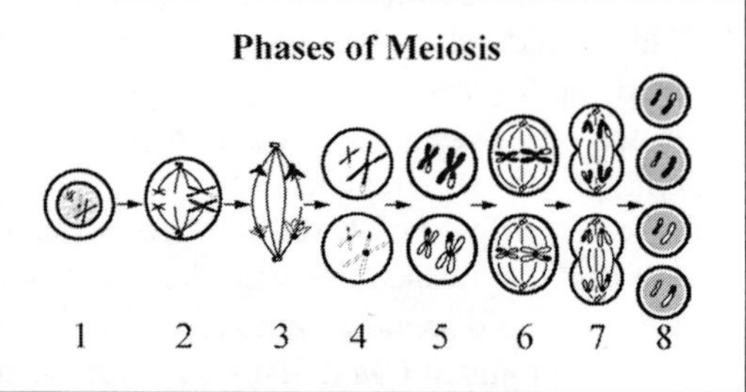

Numerical Response

5. Match the following meiotic phases with their respective numbered stage in the given diagram.

- prophase I ___1___
- metaphase II ___6___
- telophase I ___4___
- anaphase II ___7___

Use the following information to answer the next question.

The fruit fly *Drosophila melanogaster* is used frequently for genetic research. The wild type fly has red eyes, and the mutant fly has white eyes. The gene for the white eye is located on the X chromosome, so it is sex-linked. The white eye gene is also recessive.

6. If a white-eyed female is crossed with a red-eyed male, then what percentage of the female offspring will be white-eyed?
   A. 0% **B.** 25%
   C. 50% **D.** 100%

	X^R	Y
X^r	$X^R X^r$	$X^r Y$
X^r	$X^R X^r$	$X^r Y$

X^R = red
X^r = white
female = heterozygous
male = Homozygous

Use the following information to answer the next question.

> The alleles of neither black flowers (B) nor white flowers (W) are dominant in a plant. When both are present, the flower colour is grey.

Numerical Response

7. If two grey-flowered plants are crossed, then what is the **phenotypic** ratio of the progeny?

__2__ grey, __1__ black, __1__ white

BW x BW

	B	W
B	BB	BW
W	BW	WW

grey = BW
Black = BB
white = WW

Use the following information to answer the next question.

> The genotype of an individual for a given genetic loci is determined by two alleles. If the two alleles are the same, the individual is said to be homozygous. If the two alleles are different, the individual is said to be heterozygous. If the two alleles are both dominant, then the individual is said to be homozygous dominant, and if the two alleles are both recessive, the individual is said to be homozygous recessive. If, however, the individual has one dominant allele and one recessive allele, then the individual is said to be heterozygous dominant.
> The given information can be summarized in this table.

Alleles	Genotype
Both Recessive	Homozygous recessive
Both Dominant	Homozygous dominant
One of Each	Heterozygous dominant

Open Response

8. Identify which of the given genotypes is typically used in a test cross to determine the unknown genotype of an individual exhibiting a dominant trait, and explain.

____

____

____

____

____

9. Which of the following statements about meiosis is **not** correct?

A. It is a reductional division

B. It gives rise to genetic variations

C. There are two successive cell divisions

D. The chromosome number remains constant

Use the following information to answer the next question.

The chromosome theory of heredity states that genes on chromosomes are responsible for the inherited characteristics of organisms.

10. Which of the following statements summarizes the chromosome theory of heredity?

A. Genes exist in pairs

B. The human cell contains 46 chromosomes

C. Chromosomes are composed of DNA and protein

D. Genes located on chromosomes determine hereditary traits

Open Response

11. Explain why meiosis must occur before fertilization can happen.

____

____

____

____

____

____

____

12. The inheritance of the AB blood group in humans is an example of

A. dominance

B. codominance

C. polygenic inheritance

D. incomplete dominance

Use the following information to answer the next question.

Recessive traits express themselves only in the absence of dominant traits.

13. Which of the following traits is recessive?

A. Purple flowers in pea plants

B. Colour blindness in humans

C. Tallness in pea plants

D. Curly hair in humans

14. Which of the following symptoms is **not** characteristic of Down syndrome?

A. Folded skin of the upper eyelids

B. Sterile and degenerated sex organs

C. Stubby hands with single palmar fold

D. Broad skull with widely spaced nostrils

15. What term describes the process of culturing cells in glass petri dishes?

A. *In vivo*

B. *In vitro*

C. Cell staining

D. Cell incubation

Open Response

16. Production of insulin using bacteria has helped diabetic patients throughout the world. What is the name of the method used for producing insulin from bacteria?

____

____

____

____

____

____

____

ANSWERS AND SOLUTIONS — UNIT TEST

1. OR	5. 1647	9. D	13. B
2. OR	6. A	10. D	14. B
3. A	7. 211	11. OR	15. B
4. A	8. OR	12. B	16. OR

1. OR

Any 3 of the following, or any other reasonable answer.

- Gene therapy often has short-lived results due to the instability of the therapeutic DNA within the patient's genome. Consequently, patients often require multiple rounds of this very expensive therapy, ultimately causing financial strain either on the individual, their family, or the health care system.
- Viral vectors can initial mild to severe immune responses in the patient which can potentially cause the death of the patient.
- Viral vectors retain the capacity to recover their inherent pathogenicity with serious health implications for the patient.
- Many religious ideologies believe that altering the genetic make-up of an individual is interfering with or meddling with God's work or design.
- Gene therapy can potentially initiate undesired gene expression if the new gene is inserted at the wrong place in the genome. For example, tumour growth is a potential risk if the new gene is accidentally inserted into a tumour suppressor gene within the patient's genome.

2. OR

Transgenics is the science of introducing a desired gene into an organism, which normally lacks that gene, to obtain expression of a desired characteristic, such as insulin production. Currently, science is using transgenics to create safflower plants that produce human insulin in their seeds. This technology offers a less expensive, more efficient way of producing human insulin for use in treating diabetes, than any other existing human insulin production technology.

3. A

The centrioles, located near the nucleus, form the spindle fibres and separate chromosomes during meiotic and mitotic cellular division.

4. A

In addition to the normal 44 autosomes and the two sex chromosomes (46 chromosomes total), an individual with Down's syndrome has an additional chromosome number 21. This condition is termed **trisomy**; in terms of chromosomes, it is represented as $2n + 1$.

During nullisomy, the chromosomal set is missing a complete homologous pair. This is represented as $2n - 2$.

During tetrasomy, four copies of a specific chromosome are present. This is represented as $2n + 2$.

During monosomy, a specific chromosome is present only as a single copy and the other member of the pair is absent. This is represented as $2n - 1$.

5. 1647

Meiotic phases proceed in the following order: prophase, metaphase, anaphase, telophase. The first half of the illustration depicts **meiosis I**(steps 1-4) and and the second half of the illustration depicts **meiosis II**(steps 5-8). Therefore:

- **prophase I** corresponds to numbered stage 1
- **metaphase II** corresponds to numbered stage 6
- **telophase I** corresponds to numbered stage 4
- **anaphase II** corresponds to numbered stage 7

The correct numerical response is 1, 6, 4, 7.

6. A

Since the white eye gene is recessive, it means both X chromosomes of the female will carry the white eye allele. In other words, the female will be homozygous for the white eye. Since the male is red-eyed, the sole X chromosome of the male will carry the red eye allele. All the female offspring will be heterozygous and show the red-eyed phenotype. All male offspring will get their one X chromosome with the white-eyed allele from their mother, so all males will be white-eyed.

7. 211

Incomplete dominance occurs when both alleles act together to form an intermediate phenotype. Therefore, the cross between two grey-flowered plants is $BW \times BW$ (where B stands for black and W stands for white). Use a Punnett square to determine the offspring.

	B	**W**
B	*BB* black	*BW* grey
W	*BW* grey	*WW* white

The Punnett square indicates that the phenotypic ratio of the progeny is 2 grey: 1 black: 1 white

8. OR

In order to determine the genotype of an individual exhibiting a dominant trait, a test cross is performed between the individual of interest and a homozygous recessive individual. When a homozygous recessive individual is crossed with an individual that has an unknown genotype but expresses dominant phenotypic traits, all the dominant alleles will be exhibited in the offspring.

For example, a test cross is performed between a homozygous recessive genotype and an unknown genotype. If all the offspring exhibit the dominant trait, then you know that the unknown genotype was homozygous dominant, as shown in the test cross.

	b	**b**
B	*Bb*	*Bb*
B	*Bb*	*Bb*

If another test cross is performed between a homozygous recessive genotype and an unknown genotype and only half the offspring exhibit the dominant trait, then you know that the unknown genotype was heterozygous dominant.

	b	**b**
B	*Bb*	*Bb*
b	*bb*	*bb*

9. D

Meiosis is composed of two stages: meiosis I and meiosis II. During the first meiotic division, the chromosomes of each homologous pair separate and are distributed into separate cells. In the second meiotic division, the sister chromatids of each chromosome separate and are distributed to the daughter cells. Therefore, the number of chromosomes per cell does not remain constant; it is reduced to half the original number. This is known as reductional division.

10. D

The chromosome theory of heredity states that genes located on chromosomes determine hereditary traits. The various characteristics are passed from parents to offspring through genes, and genes are present on the chromosomes.

11. OR

Meiosis maintains the fixed number of chromosomes in sexually reproducing organisms. Therefore, meiosis is responsible for the maintenance of chromosome number during reproduction.

The chromosome number in humans is $2n$. If mitosis occurred in gametes, each gamete would contain $2n$ chromosomes. If the gametes were $2n$, the resultant zygote would have twice as many chromosomes as the parent. In most organisms, this would cause death.

Therefore, in order to maintain the chromosome number ($2n$) between subsequent generations, a gamete with half the number of chromosomes (n) is produced during the process of meiosis.

12. B

Human beings that belong to blood group AB exhibit the phenotypic effects of both group A and group B. The genes for groups A and B are both dominant; therefore, both are expressed when present.
This phenomenon is known as codominance.

Dominance is the phenomenon in which one characteristic is dominant over another. If present, this characteristic will always express itself, thereby masking the recessive characteristic. Polygenic inheritance is the condition in which a characteristic is expressed to varying degrees depending on the presence or interaction of two or more other genes. The inheritance of skin colour is an example of polygenic inheritance. Incomplete dominance is the condition in which the dominant characteristic does not completely mask the expression of the recessive characteristic. The phenotypic expression during incomplete dominance is a mixture of the characteristics of both parents. For example, when a red flowering plant is crossed with a white flowering plant, the resultant F_1 generation are all pink flowering plants.

13. B

Colour blindness in humans is a recessive trait.

Purple flowers in pea plants, tallness in pea plants, and curly hair in humans are all dominant traits.

14. B

Sterility is not a characteristic feature of individuals with Down syndrome because it does not affect the sex chromosomes. Down syndrome occurs because of the trisomy of the twenty-first chromosome.

15. B

When cells are cultured in glass petri dishes or test tubes rather than within living organisms, the process is referred to as *in vitro*. An example of an *in vitro* process is *in vitro* fertilization, which is often utilized to develop the embryos required by couples experiencing problems with infertility.

In vivo refers to the process of culturing cells within living organisms, such as the formation of a chicken embryo.

Cell staining is the process by which dye is added to cells in order to better view them under a microscope.

Cell incubation is the method of placing petri dishes in an oven to heat the cultures to optimal growth temperatures.

16. OR

Recombinant DNA technology is the name of the method used for producing insulin from bacteria. It involves inserting foreign DNA fragments into the bacterial cell's genome so that the bacteria will express the foreign gene and produce the desired recombinant protein product, such as insulin.

NOTES

Animals: Structure and Function

ANIMALS: STRUCTURE AND FUNCTION

Table of Correlations

	Specific Expectation	Practice Questions	Unit Test Questions	Practice Test 1	Practice Test 2
11.5.E1	analyse the relationships between changing societal needs, technological advances, and our understanding of internal systems of humans				
11.5.E1.1	*evaluate the importance of various technologies, including Canadian contributions, to our understanding of internal body systems*	1		51	
11.5.E1.2	*assess how societal needs lead to scientific and technological developments related to internal systems*	2			53a, 53b
11.5.E2	investigate, through laboratory inquiry or computer simulation, the functional responses of the respiratory and circulatory systems of animals, and the relationships between their respiratory, circulatory, and digestive systems				
11.5.E2.1	*use appropriate terminology related to animal anatomy, including, but not limited to: systolic, diastolic, diffusion gradient, inhalation, exhalation, coronary, cardiac, ulcer, asthma, and constipation*	5, 6, 7, 8	1, 2, 3	52, 53, 54	54, 55, 56
11.5.E2.2	*perform a laboratory or computer-simulated dissection of a representative animal, or use a mounted anatomical model, to analyse the relationships between the respiratory, circulatory, and digestive systems*	19	4	55, 56	57
11.5.E2.3	*use medical equipment to monitor the functional responses of the respiratory and circulatory systems to external stimuli*	20	5	57	
11.5.E3	demonstrate an understanding of animal anatomy and physiology, and describe disorders of the respiratory, circulatory, and digestive systems				
11.5.E3.1	*explain the anatomy of the respiratory system and the process of ventilation and gas exchange from the environment to the cell*	9, 10, 11	6, 7, 8	58	58, 59, 60
11.5.E3.2	*explain the anatomy of the digestive system and the importance of digestion in providing nutrients needed for energy and growth*	12, 13, 14	9, 10, 11	59	61
11.5.E3.3	*explain the anatomy of the circulatory system and its function in transporting substances that are vital to health*	15, 16, 17a, 17b, 18	12, 13, 14	60a, 60b, 61, 62, 63	62, 63, 64
11.5.E3.4	*describe some disorders related to the respiratory, digestive, and circulatory systems*	3, 4	15, 16	64	65

11.5.E1.1 evaluate the importance of various technologies, including Canadian contributions, to our understanding of internal body systems

Technology and Internal Systems

Internal systems technologies have rapidly advanced in the past two decades, and each new development improves understanding of internal systems. Some important developments in recent decades include computer axial tomography, endoscopy, radioisotopes, and laser technologies.

Internal Systems Technologies

Computer axial tomography (commonly known as a CAT scan) uses X-ray beams to display two-dimensional cross-sectional images of internal organs (such as the lungs and brain), which are then displayed on a computer screen. Visuals provided by a CAT scan can often be used instead of the more invasive procedure of surgery. By providing a detailed image of organs, internal systems can be more thoroughly examined and detecting disorders becomes easier. Scientists can use the images from the CAT scans to provide information that is not easily discerned by simply observing the physical appearance of a person alone.

Magnetic resonance imaging (MRI) is another form of non-invasive medical imaging that provides images of internal body structures. This imaging technique uses a powerful magnetic field to construct an image of the body's internal structures and provides a higher contrast between the soft tissues of the body than those images provided by a CAT scan. This particular characteristic of MRI makes it extremely useful for diagnostic imaging of the nervous, musculoskeletal, and cardiovascular systems, as well as for detecting various types of cancer.

Endoscopy is a minimally invasive imaging technology that uses a special instrument called an endoscope to view the interior surfaces of different organs by inserting it through a small incision in the skin. The endoscope is typically composed of a tube that facilitates visual inspection of the interior surface of a given organ (such as those of the digestive system), biopsy removal of tissue samples, and surgical removal of different internal system tumours.

Radioisotopes are radioactive markers injected into the blood of an individual that help to identify and combat diseases. For example, the radioisotope carbon-11 is inserted into an individual and is used to detect and diagnose cancer. This isotope can be detected by positron emission tomography (PET), a nuclear medicine imaging technique, which produces a detailed 3-D image of the body and can detect any abnormalities in the brain, heart, or other organs.

The many applications that recent advancements in laser technologies have in the medical field include cosmetic surgery, eye surgery, oral and dental surgery, tumour removal, and as a laser scalpel in general surgeries.

Canadian Contributions to the Development of Internal Systems Technologies

In 1969, five individuals founded MDS Nordion, a Canadian company that provides medical imaging technologies, such as PET scans, to countries all over the world. They also supply radioisotopes that are used to monitor and capture 3-D images. These images allow physicians to diagnose and treat a number of diseases affecting organs of the internal system, such as the heart and brain. Additionally, this technology can also be used to detect numerous types of cancers.

Open Response

1. Which imaging technique would be **most** useful in detecting cardiovascular disorders such as an aneurysm? Explain why.

____

____

____

____

____

11.5.E1.2 assess how societal needs lead to scientific and technological developments related to internal systems

Importance of Science and Technology to Human Health

The advent and further improvement of many technologies, such as televisions, computers, and video-game systems, has led to an escalation within society of the sedentary lifestyle associated with participating in these less than physical activities. Accordingly, fitness and health have become increasingly important in everyday life. There are numerous products that health-conscious consumers can buy to increase wellness. Low-fat, no-sugar foods have become the norm in supermarkets, and even fast-food outlets now provide healthier alternatives to burgers and fries. Fats are hard to break down and subsequently become stored within cells. As fat accumulates in the body, it can adversely affect internal systems. For example, fatty deposits in arteries can lead to decreased blood flow to the heart, which could potentially cause a heart attack.

Whether at the gym or at home, the popularity and complexity of fitness equipment has increased exponentially as a result of the many benefits it offers to the health-conscious individual. Weightlifting helps strengthen and tone muscles and also decreases blood pressure, reducing the risk of heart disease. Running on a treadmill helps improve your internal system by increasing blood flow to cells. This improves your metabolism since cells are able to receive oxygen more quickly, which allows the breakdown of nutrients to occur much faster. Eating well and exercising regularly can help an individual lose weight and avoid invasive procedures to remove fat, such as surgery and liposuction.

If a part of the internal system does not function correctly, the whole system is affected.
For example, the liver is an organ in the body that serves many important functions. It stores nutrients such as glucose, filters toxins from the blood, and produces bile, a substance used to help break down fats. If an individual experiences liver failure, he or she could suffer from malnutrition due to the inability to store nutrients. This affects the entire system because cells would be unable to use those nutrients. Advancements in technology have made liver donation a viable option. Liver donors donate all or part of their liver to patients who require it. Donors could be people who have died and previously consented to donate their organs or people who donate parts of their liver to another person while still alive. Because of increased societal awareness of organ donation, there have been numerous advancements of technologies to make it an increasingly effective and safe procedure.

Use the following information to answer the next question.

Scientific and technological developments have led to the progression of society such that humans can now view their internal systems and devise mechanisms and treatments to correct certain dysfunctions. Despite these advancements, people continue to suffer from ailments such as heart disease and obesity.

Open Response

2. **Describe three** technological advancements that an individual can utilize to reduce the risk of illness and poor health.

____
____
____
____
____

11.5.E3.4 describe some disorders related to the respiratory, digestive, and circulatory systems

11.5.E2.1 use appropriate terminology related to animal anatomy, including, but not limited to: systolic, diastolic, diffusion gradient, inhalation, exhalation, coronary, cardiac, ulcer, asthma, and constipation

Animal Internal Systems and Their Common Disorders

Although the variety of animals (humans included) can appear to be quite different from each other, their internal systems are organized and function similarly. An overview of basic animal anatomy reveals insight into the fundamental systems (cardiovascular, digestive, and respiratory) responsible for supplying the needs of most animals.

Circulatory System

The most basic components of the circulatory system include the heart and blood vessels (arteries and veins). The heart is a powerful pump that is responsible for movement of blood throughout the body permitting the efficient transport of substances (such as nutrients, carbon dioxide, and oxygen) between the body's tissues. Exchange of important substances between the blood and various tissues occurs by the process of **diffusion**. Specifically, the substances either enter or exit their respective tissues by flowing down the **diffusion gradient** from an area of higher concentration to an area of lower concentration. **Systole** is the phase in which the ventricles of the heart contract and pump blood out into the arteries. This creates **systolic pressure** in the arteries as blood flow increases within them. **Diastole** refers to the phase during which the heart ventricles relax following systole and blood flows back into the heart from the various tissues of the body through the veins. This creates **diastolic pressure** within the arteries as the blood pressure within them decreases.

Common Disorders of the Circulatory System

Two common disorders of the circulatory system are as follows:

- **Cardiac arrest** occurs when the heart fails to contract properly during systole and the blood within the vessels fails to flow. The consequences of cardiac arrest can be severe if blood flow is not returned to normal in a short time span because essential oxygen is no longer reaching the body's tissues, including those of the brain. Cardiac arrest can lead to brain damage in just five minutes and will ultimately lead to death if not promptly treated.
- **Arteriosclerosis** is a condition in which the arteries become stiffened. This stiffening or hardening is often due to either a decrease in the elasticity of the arteries or the development of plaques within the arteries. It can become severe enough that the lumen of the artery becomes dangerously narrowed or even blocked entirely. Some symptoms of this condition include pain, infection, angina, and an increased incidence of stroke and cardiac arrest.

Respiratory System

The body's cells and tissues require oxygen to perform cellular respiration: the cellular process that is responsible for producing the energy required for the body's basic functioning. Carbon dioxide in turn is a waste product created during cellular respiration. It is the job of the blood to transport oxygen and carbon dioxide to and from the body's tissues, respectively. However, it is the role of the respiratory system to exchange these gases with the external environment as required.

The basic components of the respiratory system include the upper respiratory system (such as the nose, turbinates, and pharynx) and the lower respiratory system (such as trachea, bronchi, lungs, and alveoli). During the inhalation (inspiration) phase of ventilation (breathing), the concentration of oxygen in the air space of the lungs is much greater than the concentration of oxygen within the blood arriving at the capillaries that surround the alveoli. As a result, oxygen enters the blood by passive diffusion (along its gradient) across the alveolar-capillary membrane. Simultaneously, carbon dioxide exits the blood (by diffusion along its gradient) and enters the air space of the lungs because the concentration of carbon dioxide within the blood arriving at the capillaries that surround the alveoli is much greater than the concentration of carbon dioxide within the air contained in the lungs. The carbon dioxide can now be expired during the exhalation phase of ventilation. Facilitation of this gas exchange is provided by the large surface area created by the numerous alveoli that create the air sacs within the lungs.

Common Disorders of the Respiratory System

Two common disorders of the respiratory system are asthma and emphysema.

Asthma is a disease that affects a person's ability to breathe. The airways swell and fill with mucus, allowing less air to travel through them. When this happens, a person suffers an asthma attack.
A person suffering from asthma may find it hard to breathe. They may wheeze as they try to breathe. Asthma attacks can happen for different reasons such as allergies, pollution, exercise, stress, and changes in ambient air temperature.

Before an Asthma Episode

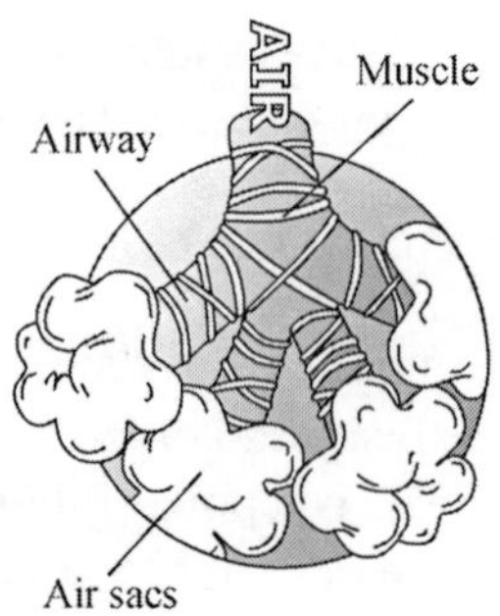

After an Asthma Episode

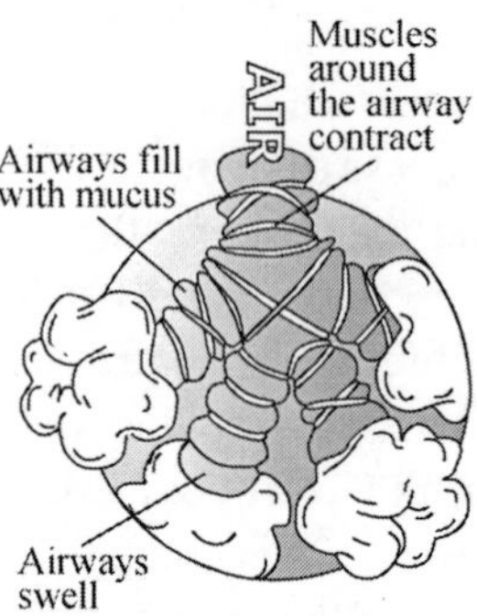

Emphysema is a disease of the lungs that can be caused by smoking or other chemical exposure. These chemicals or cigarette smoke can destroy the structures leading to the alveoli in the lungs.
They can also destroy the capillaries supplying the alveoli, resulting in less oxygen transfer to the blood during inhalation. It also makes it difficult to expel carbon dioxide from the lungs during exhalation.
A person suffering from emphysema will often display rapid breathing (hyperventilation), and they may wheeze during exhalation. They may also present subtle signs of cyanosis such as a bluish colour around the lips or finger nails.

Digestive System

It is the primary role of the digestive system to deliver essential nutrients, vitamins, minerals, and water to the body. Through the process of ingestion, food material is consumed and enters into the digestive tract where the processes of digestion and absorption can take place. The basic components of the digestive tract include the mouth, esophagus, stomach, small intestine, large intestine (colon), and anus. Additionally, there are a number of accessory glands (such as the liver and pancreas) that aid in the process of digestion by contributing various enzymes. It is primarily the role of the small and large intestines to function in nutrient and water absorption, respectively. These organs are uniquely designed to include specialized structures that absorb and transfer these essential substances to the circulatory system for transport to those body tissues that require them.

Common Disorders of the Digestive System

Some common disorders of the digestive system include ulcers, constipation, and colitis.

The term *ulcer* commonly refers to a sore or some form of damage on the interior lining of the digestive tract. It most commonly occurs due to bacterial infection by a spiral-shaped bacterium called *Helicobacter pylori* that is a normal resident within the acidic habitat of the stomach. Once the damage is present, the digestive juices of the stomach and intestine further agitate the sore by initiating digestion on the tissues in a manner similar to the digestion of food. If left untreated, ulcers can lead to serious infection and illness as the damage spreads to blood vessels and the gut cavity.

Constipation is a condition in which the feces inside the large intestine become hardened, compacted, and subsequently difficult to expel. This is typically due to an increase in the amount of water being absorbed by the large intestine when the fecal matter moves too slowly. If severe enough, elimination could be painful and may potentially lead to a complete obstruction.

Colitis refers to an inflammation of the tissues of the large intestine (colon). It is a chronic digestive disease classified among the inflammatory bowel diseases. It may be caused by any number of things including limited blood supply (possibly due to arteriosclerosis), bacterial infections, or autoimmune reactions. Typical symptoms include abdominal tenderness, pain, and diarrhea or constipation.

3. Asthma is characterized by the presence of large quantities of which of the following immunoglobulins?

A. IgA **B.** IgD
C. IgE **D.** IgG

4. What does the term hypertension refer to?

A. High pulse rate
B. High sugar level
C. Low blood pressure
D. High blood pressure

5. Which of the following stages occurs during the act of inhalation?

A. Increased volume of the thoracic cavity
B. Elastic recoil of the lung tissue and chest wall
C. Upward movement of the diaphragm due to abdominal muscle compression
D. Relaxation of the diaphragm and the regaining of its dome-shaped configuration

6. Inhalation is the movement of air from the external environment into the body. Which of the following conditions initiates the process of inhalation?

A. An increase in lung volume
B. A high oxygen level in the blood
C. A high carbon dioxide level in the blood
D. An increase in air pressure inside the thoracic cavity

7. Which of the following terms is **not** related to the human heart?
   A. Four- chambered
   B. Pacemaker
   C. Neurogenic
   D. Mitral valve

Use the following information to answer the next question.

Three Disorders of Human Internal Systems

1. aneurysms
2. ulcers
3. emphysema

Numerical Response

8. **Match** the given conditions to their respective internal system. (Record your answer as a three-digit number.)

Internal system	Disorder
Digestive	_________
Respiratory	_________
Circulatory	_________

11.5.E3.1 explain the anatomy of the respiratory system and the process of ventilation and gas exchange from the environment to the cell

Ventilation and Gas Exchange

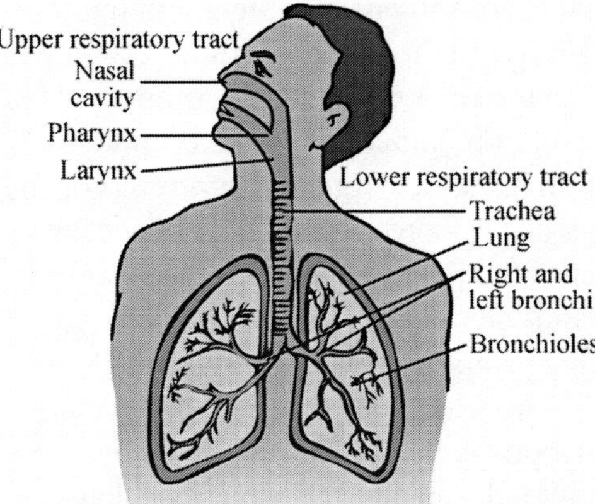

Ventilation is the process of air moving in and out of the body. During inhalation, the diaphragm contracts and moves down; during exhalation, the diaphragm relaxes and moves up. There is a higher concentration of oxygen outside of the body than inside the body, so oxygen will diffuse from the atmosphere into your lungs. Oxygen travels through your upper respiratory tract into your nostrils or mouth, past the pharynx and the larynx.
Oxygen then enters your lower respiratory tract, into a hollow tube called the trachea or windpipe, which branches into two tubes called the bronchi.
One bronchus enters the right lung, and the other bronchus enters the left lung. The bronchi branch into smaller tubes called bronchioles, and the bulbous ends of the bronchioles are called alveoli. The respiratory system is lined with hair-like cilia and mucous-producing cells. The mucous traps foreign particles (such as dirt or bacteria), and the cilia sweeps them out.

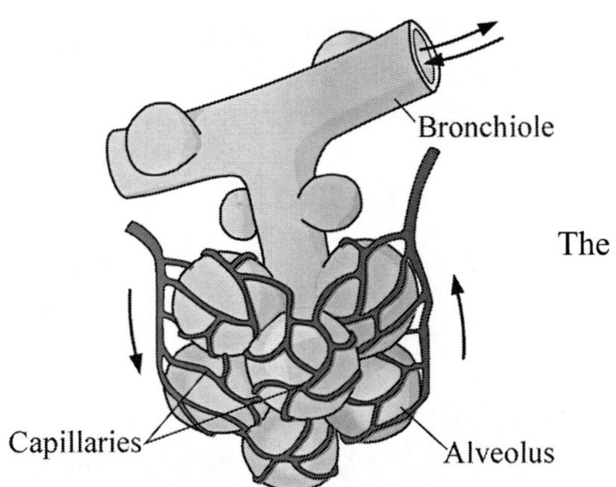

The alveoli are very thin and composed of one cell layer, so oxygen can easily diffuse out of the alveoli (where there is a high concentration of oxygen) into the surrounding capillaries (where there is a low concentration of oxygen). Once oxygen enters the bloodstream, it binds to hemoglobin, a protein that contains iron, which is found in every individual red blood cell. Once the oxygen has bound to the hemoglobin, it is transported throughout the body via the circulatory system and diffuses into cells, where it is needed to fuel the process of cellular respiration.

Use the following information to answer the next question.

Hemoglobin is a molecule with amazing qualities. For example, the affinity of hemoglobin for oxygen is dependent on the pH of the blood, which is dependent on the level of carbon dioxide in the blood.

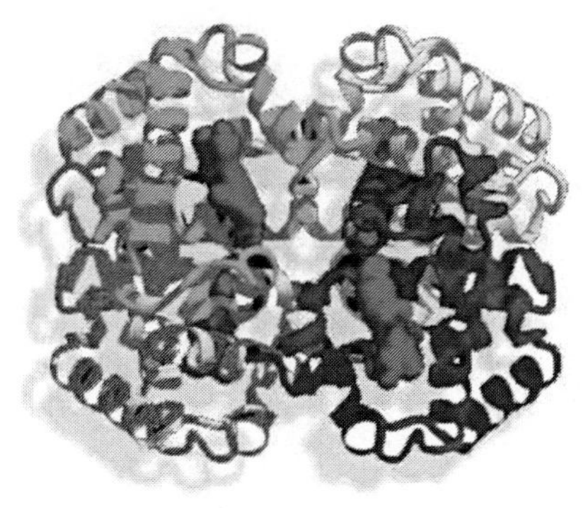

9. For blood travelling through a very active muscle in which a lot of CO_2 is being produced, the blood would have a

A. low pH and a low quantity of oxygen released by the hemoglobin

B. low pH and a high quantity of oxygen released by the hemoglobin

C. high pH and a low quantity of oxygen released by the hemoglobin

D. high pH and a high quantity of oxygen released by the hemoglobin

10. Which of the following sequences shows the pathway that oxygen travels through the respiratory tract?

A. nose → pharynx → larynx → trachea → bronchioles → bronchi → alveoli

B. nose → larynx → pharynx → trachea → bronchi → bronchioles → alveoli

C. nose → pharynx → larynx → trachea → bronchi → bronchioles → alveoli

D. nose → larynx → pharynx → trachea → bronchioles → bronchi → alveoli

Use the following information to answer the next question.

Inhaling a typical cigarette exposes one's body to over 4 000 chemical compounds, many of which are highly toxic, and 43 of which are cancer causing.
These chemicals in tobacco smoke seriously affect both the mucous and cilia lining the respiratory tract and may lead to severe coughing.

Open Response

11. Which functions in the respiratory tract would be impeded by the paralysis of cilia?

____

____

____

____

____

____

____

11.5.E3.2 explain the anatomy of the digestive system and the importance of digestion in providing nutrients needed for energy and growth

Importance of Digestion

The digestive system is an important part of your internal system. The process of digestion begins with teeth, which grind up the food into smaller pieces. Then, enzymes found in saliva digest the food. Enzymes are proteins that speed up the rate of a reaction. For example, the enzyme amylase breaks down the polysaccharide starch into smaller di- and mono-saccharides such as glucose.
If enzymes were not present, food would take much longer to break down, and cells would not be fed quickly enough to sustain the energy requirements of the body. Once the food is swallowed, peristalsis of muscles in the esophagus contract and squeeze the food downward until it reaches the stomach, where acids break the food down further.
This soggy, acid-covered food called chyme then enters the small intestine, where various enzymes released from the pancreas further break down carbohydrates, proteins, and fats in the food.
The small intestine is lined with small, hairlike villi and microvilli that absorb these nutrients and pass them to capillaries associated with the villi.
These nutrients are then transported by the circulatory system to individual cells, where they are metabolized, or to the liver, where nutrients are stored. The large intestine receives food that was not digested or absorbed by the stomach or small intestine and absorbs the water out of it.
This undigested food leaves through the anus as compact feces.

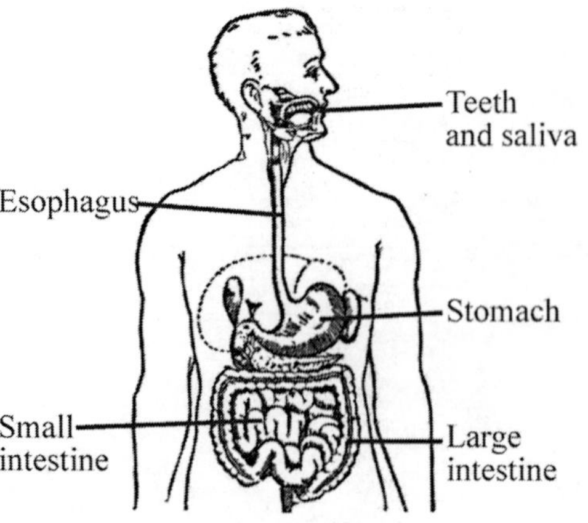

It is essential that proper nutrients are eaten daily to maintain a healthy body. This is important because without consuming nutrients such as carbohydrates, proteins, water, vitamins, and minerals, humans and animals would not be able to produce the energy required or create the building blocks necessary for growth, development, and the maintenance of homeostatic processes. For example, carbohydrates, such as glucose, are sugars that are found in breads, pastas, and a variety of other foods. In a process called cellular respiration, the mitochondria present in each cell use oxygen to break down glucose and produce carbon dioxide, water, and energy. The energy made as a product of cellular respiration is used to fuel everyday life processes such as breathing, digestion, growth, metabolic waste removal, and temperature regulation. Furthermore, proteins, such as those found in meats, fish, dairy products, beans, and lentils are components of body structures such as muscles, hair, hemoglobin, and the lens of the eye and are therefore required for their development. Fundamentally, it is the proper digestion and utilization of the nutrients an organism consumes that maintain its day-to-day functioning.

Use the following information to answer the next question.

Egg whites are rich in protein. Egg yolks are rich in fat and cholesterol.
To determine what is required to digest an egg, tubes containing different chemical reagents were set up.
To each test tube, 2 mL of raw egg were then added. All test tubes were incubated for four hours at room temperature (22°C) and shaken regularly in order to mix the contents.

The concentrations of the other additives were kept constant among all tubes.

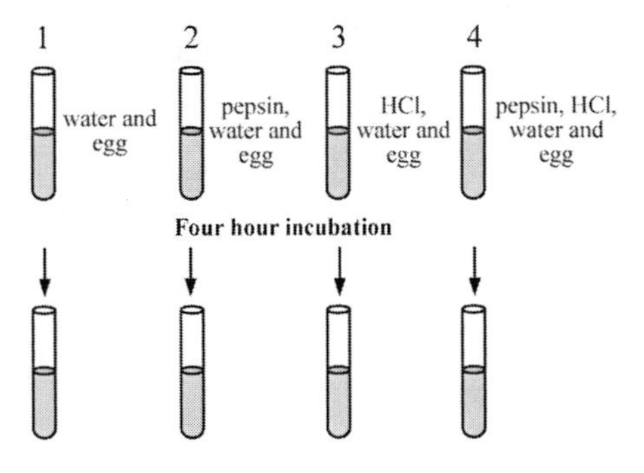

12. The part of the digestive system that is modelled in test tube 4 is the

A. mouth **B.** jejunum

C. stomach **D.** duodenum

Use the following information to answer the next question.

The human small intestine is approximately 7 m long. Yet, without its unique internal structure, it would not be able to sustain human life. The inner layer of the wall of the small intestine has a wrinkled and folded surface that contains many microscopic projections known as villi. In addition, each villus contains many extensions of its cell membrane known as microvilli.

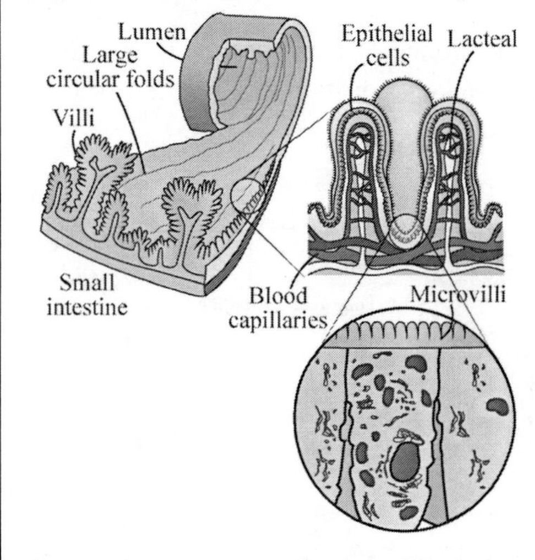

13. The purpose of the distinct internal structure of the small intestine is to increase the surface area for

A. waste formation

B. water absorption

C. oxygen absorption

D. nutrient absorption

Use the following information to answer the next question.

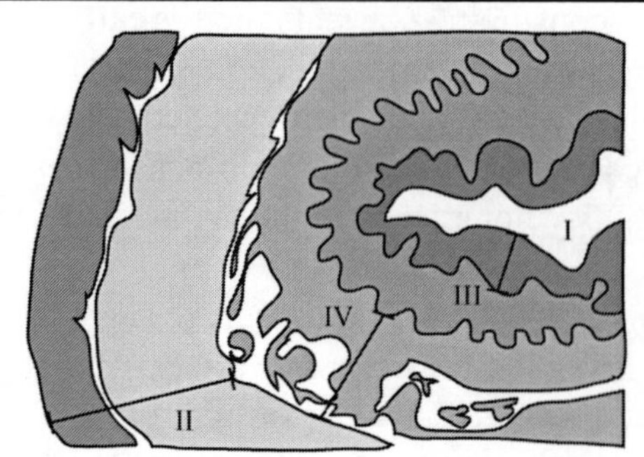

The given cross-section of the esophagus shows the mucosa, submucosa, muscularis, and lumen.

Open Response

14. **Match** each labelled region of the esophagus with it's appropriate given term.

I. __________
II. __________
III. __________
IV. __________

11.5.E3.3 explain the anatomy of the circulatory system and its function in transporting substances that are vital to health

Circulatory System Transport

An important part of your internal system is the circulatory system, also known as the cardiovascular system, which is composed of the heart (cardio) and blood vessels (vascular).

The heart is a muscular organ that pumps blood throughout the body. Oxygen-poor blood coming from the body enters the right atrium (R.A.), passes to the right ventricle (R.V.), and is then pumped to the lungs where oxygen is absorbed from the external environment. This now oxygen-rich blood then enters back into the left atrium (L.A.) of the heart, passes to the left ventricle (L.V.), and through the aorta to be pumped to the rest of the body tissues.

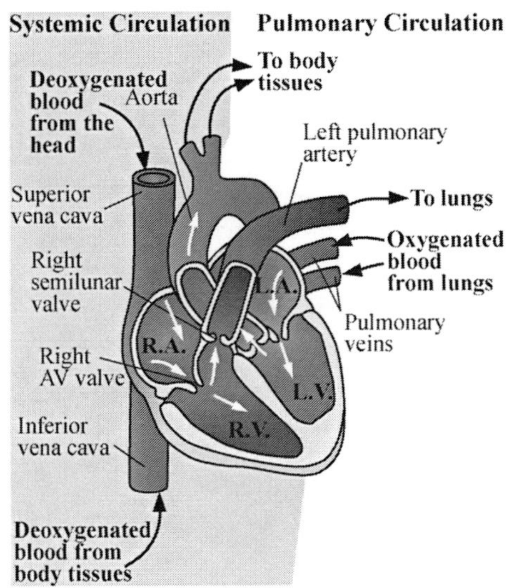

Anatomy of the human heart

Blood vessels function to transport blood, nutrients, respiratory gases, and wastes. Capillaries are the smallest blood vessels, measuring one cell layer thick. Their size allows for fast and efficient diffusion of substances. Capillaries merge into larger arterioles, which fuse to form thick, muscular arteries. All arteries in the body lead away from the heart. Capillaries also merge to form venules that eventually fuse to become larger veins. All veins in the body lead toward the heart. The pulmonary circulatory system is composed of pulmonary arteries that lead oxygen-poor blood away from the heart toward the lungs where they pick up oxygen and pulmonary veins that carry oxygen-rich blood away from the lungs toward the heart to be pumped throughout the body to all cells.

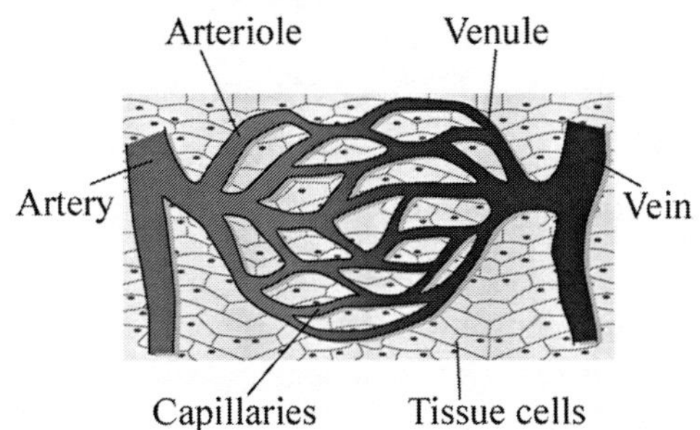

Transportation of blood cells, nutrients, gases, and wastes occurs in a complex network of blood vessels that are connected to each other in order to get substances from one part of the body to the other. For example, nutrients that are absorbed into capillaries from the small intestine have to travel through a network of arteries and veins to get to all the cells in your body, from the top of your head to the tip of your toes. Arteries connected to the heart allow oxygen to travel to all cells. Cells then use the oxygen to help break down nutrients, producing energy, water, and carbon dioxide (a waste product). Carbon dioxide is released by the cell and absorbed into veins that carry the carbon dioxide to the heart, which pumps it to the lungs where it is exhaled out of the body. Hormones travel from the organ where they are made to target cells all over the body where they produce an effect.

For example, the hormone estrogen is produced by the ovaries and absorbed into the bloodstream, where it travels and targets cells to promote hair growth, a secondary sex characteristic.

Use the following information to answer the next question.

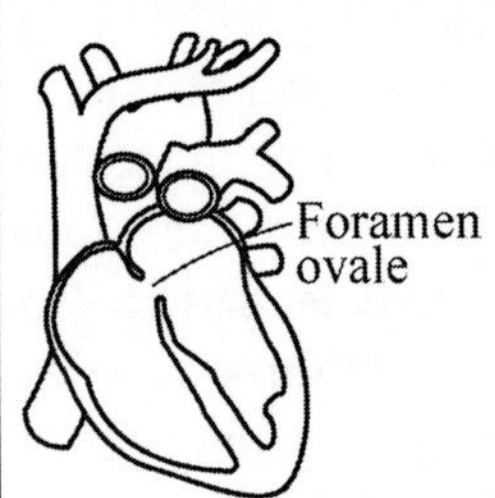

The heart of an unborn fetus has an opening called the foramen ovale that directly connects the right and left atria. If the foramen ovale (which normally closes at birth) fails to close, the baby is born with a hole in its heart.

15. Failure of the foramen ovale to close would have which of the following effects on arterial blood gas concentration?

A. A lower than normal concentration of O_2 and CO_2 in arterial blood

B. A higher than normal concentration of O_2 and CO_2 in arterial blood

C. A lower than normal O_2 concentration and a higher than normal CO_2 concentration in arterial blood

D. A higher than normal O_2 concentration and a lower than normal CO_2 concentration in arterial blood

Use the following information to answer the next question.

In order to transport and deliver needed materials to the tissues, blood moves throughout a complicated network of vessels in the body. The following structures are part of this network of vessels:

- Capillaries
- Arterioles
- Venules
- Arteries
- Veins

Open Response

16. List the given vessels in the order that oxygenated blood passes through them on its path from the heart to the tissues and back to the heart as deoxygenated blood.

Use the following information to answer the next multipart question.

17. In July 1997, the Mayo Clinic in Rochester Minnesota reported that 24 women, with no previous history of heart abnormalities, were found to be suffering from valvular disease and hypertension. All 24 women were taking, either presently or in the past, the weight loss drugs phentermine and fenfluramine

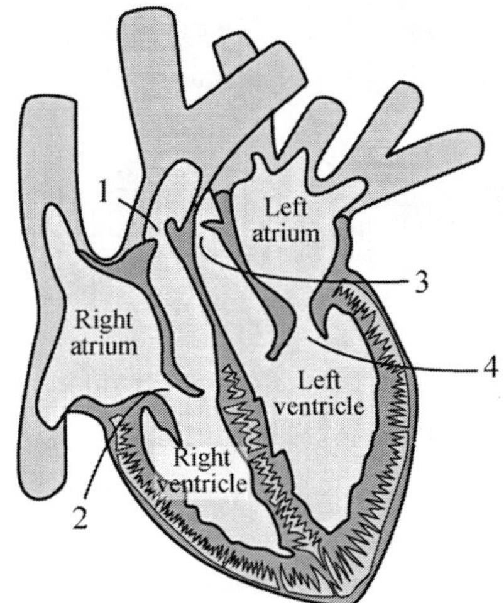

The following symptoms were identified in the 24 women:

i. Abnormally functioning weak heart valves that caused mixing of blood between the atria and the ventricles
ii. Thickening of the heart valves
iii. In a few cases, high blood pressure in the vessels carrying blood from the heart to the lungs

The Mayo Clinic report does not define a clear cause-and-effect relationship between the weight loss drugs phentermine and fenfluramine use and heart abnormalities, but the report does provide an association between phentermine and fenfluramine use and heart problems.

Open Response

a) The valves in these 24 patients were termed "regurgitating valves." From the given information, why might this term be applied?

____
____
____
____
____
____
____

b) What is the **main** artery that carries blood from the heart to the lungs?

____
____
____
____
____
____
____

Open Response

18. Explain how a damaged AV valve on the left side of the heart could cause fluids to build up in the lung tissues.

____
____
____
____
____
____
____

11.5.E2.2 perform a laboratory or computer-simulated dissection of a representative animal, or use a mounted anatomical model, to analyse the relationships between the respiratory, circulatory, and digestive systems

Analyzing the Relationships between the Organs Systems

Examination of the physical connections and relationships that exist between the digestive, respiratory, and circulatory systems can be accomplished through dissection of a representative animal or visual inspection of an anatomical model.

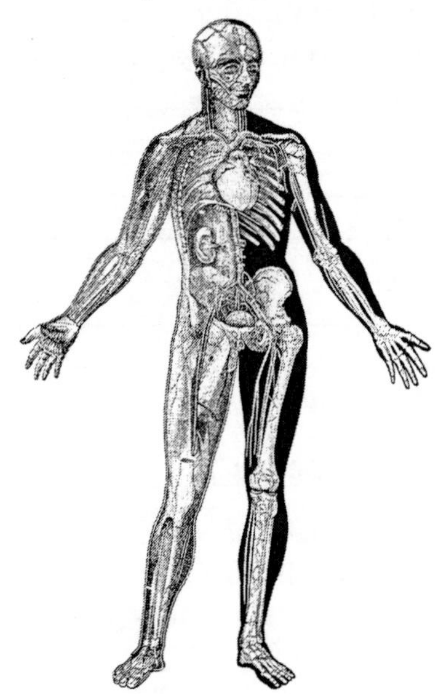

Human body systems

Respiratory System Relationships

The respiratory system aids in the exchange of oxygen and carbon dioxide between the circulatory system and external environment. Oxygen (which is necessary for life) enters into circulation, and carbon dioxide (a waste that the body does not need) is removed from circulation through the respiratory system. Specifically, the blood in the circulatory system carries carbon dioxide, released during cellular respiration, from the body tissues to the alveoli in the lungs. The alveoli then remove the carbon dioxide from the blood and replace it with oxygen from the air, through a process known as diffusion.

Investigation of the thoracic cavity by dissection or anatomical model reveals the macroscopic structure of the lungs as two spongy sacs that surround the heart and great vessels.

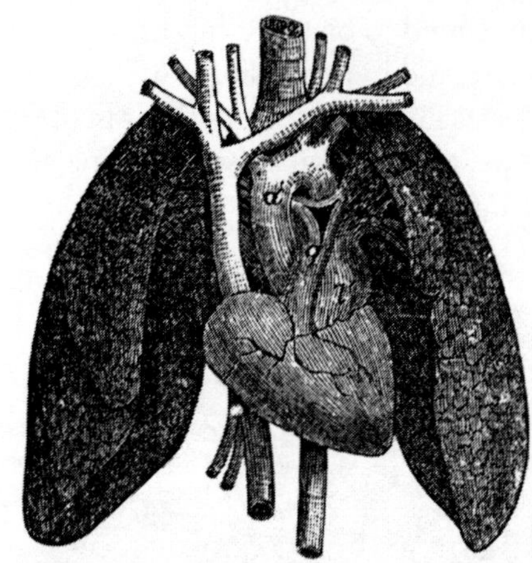

Macroscopic structure of the lungs

Further investigation into the microscopic structure reveals an inner branching network of alveoli, which are tiny bulbous air sacs. The alveoli exponentially increase the surface area of the lungs for gas exchange relative to the outside area of the lungs themselves. Each alveolus is intricately associated with capillaries belonging to the circulatory system.

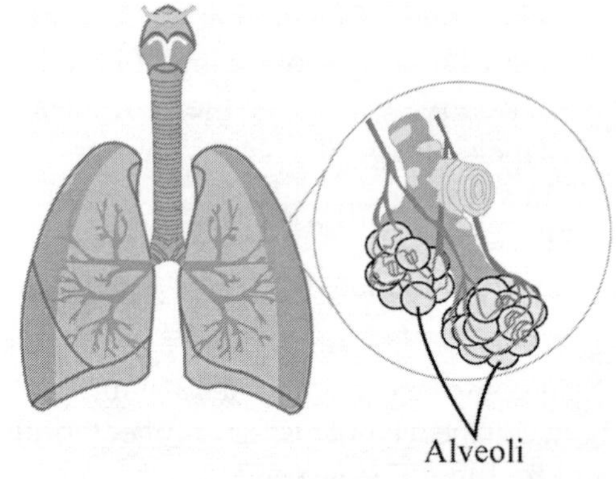

Microscopic structure of the lungs

Digestive System Relationships

The digestive system is the system of organs that takes in food (ingestion), breaks it down (digestion), and gets rid of the remaining waste (excretion). When the food is digested, the nutrients and energy then get taken up by the circulatory system (absorption) so that they can be distributed to various cells throughout the body.

Investigation of the abdominal cavity by dissection or anatomical model reveals the macroscopic structure of the intestines as a series of highly folded tubular structures extending from the stomach to the anus.

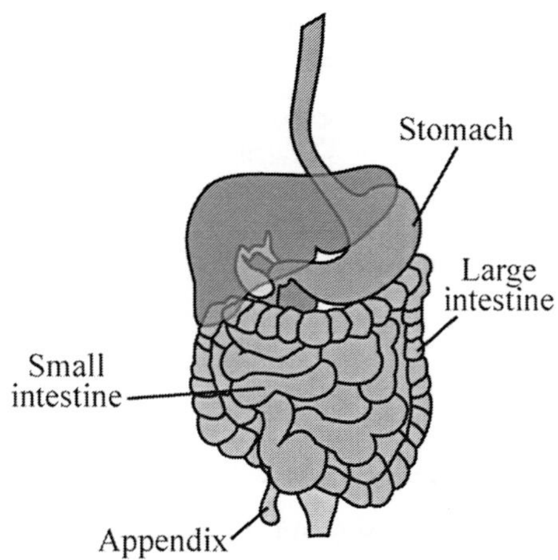

Macroscopic structure of the digestive system

Microscopically, the interior surface of the small intestine has numerous tiny projections called villi that are themselves covered in even tinier projections called microvilli. These tiny projections are designed to increase surface area for absorption of nutrients, and each one is intricately associated with a capillary vessel from the circulatory system.

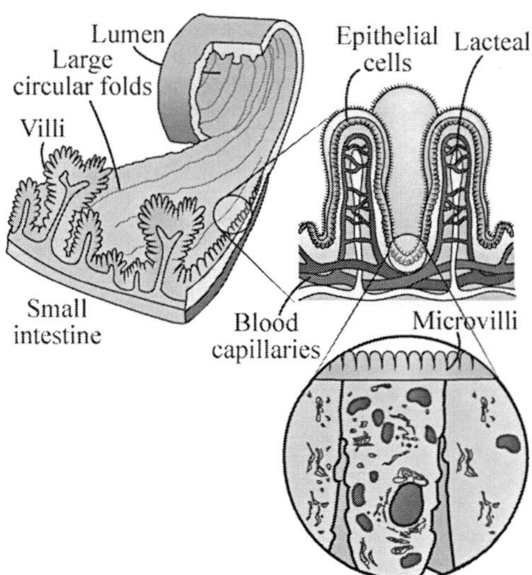

Microscopic structure of the small intestine

Circulatory System Relationships

The function of the blood (circulatory system) is to move important substances around the body so that they can be utilized by tissues or exchanged between systems accordingly. Some of these substances include the following:

- Oxygen from lungs (respiratory system) to body systems that require oxygen
- Carbon dioxide from body tissues to the lungs to be removed from the body
- Nutrients from the digestive system to body systems that require them
- Chemical waste from all body systems to the kidney to be removed from the blood
- Hormones from glands to cells that require them

Dissection of the human circulatory system would reveal a highly intricate, interconnected, branching network of vessels associated with every tissue of the body.

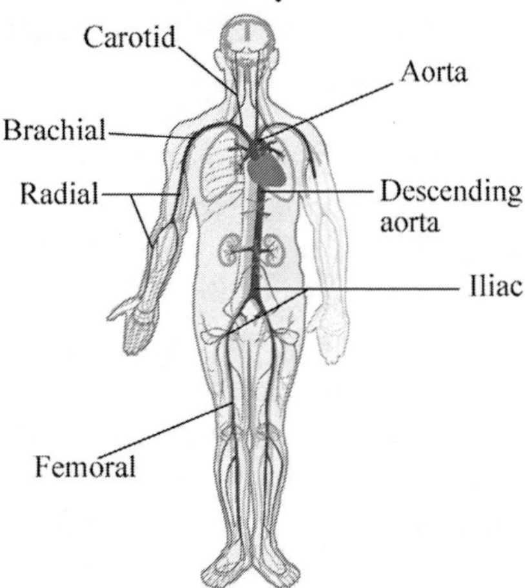

Direction of blood movement: from heart to body tissues

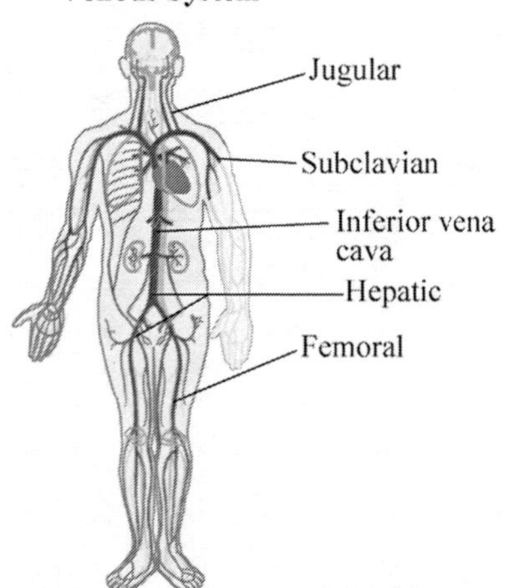

Direction of blood movement: from body tissues to heart

Use the following information to answer the next question.

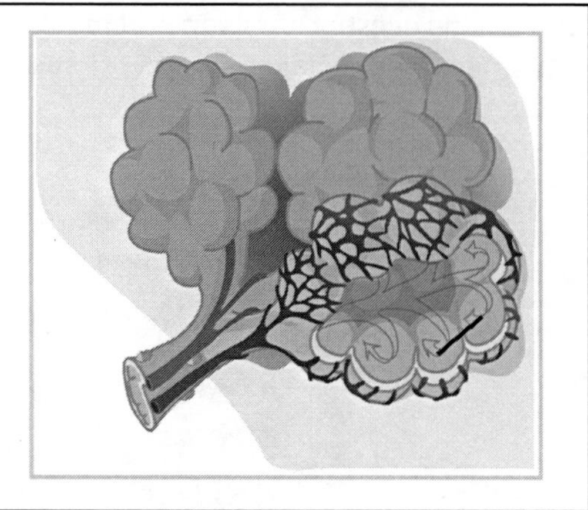

Open Response

19. Identify the **two main** structures depicted in the given diagram. Which **two** internal systems are illustrated by the picture and in what way do they work together?

____

____

____

____

____

____

____

11.5.E2.3 use medical equipment to monitor the functional responses of the respiratory and circulatory systems to external stimuli

Respiratory and Circulatory Responses

A stethoscope is the instrument that is most frequently used for listening to the internal sounds of the body, such as heart rate, breathing, and arterial blood flow. It is often used in combination with a manual sphygmomanometer (blood pressure cuff) for detecting the sounds of systolic and diastolic blood flow within the arteries of the arm.

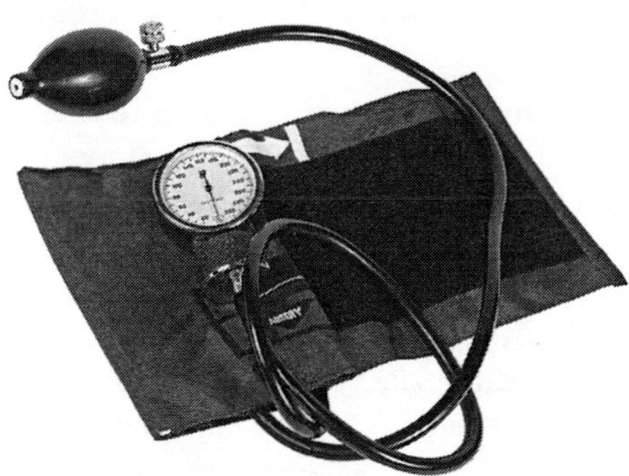

When used together, these two devices provide important information regarding responses in heart rate, breathing rate, and blood pressure in humans and animals. For example, they can be used to monitor a person's heart rate and breathing at rest and then immediately after exercise. Measurements taken by these devices indicate that exercise increases breathing, heart rate, and blood pressure. This is because blood must flow to areas where it is needed and is therefore routed in a manner to ensure that some parts of the body receive more blood flow and others receive less as different circumstances dictate. For example, during exercise, arterioles leading to muscles dilate because these cells need more oxygen and nutrients than other parts of the body. Once you are at rest, blood pressure, heart rate, and breathing decrease. Arterioles leading to muscles constrict, and arterioles leading to the stomach and small intestine dilate, allowing normal digestion to return. During exercise, you may not feel hungry, but it is common that after exercise, you become very hungry.

20. A spirometer is used to measure

A. ventilation

B. temperature

C. blood pressure

D. atmospheric pressure

ANSWERS AND SOLUTIONS
ANIMALS: STRUCTURE AND FUNCTION

1. OR	6. C	11. OR	16. OR	20. A
2. OR	7. C	12. C	17. a) OR	
3. C	8. 231	13. D	b) OR	
4. D	9. B	14. OR	18. OR	
5. A	10. C	15. C	19. OR	

1. OR

Nuclear Magnetic Resonance Imaging (NMR) would be particularly useful because it is a non-invasive imaging technique that visualizes internal body structures and provides a **high contrast image** of the different **soft body tissues**. This characteristic makes it particularly useful when detecting and diagnosing cardiovascular disorders such as aneurysms because these types of disorders occur within the soft tissues of the arteries and veins, which are embedded in soft connective, nervous and muscular tissues. NMR provides high contrast images that distinguish between these different types of soft tissues, permitting for visualization of each of the tissue types independently and providing a clearer picture to detect and diagnose from.

2. OR

Some technological advancements an individual can utilize to reduce the risk of illness and poor health are the following:

- Eat enriched and fortified foods. Many products in today's society are enriched or fortified to contain extra vitamins and supplements that many people don't get enough of in their regular diet. For example, milk has extra calcium and vitamin D added to it; orange juice is often fortified with calcium.
- Exercise regularly and more efficiently outdoors, at home, or at the gym by taking advantage of new high-tech exercise equipment and devices that improve the quality of exercise, monitor heart rate, and count calories burned.
- Visit the doctor regularly for check-ups. Advances in screening techniques provide earlier and earlier detection of diseases and enable early treatment options.
- Any other reasonable answer.

3. C

Asthma is an allergic disorder characterized by the presence of large quantities of IgE antibodies. These antibodies are called reagins or sensitizing antibodies, they bind to allergens and trigger histamine release.

IgA is an immunoglobulin found in body fluids such as tears and saliva and in the respiratory, reproductive, urinary, and gastrointestinal tracts. It defends exposed external surfaces against infectious agents. IgD is an immunoglobulin found on the surface of B cells. It is involved in activating B cells to participate in the immune response. IgG is an immunoglobulin produced late in the immune response and it forms the majority of immunity against invading pathogens.

4. D

A continuous or sustained rise in the arterial blood pressure is known as hypertension.

High pulse rate is termed tachycardia. Low blood pressure is termed hypotension. High sugar level is termed diabetes mellitus.

5. A

During the act of inhalation, the diaphragm and external intercostal muscles contract, causing the diaphragm to flatten and the rib cage to expand. This creates an overall increase in the volume of the thoracic cavity. This action causes the lung pressure to decrease below atmospheric pressure, resulting in air passively entering the airspaces within the lungs.

Elastic recoil of the lung tissue and chest wall occurs during exhalation as the diaphragm relaxes and regains its dome-shaped configuration. Compression of intestinal structures by abdominal muscles occurs during the exhalation phase of forced (heavy) breathing.

6. C

When the level of carbon dioxide in the blood rises, the medulla oblongata stimulates the intercostal muscles and causes the diaphragm to contract, thereby causing the expansion of the lung cavity.

An increase in lung volume and in air pressure inside the thoracic cavity initiate exhalation. A high level of oxygen in the blood does not initiate inhalation.

7. C

Neurogenic is a term related to a type of heart found in some annelids and arthropods where the cardiac impulse originates in the nervous system. In the human heart the cardiac impulse originates in the heart itself at a patch of modified heart muscle called the sinoatrial node which is often referred to as the pacemaker. The human heart is four-chambered with two auricles (atria) and two ventricles. A mitral valve is also called the bicuspid valve or left atrioventricular valve which guards the opening between the left atrium and left ventricle.

8. 231

Internal system	Disorder
Digestive	2
Respiratory	3
Circulatory	1

Ulcers (2) are a digestive condition. Emphysema (3) is a respiratory condition. Aneurysms (1) are a circulatory condition. The correct numerical response is 2, 3, 1.

9. B

Gas exchange in the human body occurs by diffusion. The direction of diffusion is dependent on partial pressures of the individual gases both at the lungs and at the tissues. At the lungs, the partial pressure of oxygen (O_2) in the lung air spaces is higher than in the blood, so O_2 diffuses into blood and binds with hemoglobin in red blood cells. Conversely, the partial pressure of carbon dioxide (CO_2) at the lungs is higher in the blood than in the lung air spaces, so CO_2 diffuses from the blood into the lungs and is exhaled.

In the capillaries of the body tissues, such as active muscles, the situation is the opposite. Carbon dioxide released from the cells during cellular respiration diffuses into the blood and reacts with water (H_2O) in the red blood cells to form carbonic acid. $H_2O + CO_2 \rightarrow H_2CO_3$

Carbonic acid is unstable and breaks down into hydrogen ions $\left(H^+\right)$ and bicarbonate ions $\left(HCO_3^-\right)$.

The H^+ ions cause the blood to become more acidic by lowering the blood pH, and they bind and reduce hemoglobin, causing the hemoglobin to release its O_2. The O_2 is then free to diffuse into surrounding tissues.

Therefore, the blood travelling through a very active muscle will have a low pH and a high quantity of oxygen released by the hemoglobin.

10. C

Air travels through the nose, enters the pharynx, then the larynx, where it then enters the trachea. Air then passes into the bronchi, which branch off into smaller bronchioles. Bronchioles end at bulbous sacks called alveoli.

11. OR

As air travels through the nose and enters the body, it passes through the nasal passages, which are coated with mucous and the thin, hair-like structures called cilia. Mucous traps dust and bacteria and other small materials, while the motion of the cilia sweeps the mucous away from the lungs and toward the pharynx so it may be swallowed. If the cilia are not functioning, the mucous will build up on the lungs and cause severe coughing. Some mucous will remain on the lungs.

12. C

Test tube 4 models the stomach.

Both pepsin (a hydrolytic enzyme that digests protein) and HCl (hydrochloric acid—secreted in the stomach and responsible for the acidic pH of gastric juice) are major components of gastric juice. None of the other digestive organs normally secrete and possess high concentrations of these two substances.

13. D

The small intestine is responsible for the absorption of nutrients, such as simple sugars, fatty acids, glycerol, and amino acids.

Both waste formation and water absorption occur in the large intestine, where most of the water is reabsorbed, leaving the solid waste matter (feces), which cannot be used by the body. O_2 absorption is done in the alveoli of the lungs.

14. OR

I. Lumen
II. Muscularis
III. Mucosa
IV. Submucosa

15. C

Blood that passes from the right atrium through the foramen ovale into the left atrium does **not** enter the right ventricle and passes directly into the left side of the heart.

This blood therefore bypasses the lungs. Recall the cardiac cycle:
Right atrium → right ventricle → pulmonary artery → lungs → pulmonary veins → left atrium → left ventricle → arteries → body tissues

In the lungs, gases are exchanged. Oxygen is taken up by the blood out of the lungs, and carbon dioxide is released by the blood into the lungs. Therefore, bypassing the lungs would cause blood in arteries to have a lower concentration of oxygen and a higher concentration of carbon dioxide waste derived from cellular respiration in body tissues.

16. OR

Oxygenated blood is pumped from the left ventricle of the heart through the aorta to the arteries. The arteries distribute the oxygenated blood to the various parts of the body through a branching network of smaller vessels called arterioles. The arterioles deliver the blood to the capillary beds at the tissues. Fluid exchange occurs in the capillary bed, where the blood delivers the needed materials to the tissues.

The blood becomes deoxygenated in the capillaries. The blood then travels back to the heart from the capillaries into the venules and then into the veins. Eventually, the blood passes into the superior and inferior vena cava before reentering the right atrium of the heart.

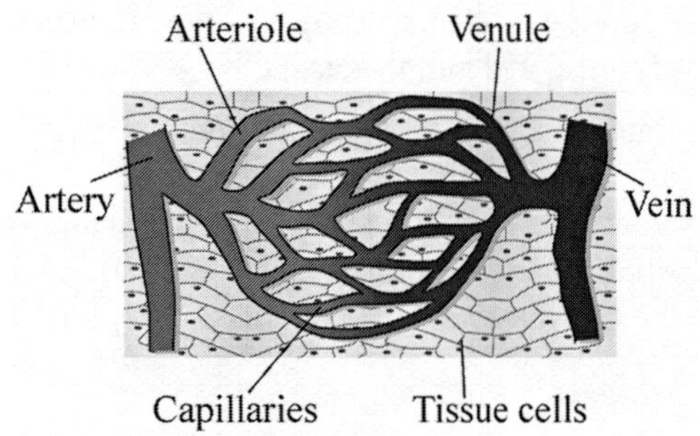

Blood vessels

The correct order blood passing through the given vessels is arteries→arterioles→capillaries→ venules → veins.

17. a) OR

Normally, once blood flows into the ventricle and the ventricles begin to contract, the AV valves (between the atria and ventricles) close, preventing backflow of blood into the atria. The term "regurgitating" refers in this case to the weak AV valves (tricuspid and mitral) that fail to close completely, thereby allowing blood between the atria and the ventricles to mix. Mixing of blood is an indication that backflow is occurring.

b) OR

All arteries take blood away from the heart. The artery that takes blood from the heart to the lungs is the **pulmonary artery**.

This artery takes oxygen-poor blood from the heart to the lungs where the blood is reoxygenated. The blood is then returned to the heart by the pulmonary vein and sent to the cells of the body. Hypertension caused by a defect in the pulmonary artery may be fatal.

18. OR

A damaged AV valve could leak, causing a back flow of blood into the left atrium, which would cause blood pressure buildup in the pulmonary vein. This backup could result in high blood pressure at the venule end of the capillary bed and in the alveoli. High blood pressure would prevent fluids of the lung tissue (forced out of the capillary at the high pressure arteriole end) from re-entering the blood as it normally would, causing an increase in fluid buildup in the lung tissues.

Furthermore, the higher than normal blood pressure at the venule end of the capillary beds would have a greater impact on waste movement between the tissues and blood than the osmotic pressure in the capillary beds. This would result in a reduced amount of waste entering the blood from the tissues. With a greater amount of waste remaining in the tissues, the osmotic pressure of the tissues would be higher than the blood pressure, and fluid would be drawn into the tissues by osmosis, causing the tissues to swell further.

19. OR

The structures in the diagram are *alveoli* and their associated *capillaries*. The two internal systems illustrated are the *respiratory* and *circulatory*. These two systems work together to exchange respiratory gases such as carbon dioxide and oxygen between the external environment and the internal tissues.

20. A

A spirometer is an instrument that is used to measure ventilation, which is the movement of air into and out of lungs. A spirometer can be used to measure ventilation at rest (tidal volume) or ventilation during exercise, where an individual may experience maximum inhalation and exhalation (vital capacity).

UNIT TEST — ANIMALS: STRUCTURE AND FUNCTION

1. Which of the following statements about systolic and diastolic pressure is **true**?
   A. Systolic pressure is same as diastolic pressure.
   B. Systolic pressure is lower than diastolic pressure.
   C. Systolic pressure is higher than diastolic pressure.
   D. Systolic pressure can be higher or lower than diastolic pressure, depending upon the conditions.

2. The function of the coronary arteries is to supply blood to the muscles of the
   A. stomach **B.** arms
   C. heart **D.** face

Open Response

3. The term cardiac **typically** refers to which organ and body system?

____

____

Use the following information to answer the next question.

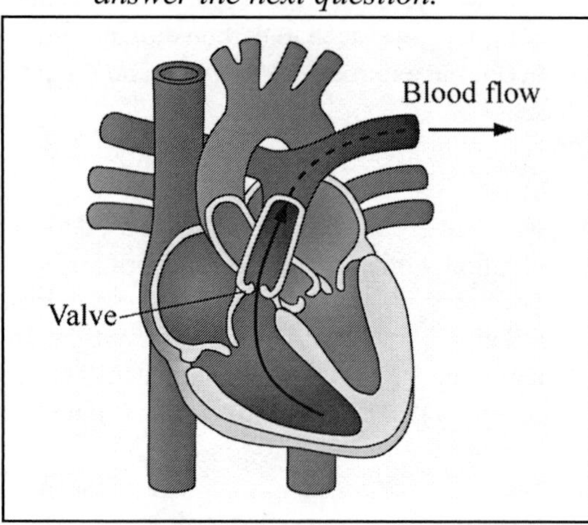

4. Blood flowing in the direction depicted in this illustration of the heart will travel to structures of which internal system **next**?
   A. Musculoskeletal
   B. Respiratory
   C. Digestive
   D. Urinary

Open Response

5. While measuring blood pressure with a sphygmomanometer, the stethoscope is placed on which blood vessel?
   Briefly explain the process by which the sphygmomanometer works.

____

____

____

____

____

Use the following information to answer the next question.

Partial Pressure of Gases at Sea Level (mmHg)			
Gas	Alveolar Air Space	Blood Entering Lungs	Blood Leaving Lungs
Oxygen	100	40	95
Carbon Dioxide	40	45	40

Numerical Response

6. According to the data in the given table, the change in the partial pressure of oxygen in the blood as it moves through the lungs is __________ mmHg.

Open Response

7. List four events that occur during exhalation after the respiratory centre in the brain is stimulated by the stretch receptors in the thoracic wall to stop inhalation.

____
____
____
____
____

Open Response

8. What is the oxygen-carrying molecule that $CO_{(g)}$ competes for? **Explain** its functions.

____
____
____
____
____

Use the following information to answer the next question.

The cross section of the stomach shows the lumen, the muscularis, the submucosa, the mucosa, and rugae.

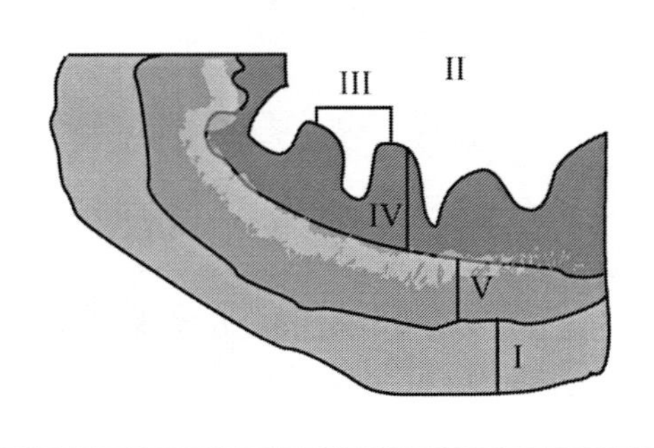

Open Response

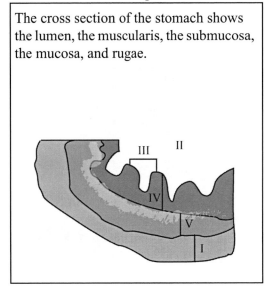

9. **Match** each labelled region of the stomach with its appropriate given term.

I. __________
II. __________
III. __________
IV. __________
V. __________

Open Response

10. **Explain** how the structure of the small intestine facilitates the efficient absorption of nutrients.

____
____
____
____
____
____
____

Use the following information to answer the next question.

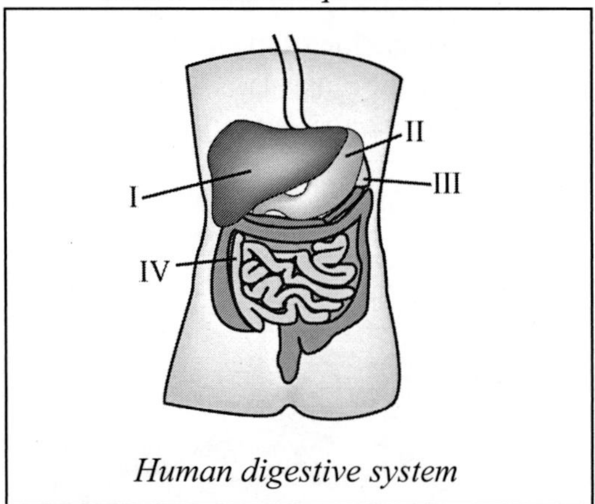

Human digestive system

11. Which of the following enzymes is produced by structure II?

A. Peptidase **B.** Amylase

C. Trypsin **D.** Pepsin

12. Which of the following statements **best** completes the following phrase? Capillaries are a network of vessels _________

A. with thick walls

B. connecting arterioles with venules

C. comprising a small surface area in the body

D. whose diameter can be automatically changed to control blood pressure

Use the following information to answer the next question.

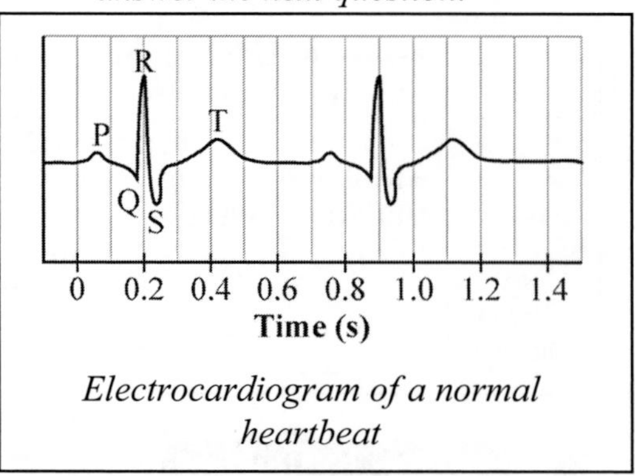

Electrocardiogram of a normal heartbeat

Numerical Response

13. The stroke volume of the patient whose electrocardiogram is shown above is 66 mL/beat. What is the patient's cardiac output? _________ mL/minute

Use the following information to answer the next question.

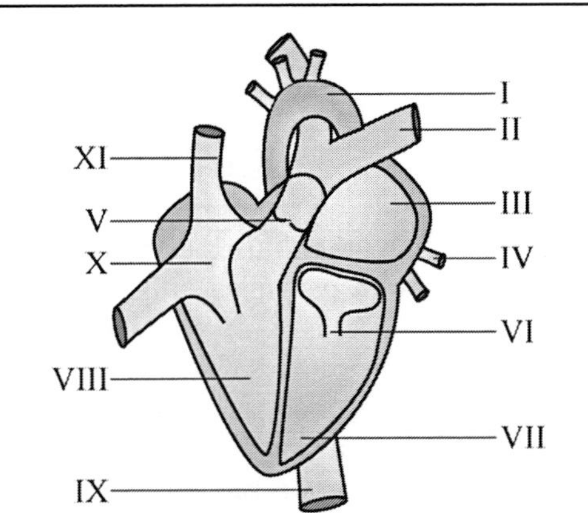

In the given illustration of a mammalian heart, the right atrium and left atrium, right ventricle and left ventricle, aortic arch, pulmonary artery, pulmonary vein, semilunar valve, atrioventricular valve, descending aorta, and superior vena cava are labelled.

Open Response

14. **Match** each labelled part of the mammalian heart to the appropriate given term.

I. ________
II. ________
III. ________
IV. ________
V. ________
VI. ________
VII. ________
VIII. ________
IX. ________
X. ________
XI. ________

Use the following information to answer the next question.

Angina pectoris is a heart condition in which afflicted individuals have a decreased tolerance for exercise due to severe pain in the chest upon physical exertion.

15. The deficiency of the blood supply to heart muscles that causes angina pectoris is called
   A. myocardial infarction
   B. myocardial ischemia
   C. cardiac arrest
   D. endocarditis

Open Response

16. **Hypothesize** how being overweight can cause an increased heart rate and hypertension (high blood pressure).

____
____
____
____
____

ANSWERS AND SOLUTIONS — UNIT TEST

1. C	**5. OR**	**9. OR**	**13. 6600**
2. C	**6. 55**	**10. OR**	**14. OR**
3. OR	**7. OR**	**11. D**	**15. B**
4. B	**8. OR**	**12. B**	**16. OR**

1. C

The systolic pressure is normally 120 mm of Hg whereas diastolic pressure is normally 80 mm of Hg. The former is higher than the latter because blood is forcefully pumped into the arteries by the heart during systole.

2. C

The coronary arteries, found on the outside of the heart, supply blood to the heart muscles.
The subclavian artery supplies blood to the arms. The carotid artery supplies blood to the head and face. The gastric artery supplies blood to the stomach.

3. OR

The term cardiac typically refers to the *heart* and *cardiovascular* system.

4. B

The direction of blood flow depicted in the given illustration is travelling from the right ventricle into the pulmonary arteries. It will be delivered to structures (lungs and alveoli) of the **respiratory system** next where it will be oxygenated and then returned to the heart by way of the pulmonary veins so that it may be delivered to the rest of the body. Blood flowing to the digestive, musculoskeletal, and urinary systems would exit the heart from the left ventricle, not the right.

5. OR

The stethoscope is placed on the *brachial artery* of the same arm upon which the sphygmomanometer is placed. This is usually the left arm.

Once in place on the left arm, at around the same vertical level as the patients heart, the cuff of the sphygmomanometer is pumped and inflated so that the air pressure overcomes the arterial pressure and the brachial artery is compressed to the point that it is completely occluded and no blood can flow into it. Because blood flow is prevented, no sound is heard when listening to the brachial artery with a stethoscope. As the pressure in the cuff is slowly released blood begins to flow into the artery again and a sound is heard through the stethoscope.
The pressure at which the first sound is noted is referred to as the systolic blood pressure. As the pressure in the cuff continues to be released the pressure in the artery changes and eventually no sound is heard. The point at which a sound is no longer heard is referred to as the diastolic blood pressure.

6. 55

Partial pressure is the air pressure contributed by a specific gas when a combination of gases is contributing to total pressure (e.g., oxygen in the blood). In the given table, the partial pressure of oxygen entering the lungs is 40 mmHg. This is lower than the partial pressure of oxygen (100 mmHg) in the alveoli—tiny air sacs at the ends of bronchioles —so oxygen diffuses into blood. (Recall that a gas diffuses from an area of high partial pressure to an area of lower partial pressure.)

As a result, blood leaving the lungs has a higher partial pressure of oxygen (95 mmHg). The increase in the partial pressure of blood oxygen between oxygen entering and leaving the lungs is
95 mmHg – 40 mmHg = 55 mmHg.

7. OR

1. Rib and diaphragm muscles stop contracting and relax
2. Diaphragm returns to the original position (dome-shaped)
3. Thoracic volume is decreased both horizontally and vertically
4. Thoracic pressure increases as thoracic volume decreases in order to force the air from the lungs to the environment

8. OR

An iron-protein compound called **hemoglobin** transports oxygen in the body. Hemoglobin **transports oxygen** from the lungs to the body cells. Then, after oxygen is released, hemoglobin reverses function and picks up **carbon dioxide** and carries it to the lungs to be exhaled. Some molecules, such as carbon monoxide, can bind tightly to hemoglobin molecules, preventing them from transporting oxygen, which then causes severe oxygen deprivation.

9. OR

I. Muscularis
II. Lumen
III. Rugae
IV. Mucosa
V. Submucosa

10. OR

The small intestine has numerous finger-like projections called *villi* each with even smaller epithelial projections called *microvilli*, which increase the surface area for absorption by the small intestine. Each villus contains *capillaries* and *lacteals*, which take part in the absorption of nutrients and fats, respectively. Also, the *epithelium* of the small intestine is thin and moist, allowing for easy diffusion of nutrients across the epithelial membrane. The cells of the small intestine also contain numerous *mitochondria* that provide energy to carry out active transport.

11. D

Structure II is the stomach. The gastric glands of the stomach produce the enzyme pepsin. Pepsin takes part in the digestion of proteins.

The pancreas secretes peptidase, which helps digest small peptide chains, and trypsin, which helps digest proteins.

The pancreas secretes pancreatic amylase, which helps digest starch.

12. B

Capillaries are fine, thin-walled vessels that form a network with a very large surface area responsible for connecting arterioles with venules and for delivery and removal of materials between the blood and body tissues. The automatic change in diameter of arterioles is responsible for controlling blood pressure, not capillaries.

13. 6600

Stroke volume is the volume of blood that is pumped with each beat of one ventricle and is therefore measured in mL per beat.

Cardiac output is the volume of blood that flows from each ventricle per minute, expressed in mL per minute.

Heart rate is the number of times the heart contracts per minute. The formula that relates these three measurements is
Cardiac output = heart rate × stroke volume.

For this question, the stroke volume (66 mL / beat) is provided, and the heart rate can be inferred from the electrocardiogram (ECG). On an ECG, one heartbeat begins when the sinoatrial node (pacemaker) initiates a nerve impulse at the base of the P-wave. The P-wave represents the resulting contraction of the atria.

The heartbeat ends when the ventricles are fully recovered at the end of the T-wave. In the electrocardiogram shown, there are 2 full beats per 1.2 seconds, which represents the heart rate. Plugging the heart rate and stroke volume into the equation above (and converting seconds to minutes), you get

$$\frac{2\text{ Beats}}{1.2\text{ Second}} \times \frac{60\text{ Seconds}}{\text{Minute}} \times \frac{66\text{ mL}}{\text{Beat}} = \frac{6\ 600\text{ mL}}{\text{Minute}}$$

.

The solution to this question can also be derived by solving for the correct units of mL/minute.

$$\frac{\text{Beats}}{\text{Second}} \times \frac{\text{Seconds}}{\text{Minute}} \times \frac{\text{mL}}{\text{Beat}} = \frac{\text{mL}}{\text{Minute}}$$

14. OR

I. Aortic arch
II. Pulmonary artery
III. Left atrium
IV. Pulmonary veins
V. Semilunar valve
VI. Atrioventricular valve
VII. Left ventricle
VIII. Right ventricle
IX. Descending aorta
X. Right atrium
XI. Superior vena cava

15. B

Myocardial ischemia occurs due to deficiency of blood supply to heart muscles, causing angina pectoris.

Myocardial infarction is the death of a part of heart muscle due to lack of blood supply following blockage of the coronary artery, it can lead to cardiac arrest which is the cessation of the rhythmic activities of the heart. Endocarditis is inflammation of the endocardium, usually caused due to rheumatic fever.

16. OR

Obesity forces the heart to work harder because there are more cells to feed. The heart rate increases, which causes a subsequent increase in blood flow to cells to ensure they receive the nutrients and oxygen they demand. Consequently, as the amount of blood flow increases, the amount of pressure on arterial walls also increases.

Plants: Anatomy, Growth, and Function

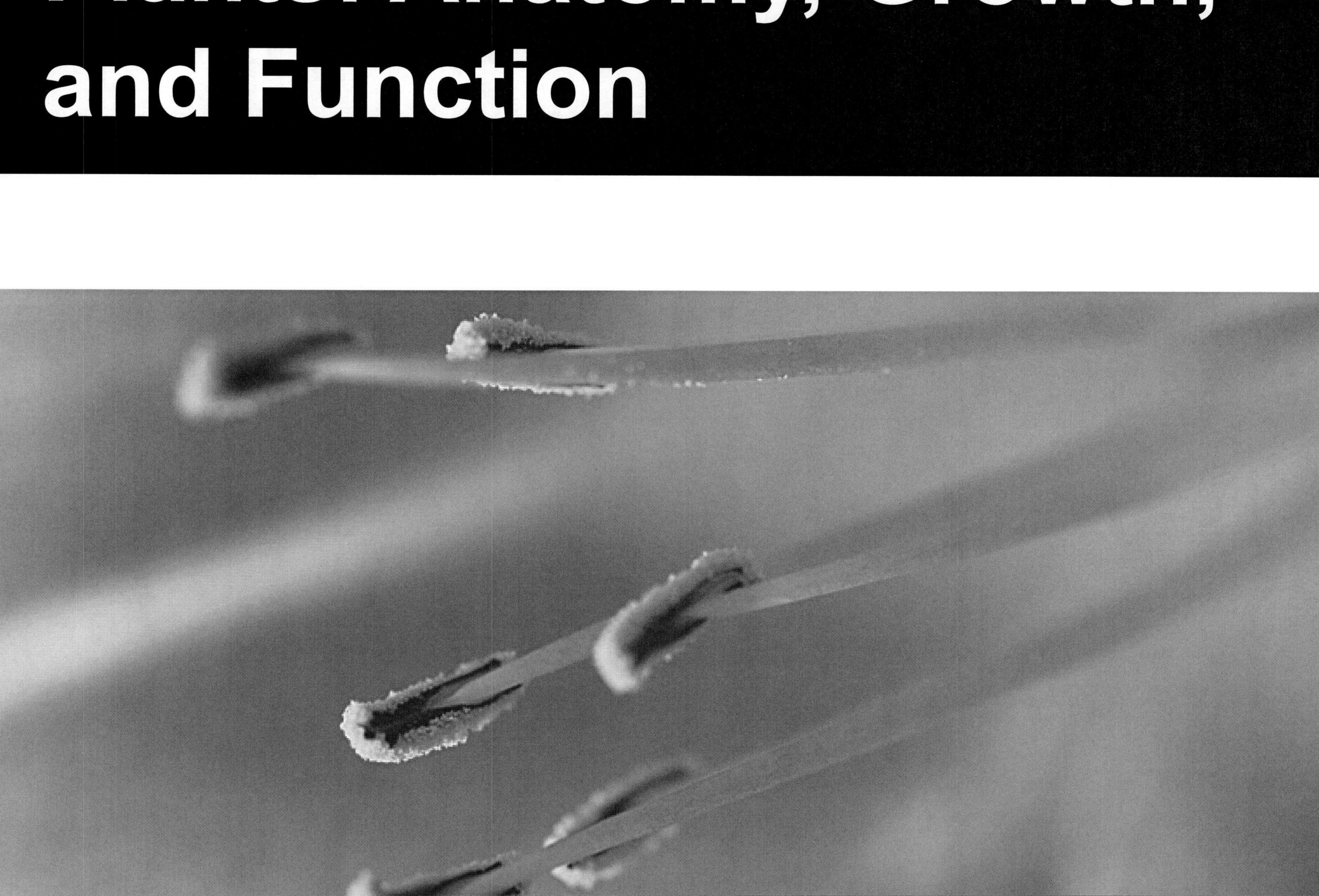

PLANTS: ANATOMY, GROWTH, AND FUNCTION

Table of Correlations

	Specific Expectation	Practice Questions	Unit Test Questions	Practice Test 1	Practice Test 2
11.6.F1	evaluate the importance of sustainable use of plants to Canadian society and other cultures				
11.6.F1.1	*evaluate, on the basis of research, the importance of plants to the growth and development of Canadian society*		11		66
11.6.F1.2	*evaluate, on the basis of research, ways in which different societies or cultures have used plants to sustain human populations while supporting environmental sustainability*	1			67
11.6.F2	investigate the structures and functions of plant tissues, and factors affecting plant growth				
11.6.F2.1	*use appropriate terminology related to plants, including, but not limited to: mesophyll, palisade, aerenchyma, epidermal tissue, stomata, root hair, pistil, stamen, venation, auxin, and gibberellin*	5, 6	12, 13, 14	65, 66, 67	68, 69
11.6.F2.2	*design and conduct an inquiry to determine the factors that affect plant growth*	13			
11.6.F2.3	*identify, and draw biological diagrams of, the specialized plant tissues in roots, stems, and leaves, using a microscope and models*	4			70
11.6.F2.4	*investigate various techniques of plant propagation*	10	15	68	71
11.6.F3	demonstrate an understanding of the diversity of vascular plants, including their structures, internal transport systems, and their role in maintaining biodiversity				
11.6.F3.1	*describe the structures of the various types of tissues in vascular plants, and explain the mechanisms of transport involved in the processes by which materials are distributed throughout a plant*	2, 3	1, 2, 3	1, 2, 3	1, 2
11.6.F3.2	*compare and contrast monocot and dicot plants in terms of their structures and their evolutionary processes (i.e., how one type evolved from the other)*	7, 8	4, 5	4	3
11.6.F3.3	*explain the reproductive mechanisms of plants in natural reproduction and artificial propagation*	9	6	5	4
11.6.F3.4	*describe the various factors that affect plant growth*	11, 12	7, 8	6, 7, 8a, 8b	5, 6, 7
11.6.F3.5	*explain the process of ecological succession, including the role of plants in maintaining biodiversity and the survival of organisms after a disturbance to an ecosystem*	14, 15, 16	9, 10	9	8

11.6.F1.2 evaluate, on the basis of research, ways in which different societies or cultures have used plants to sustain human populations while supporting environmental sustainability

11.6.F1.1 evaluate, on the basis of research, the importance of plants to the growth and development of Canadian society

Contributions of Plants to Society and Sustainable Agricultural Practices

Canadians come into contact with plants and plant products every day. Plants are vital for food, construction, fibre, fuel, and medicines. Plants are also important for the role they play in the environment.

Most of the world's food supply comes from seven major plant crops. These crops include, but are not limited to: wheat, potatoes, barley, maize (corn), and rice.

There are a number of techniques employed to promote environmental sustainability in agriculture. The following is a list of some different techniques adopted and employed by different countries participating in sustainable agricultural practices:

- Crop rotation is an agricultural technique that functions to maintain the nutrient quality of the soil in a given area by alternating the type of crop planted in sequential seasons. It increases yields naturally and decreases the need for artificial fertilizers, thereby limiting further agricultural clearing and environmental pollution.
- Seed saving is an agricultural technique designed to maintain the integrity of the world's major crops. Traditional harvesting procedures involve collecting the seeds or reproductive structures of plants from a current crop for use in next year's rotation. This technique promotes highly adapted crops with improved yields and avoids the need for purchase of seeds from a supplier, an important economic factor in developing countries.
- Companion planting is a technique that promotes the development of polyculture practices in which multiple crop plants are planted together on the same patch of land. Not only does this method increase overall production relative to land area because multiple crops are being grown at once, but it is also thought to improve the yields of the different crops because they inadvertently benefit each other. For example, traditional aboriginal corn production practices such as the Three Sisters technique employed by Native Americans utilized three different crops: squash, corn, and beans. In this combination, the beans utilize the corn stalk for climbing, the corn and squash utilize the nitrogen returned to the soil by the beans, and the squash grows close to the ground, inhibiting the growth of nutrient-depleting weeds by capturing the incoming sunlight.

Other resources valuable to society that come from plants include wood, oils, fruits, vegetables, and fibres. Olive oil, a very healthy and important source of monounsaturated fats (oleic acid), comes from the olive tree. Wood from a variety of tree species is used to build houses. About 90% of all homes in North America are made from wood. Fruits and vegetables provide some of the sustenance and energy required by people for day-to-day living as well as vital vitamins and nutrients. Natural cotton fibre is found around the seeds of the cotton plant. This is a fiber that has been used by humans for centuries. Today, cotton is used in textile products, such as terrycloth and denim, and for the production of coffee filters, fishnets, and paper.

Coal is an example of an important fuel that originates from plants. Farmers are turning to energy crops rather than food crops because environmental concerns have grown in popularity over the last 10 years. In Europe, rapeseed is used for oil and energy. In Canada, the variety of rapeseed grown is called canola. Canola is becoming an accepted biodiesel fuel, and it is valued for its high oil content, better fuel pump response, and improved performance in cold climates.

In ancient times, medicines were mostly derived from plants and their byproducts. Aboriginal people used parts of aspen trees as a means of pain relief long before the substance was refined and used in aspirin. There are many useful plant products that are used as medicines today. For example, morphine, a very strong and important pain medication that is frequently used in hospitals, comes from the poppy flower. The poppy is also responsible for codeine, which is used in cold medication.

The inherent environmental role of plants is also important. Photosynthetic activity by plants functions to help remove carbon dioxide from the atmosphere while at the same time replenishing life-sustaining oxygen. Additionally, plant root systems are important contributors to the quality and quantity of soil in a given area. They play a role in the formation of soil through the breakdown of bedrock. Also, they add nutrients to the soil through their decay and help to prevent erosion by protecting the soil from wind and flooding effects.

Protecting large, intact, forested areas by establishing national and provincial park systems provides people with the opportunity to enjoy outdoor recreational and ecotourism activities. Not only are these areas important economic generators, but they help to maintain ecosystem biodiversity.

Open Response

1. What type of planting does the Aboriginal corn production practice known as the *Three Sisters* demonstrate? How does this practice promote environmental sustainability within agricultural development?

____

____

____

____

____

____

____

11.6.F3.1 describe the structures of the various types of tissues in vascular plants, and explain the mechanisms of transport involved in the processes by which materials are distributed throughout a plant

11.6.F2.1 use appropriate terminology related to plants, including, but not limited to: mesophyll, palisade, aerenchyma, epidermal tissue, stomata, root hair, pistil, stamen, venation, auxin, and gibberellin

11.6.F2.3 identify, and draw biological diagrams of, the specialized plant tissues in roots, stems, and leaves, using a microscope and models

Anatomy and Function of Plant Tissues

Plants are made up of two main systems: the shoot system and the root system. The shoot system is further divided into two subsystems: the leaf and the stem. Water and nutrient transport take place within specialized vascular tissues located throughout the plant.

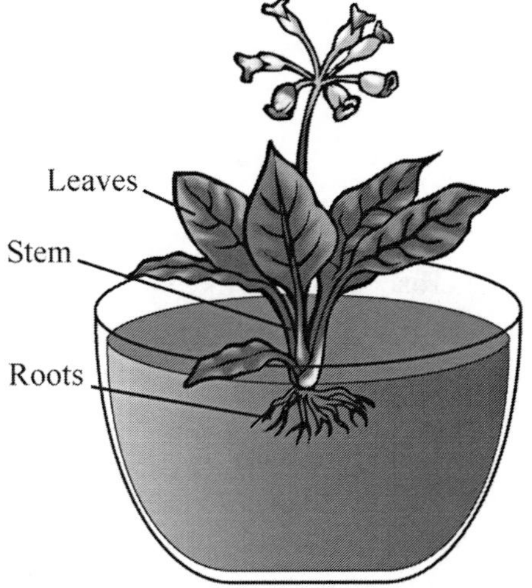

Basic Plant Morphology and Anatomy

The main parts that make up a plant are the leaf, stem, root, and flower.

Leaf

Structure

- Flattened, broad blade usually attached to the stem by a stalk called the petiole.
- Typically green, due to the pigment chlorophyll inside the chloroplasts embedded within the parenchyma cells of the ground tissue, called the mesophyll. The mesophyll is often separated in dicots to include an upper palisade (columnar) layer of cells and a lower spongy layer.
- Small openings within epidermal tissue on the underside of the leave called stomata.
- Reticulated or parallel venation. Veins composed of xylem and phloem vascular tissues.
- Waterproof cuticule, secreted by epidermal tissue, as a protective covering.

Function

- Increases surface area for more light absorption.
- Chloroplasts are the site of photosynthesis; chlorophyll is a pigment that absorbs sunlight.
- Openings (stomata) allow carbon dioxide gas into the leaf and oxygen out; also, they aid in transpiration (pull of water through the plant).
- Xylem brings water and minerals absorbed from the roots into the leaf, and phloem translocates food produced in the leaf to the roots and other non-photosynthetic parts of the plant.
- Cuticle prevents water loss and wilting of the leaves and plant.

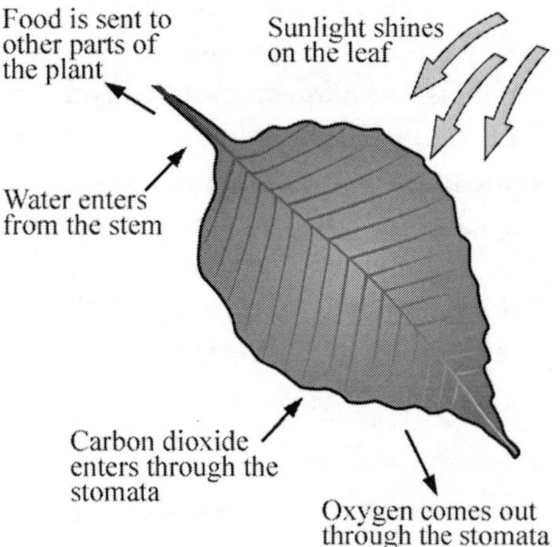

Basic leaf structure and function

Stem

Structure

- Tissues are made of cells with thick cell walls. Outer layer dies, hardens, and remains a part of the stem. Stems are strengthened by collenchyma cells.
- Contains tube-like xylem and phloem arranged into vascular bundles surrounded by ground tissue.
- Alternates between nodes and internodes.

Function

- The stem offers structure and support to the plant. The outer, dead layer gives support to larger plants.
- The xylem transports water and minerals from the roots to the leaves, and phloem translocates the food from the leaves to the rest of the plant.
- Nodes are the site of leaf attachment and internodes are the stem segments between the nodes.

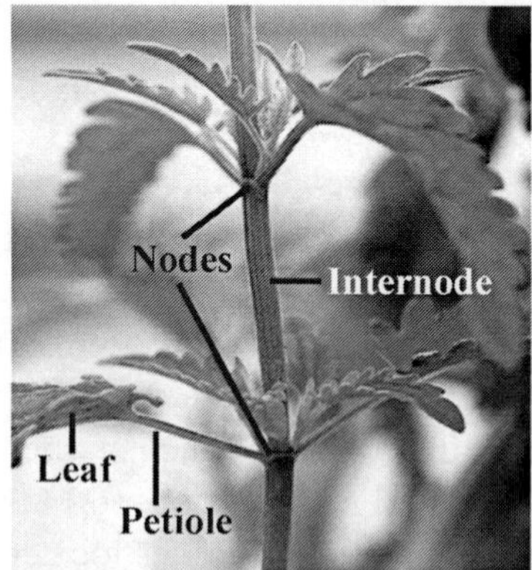

Generalized plant stem demonstrating nodes and internodes

Root

Structure

- Long, microscopic, hair-like epidermal tissue extensions off the root (called root hairs) create a large surface area.
- Roots contain both xylem and phloem arranged within a central cylinder called a stele. The stele is surrounded by the cortex (ground tissue), and the entire root is covered by an epidermal layer. In some roots exposed to anaerobic (no oxygen) conditions, the ground tissues develop into aerenchyma tissues with large air cavities that aid in the exchange of gases between the shoot and the hypoxic root.

Function

- Roots absorb water and nutrients from the soil. The large surface area makes this function more efficient.
- Xylem transports the water and minerals absorbed at the root to the rest of the plant. Food made at the leaves and translocated to the roots by the phloem is sometimes stored by the roots as starch (e.g., peanuts, potatoes, carrots, and beets).

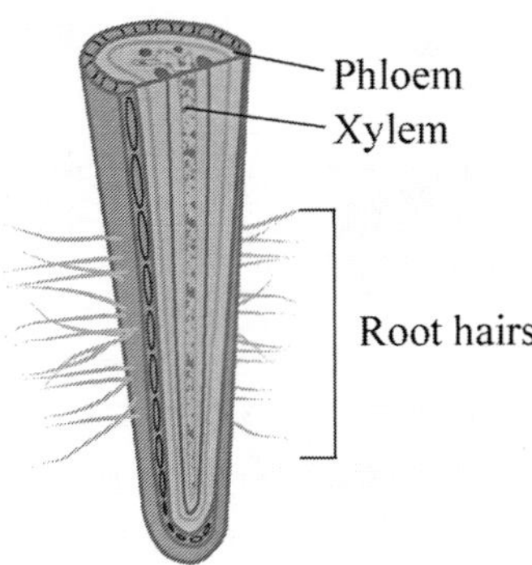

Basic root structure

FLOWER

Structure

- The reproductive female part is called the pistil (or carpel) (1), which includes the stigma (3), style (4), ovary (5), and ovule (6).
- The reproductive male part is called the stamen (2), which includes the anther (8) and filament (9).
- The non-reproductive structures include the petals (7), sepals (10), and receptacle (11).

Function

- The stigma is the sticky female part of the pistil where the pollen attaches. The style functions to transport the pollen down its long tube into the ovary. The ovary holds the ovules (eggs). The ovules are the eggs. When fertilized, this area develops into fruit or seeds.
- The anther is the bulbous male end of the stamen that holds the pollen. The pollen is yellow or orange. The filament is the long stalk of the stamen that supports the anther.
- The petals are typically used to attract insects to pollinate the plant. The sepals are the green part under the flower that protects the ovary. The receptacle is the base of the flower where all the parts attach.

Bracketed numbers correspond to labels in the diagram of the generalized structure of a flower.

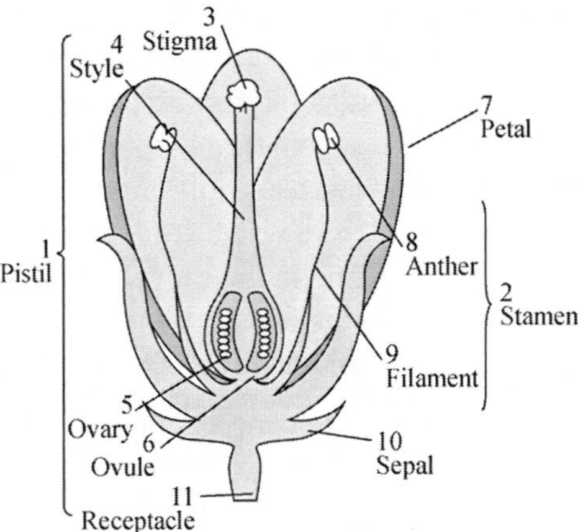

Generalized structure of a flower

Water and Food Transport in Plants

There are three main forces that move water within a plant: root pressure (osmosis), adhesion and cohesion, and transpiration.

1. **Root pressure**—water enters a plant through the hairs via osmosis because the root cells are hypertonic to the water of the surrounding soil. The force of the water moving into the plant by osmosis is called root pressure, and it pushes the water through the xylem of the roots.
2. **Adhesion/cohesion**—the xylem is composed of tiny non-living tube-like cells called tracheids and vessel elements. The force of attraction that exists between the water molecules and the inside surface of these tubules is called adhesion, and it causes water to creep up the xylem the way water would creep up the inside of a drinking straw. The force of attraction that exists between two or more molecules of water is called cohesion, and it further causes water to be pulled up the xylem throughout the plant.
3. **Transpiration**—water is pulled up to the leaves by the evaporation of water at the stomata. In addition to aiding in the movement of water from the roots to the leaves, transpiration also cools the leaves on hot days. This is accomplished through the action of the guard cells that surround the stomata. They swell to open the stomata on hot, sunny days and shrink to close the stomata at night or on cold days. Lenticels are pores on the stems of some plants that serve the same function as the stomata of leaves.

Phloem is the specialized network of sieve tubes that transport food made through photosynthesis in the leaves to the roots and other non-photosynthetic tissues of the plant. The movement of food materials through the phloem is referred to as translocation. Unlike xylem, which is composed of the non-living vessel elements and tracheids, phloem is composed of living cells.

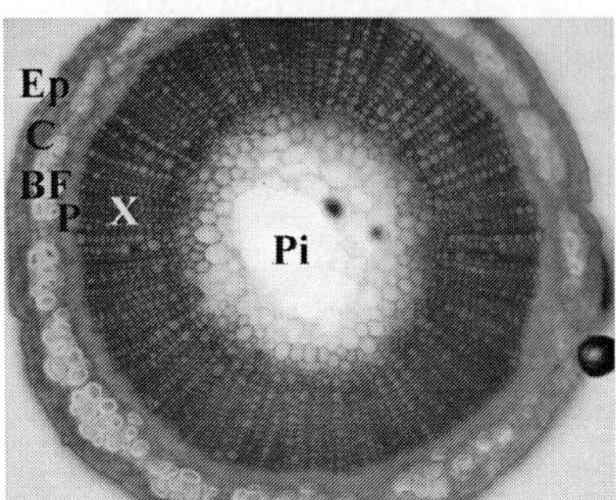

Cross section of a flax stem showing xylem (X) and phloem (P)

2. A vascular bundle in the stem of a plant contains

A. xylem and phloem

B. phloem and root hairs

C. guard cells and xylem

D. root hairs and stomates

3. The function of the endarch xylem is to

A. translocate food

B. provide protection

C. absorb water and minerals

D. provide strength and mechanical support

Use the following information to answer the next question.

The given figure represents a detailed view of the cross section of a plant stem.

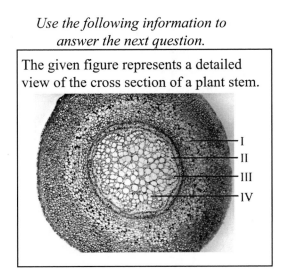

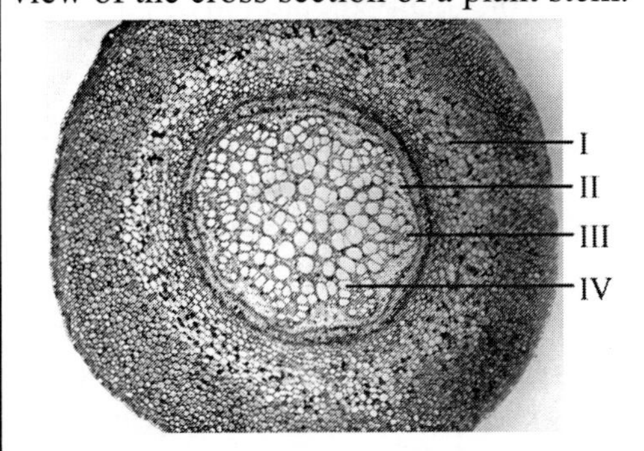

4. In the given figure, the pericycle is labelled

A. I **B.** II

C. III **D.** IV

5. When green plants synthesize complex compounds during photosynthesis, they are trapping solar energy and storing it as chemical energy. The site of photosynthesis in cells is the

A. mitochondria **B.** chloroplasts

C. ribosomes **D.** cytoplasm

Use the following information to answer the next question.

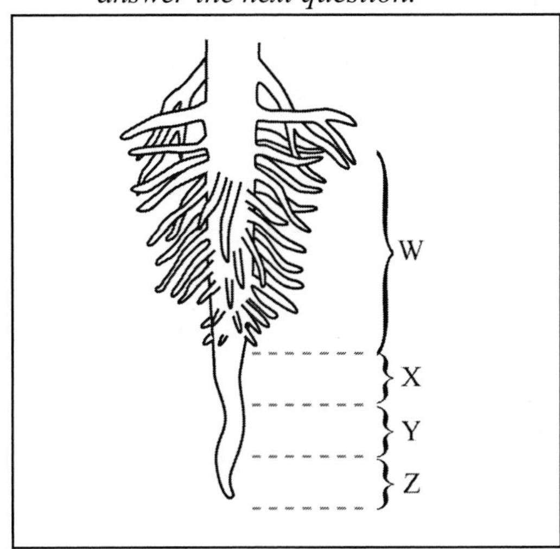

6. In the given diagram, which label represents the region where the root hairs grow?

A. W **B.** X

C. Y **D.** Z

11.6.F3.2 compare and contrast monocot and dicot plants in terms of their structures and their evolutionary processes (i.e., how one type evolved from the other)

Monocots and Dicots

Structure

Cotyledons are the seed leaves produced by the embryo. Monocots have one cotyledon, and dicots have at least two cotyledons. These seed leaves absorb nutrients from the seed until the plant's true leaves are formed.

The arrangement of vascular bundles in the stem of a monocot is scattered, whereas in the stem of dicots, vascular bundles are found in concentric circles.

A simple way to differentiate between a dicot and a monocot is to look at the pattern of veins in the leaves. Generally, monocots have veins that run parallel to the length of the leaf. Examples of monocots with parallel leaves include most types of grasses. Dicots, by contrast, have smaller veins that reticulate between the major veins in a net-like pattern. Examples of dicot leaves include grape and maple leaves.

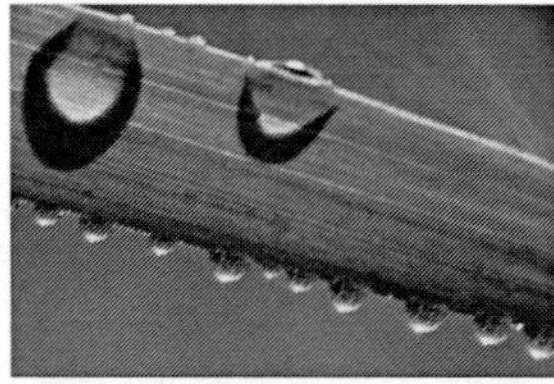

Monocot (grass) leaf with parallel veination

Dicot leaf with net-like veination

The number of flower parts in monocots and dicots also differ. Monocots tend to have flower parts that are divisible by three; for example, most have three or six petals. Dicots have flower parts that are in multiples of four or five.

A monocot has vascular bundles spread throughout the root in a loose ring. The xylem is found closer to the centre of the root, and the phloem is located around it, closer to the outside of the root. In a dicot root, the xylem is packed closely together in the centre of the root and arranged as radiating arms that resemble a cross. The phloem is found between the arms of the xylem.

Evolutionary History

Traditionally, monocots and dicots have been separated into two distinct groups of flowering plants, each originally thought to be monophyletic. Each of the groups was thought to include a common ancestor and all the ancestor's descendants. However, recent theories propose that dicots are actually the older of the two groups, and that monocots evolved from an early line of dicots. In this view, dicots comprise a paraphyletic group because the group includes a common ancestor, and all groups of flowering plants descendant from that ancestor, except for the monocots. The monocots remain a monophyletic group because the group still includes a common ancestor and all the ancestor's descendants.

7. Which of the following images of a leaf does **not** represent a dicot?

   A. 

   B. 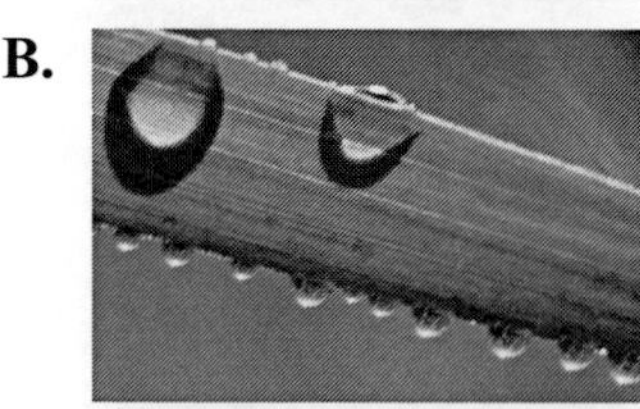

   C. 

   D. 

Use the following information to answer the next question.

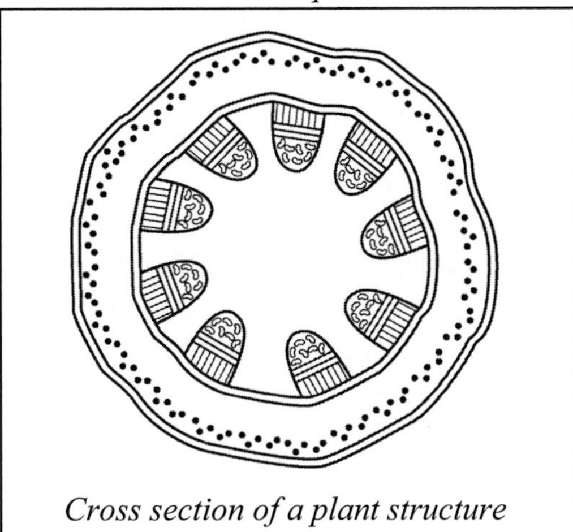

Cross section of a plant structure

Open Response

8. Which of the following structures is represented by the given cross section? Explain how you came to this conclusion.

- Dicot root
- Dicot stem
- Monocot root
- Monocot stem

____
____
____
____
____
____
____

11.6.F3.3 explain the reproductive mechanisms of plants in natural reproduction and artificial propagation

11.6.F2.4 investigate various techniques of plant propagation

Methods of Plant Propagation

Many plant species have the ability to reproduce through both sexual and asexual reproduction. The various reproductive mechanisms used by plants to ensure successful propagation in the wild have inadvertently provided humans with a range of artificial techniques for plant propagation. These techniques function to enhance agricultural plant propagation by exploiting the plant's natural reproductive processes.

Natural Modes of Propagation in Plants

Natural modes of propagation, or reproduction in plants, can be either sexual (with subsequent seed germination) or asexual.

Sexual Reproduction

Sexual reproduction occurs in plants when **pollination** of a female gamete by a male gamete is successful. Once pollination has occurred, a seed grows within the ovule until it is mature and can be released into the environment for dispersal. Embryonic development takes place within the seed's protective package that houses both the embryo and its food supply. Sexual reproduction is advantageous because it promotes genetic diversity and produces seeds. Seeds have dispersal and dormancy properties that allow for great dispersal distances and delay of germination until habitat conditions are favourable for seedling survival.

SEED GERMINATION

Once both internal and external conditions are favourable, the mature, dry seed initiates germination by absorbing ambient water. This is referred to as **imbibition**. The water causes the internal seed tissues to swell and stimulates embryonic growth through the activation of hydrolytic enzymes within the seed that function to break down the seed coat and to mobilize stored food reserves. These food resources are required for cellular respiration, which is in turn responsible for providing the embryo with the energy necessary for mitotic growth into a seedling. Other factors that can affect germination, depending on the species, include temperature, the amount of oxygen present, and the presence or absence of dormancy-ending stimuli such as light, heat from a forest fire, or ingestion by an animal.

Monocot versus Dicot Germination

Different plant groups display different patterns of germination that can be generalized based on whether the plant is a dicot or monocot.

- Monocot germination involves growth of an embryonic root (radicle) sheathed by a **coleorhiza**, followed by growth of an embryonic shoot sheathed by a **coleoptile**. Once the coleoptile breaks the soil surface, light signals the emergence of leaves on the shoot and photosynthesis begins.
- Dicot germination typically involves one of two processes, depending on the plant group: **epigeal** germination or **hypogeal** germination. In both types of germination, the radicle emerges first and begins absorbing water, signalling the growth of the embryonic shoot. The embryonic shoot is composed of three sections: the cotyledons, the epicotyl (portion above the cotyledons), and the hypocotyl (portion below the cotyledons). In epigeal germination, the shoot breaks the soil's surface via elongation and straightening of a hook, or bend, in the hypocotyl. This type of germination functions to pull both the epicotyl and cotyledons through the soil such that both surface along with the hypocotyl (e.g., bean plants). In hypogeal germination, the shoot breaks the soil's surface via elongation and straightening of a hook in the epicotyl. In this manner, only the epicotyl breaches the surface, while the hypocotyl and cotyledons remain underground (e.g., pea plants).

Asexual Reproduction

Some plants reproduce asexually. Asexual reproduction is also called vegetative reproduction and results in the creation of a population of genetically identical plants, or clones. There are a number of different plant structures that contribute to vegetative reproduction.

1. **Rhizomes:** underground horizontal stems that give rise to a new plant by producing roots and shoots from their nodes (e.g., bamboo).
2. **Runners:** horizontal branches of the stem sent out from the base of the plant that run above ground. These runners form roots where they touch the soil, from which new plants can begin to grow (e.g., strawberries). Technically, a type of stolon.
3. **Stolons:** above-ground branches of the stem that grow laterally to reach the soil where they give rise to roots and shoots that can form new plants (e.g., many types of grasses).
4. **Tubers, bulbs, corms:** specialized stem structures that function in carbohydrate storage and can participate in vegetative reproduction through the formation of new plants from vegetative eyes, bulbets, and cormels (e.g., potatoes, onion, and crocuses).
5. **Suckers:** roots sprouted from adventitious buds on existing root systems that exhibit horizontal growth until they are some distance from the original plant. They produce new shoots that travel to the surface to form a new plant (e.g., roses).

Artificial Modes of Propagation in Plants

Human exploitation of a number of different natural modes of propagation in plants has led to a variety of different artificial methods by which to manipulate plant reproduction for human benefit. Seed propagation and grafting are two artificial modes of plant propagation practised by humans.

Seed Propagation

Seed propagation involves planting desired seed varieties in areas that provide ideal environmental conditions for seedling growth. The disadvantages to the approach include seed collection costs, loss of desirable characteristics due to unintentional genetic recombination while selecting for others, and slow growth of fragile and susceptible seedlings.

Vegetative Propagation

Vegetative propagation improves the speed and certainty of agricultural crop propagation. This is because since each plant in the population is genetically identical, the exact tolerance to environmental conditions is consistent among all plants and they can be grown in ideal conditions. Additionally, the plants will all respond to environmental conditions in the same way, developing at similar rates, flowering around the same time, and dying around the same time. On the other hand, this lack of genetic variability also poses a serious disadvantage in the face of unfavourable environmental changes because the crop may lack phenotypic adaptability.

Plant cuttings and grafting provide two examples of vegetative propagation.

- **Cuttings** (leaf, stem, root)—this method involves stimulating the growth of plant fragments such as leaf, stem, or root cuttings, or associated storage structures, by placing them in favourable conditions for development. These fragments are capable of producing new plants due to the establishment of root and shoot systems through mitotic division of existing tissues. For example, a stem cutting will sprout roots from an undifferentiated mass of cells called a **callus** when placed in water (e.g., black berries). Tubers can be cut up into small pieces, each piece with its own vegetative bud, that will grow into a new plant when planted in soil (e.g., potatoes).
- **Grafting**—this technique involves attaching the stem, called the **scion**, of one variety of plant to the root, called the **stock**, of another variety. This is typically done to combine the best qualities of different plants into a single variety and usually helps improve the durability of the scion plant. In order for this to be successful, the vascular tissues of the two plants must fuse properly so that the nutrients and water absorbed by the stock plant can reach the scion and the photosynthetic products created by the scion can reach the non-photosynthetic parts of the stock plant (e.g., many fruit trees).

Open Response

9. Describe the technique of grafting as it is used in the artificial propagation of plants. Include a discussion of what **must** occur in order for a graft to be successful.

____

____

____

____

____

____

____

10. While the flower plays a role in the sexual reproduction of plants, the part of the plant that **most commonly** plays a role in asexual plant propagation is the

A. leaf **B.** root

C. fruit **D.** stem

11.6.F3.4 describe the various factors that affect plant growth

11.6.F2.2 design and conduct an inquiry to determine the factors that affect plant growth

Environmental Conditions Important to Plants

The photosynthetic activity performed by plants is essential to all life on Earth. It is therefore critical to understand plants and the factors that impact their health, growth, and reproduction.

Factors That Affect Plant Growth

Nutrients in Soil

Soil is a naturally occurring land covering that is made up of tiny rock particles and decaying organic matter. Nutrient-rich soil is capable of supporting life, and it is the medium from which plants are sustained. A nutrient is a substance that organisms require to live, reproduce, and grow. Some nutrients are found naturally as they erode out of rocks found in or near the soil. Plants are able to absorb nutrients that are dissolved in water, which enters their root systems.

Plants generally need six nutrients in large amounts (**macronutrients**) and about six in smaller amounts (**micronutrients**) to grow and thrive.
The micronutrients needed by a plant include boron, copper, iron, chloride, manganese, molybdenum, and zinc. Decaying grass, leaves, and other organic matter in the soil provide macronutrients. Nitrogen, phosphorus, and potassium (the three most important macronutrients), along with sulfur, calcium, and magnesium (secondary macronutrients) are critical for plant survival.

Functions of Nutrients

Nutrient	Function
Nitrogen (N)	Stem and leaf growth; produces vegetative or top growth; improves quality of forage crops; composition of chlorophyll and protein
Phosphorus (P)	Root growth; flower growth; fruit development; aids in the formation of oils, sugars, and starches; cellular respiration and photosynthesis
Potassium (K)	Stimulation of early growth; disease resistance; production of chlorophyll; tuber formation; production of starches and proteins; movement of sugar

Sunlight and Water

There are many factors involved in a plant achieving optimum growth. Sunlight and water are basic plant needs. Plants use solar energy and water to convert carbon dioxide into oxygen and simple sugars. Oxygen is another basic need required for the process of cellular respiration. Each plant has specific ideal conditions under which its growth will be optimal. If a plant is grown in unsuitable conditions, it will react negatively. For example, if there is not enough light, the leaves will be small, and plant growth will be slow. However, if there is too much light, the leaves can drop off entirely.

Soil pH

Soil pH is one factor that affects plant growth. Most plants have a range of soil pH tolerance under which they are best suited to grow. Typical soil pH values of optimal growth are in the slightly acidic to neutral to slightly basic range. However, extremely low soil pH, or high acidity, can impact growth in a number of ways. Extreme soil acidity can negatively impact both the biological activity of soil organisms and overall nutrient availability in the soil. This decrease in overall quality of the soil may result in stunted growth and decreased productivity of the plants found in that soil.

Growth Hormones (Regulators)

Another factor that affects the growth of plants is hormones. Plant hormones are chemicals that are manufactured naturally by plants in extremely small amounts. Even though hormones will influence growth, they are not nutrients. These chemicals are used to regulate plant growth at very specific parts of the plant and at very specific stages of their development. Hormones also have to disengage their effects when they are no longer needed or when they have served their purpose. For example, plant hormones affect seed growth, decide which tissues grow upward (stems) and which grow downward (roots), and determine when fruit will develop and ripen.

There are various types of plant hormones including auxins, gibberellins, and cytokinins.

Auxins, the first kind of growth regulators discovered, affect the plant in a positive manner. Auxins are mostly produced in the apical meristem and sometimes in the shoots of plants.
They influence things like root initiation and bud formation. In a strawberry plant, auxins are produced in the seeds and stimulate the development of fruit. They are also responsible for flower development in some plant types. Indoleacetic acid, a type of auxin, is responsible for the elongation of cells because it causes plant cell walls to become softer and more flexible.

Cytokinins are responsible for the regulation of cell division and the formation of shoots. They are also helpful to a plant because they delay the breakdown of tissue, making the plant healthier for longer periods of time. Cytokinins are produced in the roots.

Gibberellins are also needed for proper cellular division. They promote flowering, and are very important during the time of seed germination. Gibberellins help in the breakdown of the food reserves in a seed so that it may be used by the seedling. They are produced in the root and shoot of the plant.

Control Systems in Plants

When plants grow, they respond to environmental factors. These growth patterns are called tropisms.

Phototropism—Most plants grow toward sunlight, with the light (*photo*) being the stimulus and the movement (*tropism*) being the response. Stems and leaves normally have a positive reaction to light, but roots grow in the opposite direction (negative phototropism).

Gravitropism (geotropism)—Plant growth in response to gravity can also be positive or negative. Putting a plant on its side will result in the stem and leaves bending away (negative) from the earth and the roots turning to grow toward (positive) Earth's center. This growth is a result of the detected movement of large starch molecules at the bottom of cells.

Thermotropism—Plants will also respond to changes in temperature. When a plant is warmed, it will continue to grow where it is warm. If conditions are too hot, plants will grow away from the heat before they dry out and die.

Chemotropism—Plants grow toward areas with high concentrations of nutrients. Their roots detect these chemicals, and branches are sent out toward the source. If unwanted chemicals are found close to some plants, they will send roots out in the opposite direction to avoid the chemicals.

Hydrotropism—Desert plants are famous for long root systems that grow great distances down to find water. Plants are able to grow toward soils with higher water concentrations. In swamps, plants actually send their roots upward and outward to find an area that has little water. In this way they spread across swampy areas, crossing from one dry patch to the other.

Investigating Plant Growth Factors

It is possible to conduct an experiment to examine the factors that affect plant growth. This experiment investigates the effects of some different factors on the overall height of pea plants. Some of the variables in the experiment are fertilizer (nutrients), water, temperature, light, soil, and plant type.

A series of experiments can be conducted that involve growing and measuring the heights of multiple pea plants under altered conditions for each of the independent variables separately, so that it is clear which variable is affecting the outcome of the experiment. For example, if the experiment is investigating the affect the quantity of nutrients has on plant growth, then the amount of fertilizer given should be the only variable to change in that experiment. The other variables must remain constant, because some plants may respond and grow taller not because they receive more or less fertilizer, but because they receive more water or less light. The plants can then be compared with a control group to draw a conclusion about the effect that the independent variable had on plant height, and therefore overall plant growth.

11. Mustard seedlings are placed in a small bottle containing water. This bottle is kept inside a wooden box with a hole on one side directly facing a light source. Which of the following events is a probable outcome of this experiment?

A. Both the stems and roots will grow toward the light.

B. Both the stems and roots will grow away from the light.

C. The stems will grow away from the light while the roots will grow toward it.

D. The stems will grow toward the light while the roots will grow away from it.

Use the following information to answer the next question.

The diagram illustrates a shoot of a plant bending toward light as it grows.

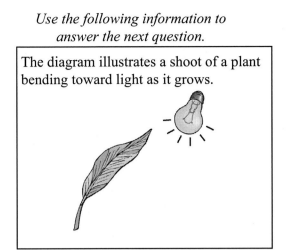

12. This phenomenon occurs because the plant hormone auxin

A. promotes growth on the side closest to the light

B. promotes growth on the side opposite the light

C. inhibits growth on the side closest to the light

D. inhibits growth on the side opposite the light

Open Response

13. While carrying out an experiment to determine the effects of nutrients on plant growth, magnesium is withheld to observe its effects. It is observed that leaves turn yellow without magnesium, indicating its role in photosynthesis, but older leaves turn yellow before young leaves.
Based on these results, explain whether magnesium is transported freely through the plant.

____

____

____

____

____

____

____

11.6.F3.5 explain the process of ecological succession, including the role of plants in maintaining biodiversity and the survival of organisms after a disturbance to an ecosystem

The Process of Ecological Succession

Succession is a fundamental concept in ecology that refers to the gradual and predictable changes in the makeup of a community. Succession may be initiated either by the development of a new, deserted habitat or by some form of disturbance such as the clear-cutting of an existing community. There are two types of succession.

The first type of succession, which is known as **primary succession**, can be defined as a series of changes that take place on an entirely new habitat that has never been occupied. These areas do not have soil. Primary succession begins when plants first start to colonize a deserted area. A sand dune and an unused paved road are examples of areas where primary succession would take place. Examples of the first colonizers include mosses and lichens. These initial colonizers are known as **pioneer species**. The pioneer species are dependent on the geology and history of the area, climate, soil type, and other environmental factors. In most cases where primary succession begins on bare rock, lichens are the pioneer species.

Secondary succession usually occurs at a faster rate than primary succession for a number of reasons. The soil that is present in areas going through secondary succession is capable of sustaining new growth and already contains a collection of seeds from suitable plants. Stumps, root systems, and other parts of the plant that managed to survive the disturbance are now able to grow and regenerate.

In both primary succession and secondary succession, as the plant communities change, so will the animal species that are associated with the vegetation. Both types of succession involve the whole community, not just the flora. In that manner, ecological succession functions to promote the biodiversity of an ecosystem.

Communities change gradually during succession and eventually result in a **climax community**. This is the final stage of both primary and secondary succession. A climax community is a stable, biologically diverse community, where species of plants and animals become well adapted to their new environment. Examples of climax communities include tropical rain forests and tundra.

14. During the process of succession on a bare rock, the pioneer species that will **most likely** appear first is a

A. grass **B.** shrub

C. fungi **D.** lichen

Open Response

15. What is the term used to describe the change that occurs in a community following a forest fire? What factor distinguishes this type of succession from the type that occurs following glacial retreat?

____

____

____

____

____

Open Response

16. In a certain community, species diversity is low during the early stages of succession, increases during the middle stages of succession, and declines in the late stages of succession. Explain why this pattern may emerge.

____

____

____

____

____

____

____

ANSWERS AND SOLUTIONS
PLANTS: ANATOMY, GROWTH, AND FUNCTION

1. OR	5. B	9. OR	13. OR
2. A	6. A	10. D	14. D
3. D	7. B	11. D	15. OR
4. B	8. OR	12. B	16. OR

1. OR

The traditional *Three Sisters* Aboriginal corn production practice demonstrates **companion planting** of three different crops: squash, corn, and beans. This technique promotes environmental sustainability during agricultural development because it involves the growth of different types of plants together on the same piece of land. Because multiple crops are grown at once, the method both **protects against pests and disease**, and **increases overall production** relative to land area. Additionally, it can **increase the yields** of the different crops because cohabitation has mutual benefits for each. The beans utilize the corn as support for climbing, the corn and squash utilize the nitrogen returned to the soil by the beans, and the squash inhibits weed growth by growing close to the ground and capturing any incoming sunlight.

2. A

Vascular tissue transports materials composed of xylem and phloem. Xylem and phloem both exist as tubes. Tiny tubes have a greater surface area relative to their diameter than large tubes do. A vascular bundle is a bundle of tiny xylem and phloem tubes. In a leaf, vascular bundles appear as veins.

3. D

The endarch xylem provides strength and mechanical support to the plant. It prevents rupturing in case of unequal pressure and also supports the conduction of water and minerals from the root to the leaf.

4. B

In the given figure, the pericycle is labelled II. The pericycle lies below the endodermis and forms the outer boundary of vascular tissues. The pericycle protects vascular tissues and strengthens the stem.

Label I represents the cortex, which is the part of the stem that functions in photosynthesis and food storage in plants with green stems. Label III represents the phloem tissue, which conducts glucose and other products of photosynthesis from the palisade parenchyma to the rest of the plant. Label IV represents the xylem tissue, which provides the mesophyll tissues with water and dissolved ions for use in photosynthesis.

5. B

Chloroplasts are organelles found in the cells of green plants. They are the main site of photosynthesis in cells. They are primarily located in the mesophyll tissue of leaves.

6. A

Label W represents the root hairs, which are 1 to 6 cm long each. This region is covered by numerous fine, unicellular hairs, which help in the absorption of water and solutes from the soil, as well as helping to anchor the plant.

7. B

The image depicting a blade of grass does not represent a dicot. Grasses are *monocots*, not dicots. The venation in monocots is parallel while the venation in dicots is net-like. A comparison of the venation patterns in the images of the given leaves reveals that only the grass leaf's pattern is parallel.

8. OR

The diagram depicts the cross section of a *dicot stem*.

The cross section can be identified as a dicot stem by the absence of root hairs, the occurrence of vascular bundles having both xylem and phloem, and the arrangement of vascular bundles in a ring around the pith.

Root hairs are present in dicot roots and monocot roots. In a monocot stem, the vascular bundles lie scattered throughout the pith.

9. OR

Grafting involves attaching the stem (called the *scion*) of one variety of plant to the root (called the *stock*) of another variety of plant. This is done in order to combine the best qualities of two different plants into a single variety. In order for this technique to be successful, the vascular tissues of the two plants must fuse together so that the nutrients and water absorbed by the root plant can reach the stem plant and the photosynthetic products created by the stem plant can reach the non-photosynthetic parts of the root plant.

10. D

Asexual reproduction in plants occurs mainly by vegetative propagation of the stem, which grows a variety of different asexual structures including rhizomes, runners, stolons, tubers, bulbs, and corms. Each of these can either develop into or sprout a new plant.

11. D

A plant stem shows positive phototropism and thus will grow toward a source of light. On the other hand, plant roots show negative phototropism and thus will grow away from light.

12. B

Auxin is a growth hormone that weakens the cell wall. As a result, turgor pressure forces the cell to enlarge. More auxin is produced on the side of the stem that is shaded. Less auxin is produced on the side of the stem that is close to the light.

13. OR

These results show that magnesium can move freely in the plant. If it could not move freely, the older leaves would not turn yellow first, as they would be able to use stored magnesium to carry out photosynthesis. By moving magnesium freely through the plant, it is transported preferentially to young leaves.

14. D

Lichens are the pioneer species in the process of succession on a bare rock. Lichens are composed of algae and fungi living together in a symbiotic relationship. The algae provide the fungi with food via photosynthesis, while the fungi protect the algae from the environment. Lichens can live on bare rock. They secrete chemicals that break down the rock, thereby leading to the accumulation of soil particles on the rock surface. Eventually, enough soil and organic matter accumulate that fungi, mosses, and small plants can grow and further break down the rock into more soil.

15. OR

The term used to describe the change that occurs in a community following a forest fire is **secondary succession**. The factor that distinguishes this type of succession from the type of succession that occurs following glacial retreat is the **presence of an established soil layer**. In the type of succession that occurs following glacial retreat (that is, in primary succession), there is no soil for seeds to germinate in and for seedlings to take root in so these areas are typically colonized first by pioneer species such as lichens. This is different than in an area ravaged by forest fire where the soil layer is still intact and may even already be host to a number of dormant seeds waiting for the right type of environmental conditions to germinate.

16. OR

During the early stages of succession, only a few pioneer species are capable of surviving in the environment. As these species become established, they change the conditions by providing food and microclimates. This lets more species enter the community. The midpoint of maximum species diversity results when conditions still allow for the early species to survive, but can also support later successional species. Diversity declines as competition for resources causes the loss of some species, and environmental conditions favour the survival of later successional species over early successional species.

UNIT TEST — PLANTS: ANATOMY, GROWTH, AND FUNCTION

1. Which of the following functions do plant roots **not** perform?
   A. Store food
   B. Absorb water
   C. Produce food
   D. Anchor the plant

2. Which of the following structures is **not** a vascular tissue?
   A. Xylem **B.** Phloem
   C. Cuticle **D.** Tracheid

Use the following information to answer the next question.

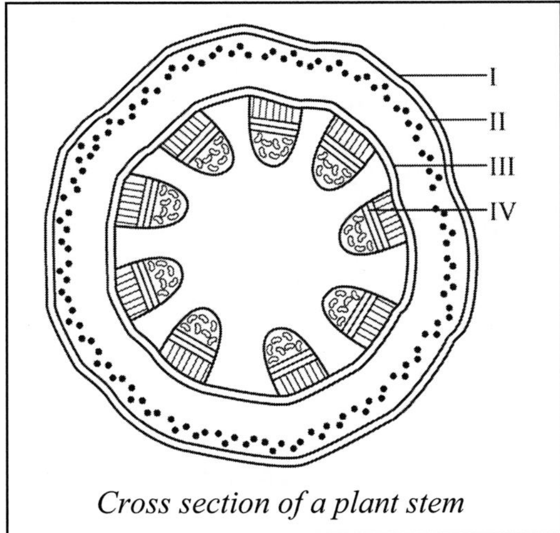

Cross section of a plant stem

3. In the given figure, vascular tissue is labelled
   A. I **B.** II
   C. III **D.** IV

4. Which of the following statements about monocot and dicot roots is **true**?
   A. Only dicots have root hairs.
   B. Only monocots have root hairs
   C. Monocots have pith in the centre of the vascular cylinder
   D. Dicots have branching arms of xylem surrounded by phloem

Open Response

5. List three ways in which monocot and dicot seeds are different from each other.

____
____
____
____
____
____
____

Use the following information to answer the next question.

Grafting is the transfer of the _________ from a plant with desirable properties onto the _________ of another plant which is well established and hardy.

Open Response

6. Use two of the following plant terms to **best** complete the given statement.

- buds
- scion
- stock
- leaves
- roots

____
____
____
____
____

Use the following information to answer the next question.

In an experiment, four grains of maize are placed vertically on a cotton pad in a petri dish. The radicle of each grain is oriented in a different direction. After several days, it is observed that irrespective of their positions, the radicles of all the seeds grow in a downward direction while the coleoptiles of the seeds grow in an upward direction.

7. This experiment demonstrates that

A. roots are positively geotropic

B. stems are positively geotropic

C. both stems and roots are negatively geotropic

D. neither stems nor roots are negatively geotropic

Use the following information to answer the next question.

2,4-D is the most widely used herbicide in the world. It is a synthetic auxin that is used to kill broadleaf weeds.

Open Response

8. Hypothesize the mechanism by which 2,4-D kills weeds.

____

____

____

____

____

____

____

Use the following information to answer the next question.

Primary succession would occur ____1____, where the first organisms present are called a ____2____ community. During the first 20 years in the development of a community, the number of species would be expected to ____3____.

9. Which of the following rows completes the given statement?

A.

1	2	3
in an area clearcut by logging	pioneer	increase

B.

1	2	3
on land where a glacier has retreated	pioneer	increase

C.

1	2	3
on land cleared by a forest fire	climax	decrease

D.

1	2	3
on weathered land	climax	decrease

Open Response

10. Does a mature forest remain unchanged once it has reached its climax stage? **Explain** your reasoning.

____

____

____

____

____

____

____

Use the following information to answer the next question.

Canada is an international leader with regards to the establishment of National Parks System such as Banff NP in Alberta, Glacier NP in British Colombia, and St. Lawrence Islands NP in Ontario.

Open Response

11. List three ways in which development of a National Parks system can contribute to the growth and development of Canadian society.

____

____

____

____

____

Use the following information to answer the next question.

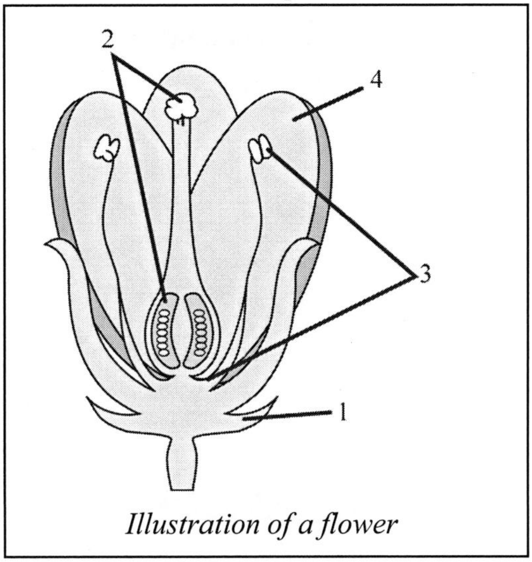

Illustration of a flower

Numerical Response

12. Match the labels in the given illustration with the morphological terms for the structures they identify. (Record your answer as a four-digit number.)

Morphological Term	Numerical Label
Carpel	________
Sepal	________
Stamen	________
Petal	________

13. Parenchyma, collenchyma, and sclerenchyma are the constituent cells of

A. ground tissue

B. muscle tissue

C. vascular tissue

D. connective tissue

Use the following information to answer the next question.

Vertical Section of a Leaf

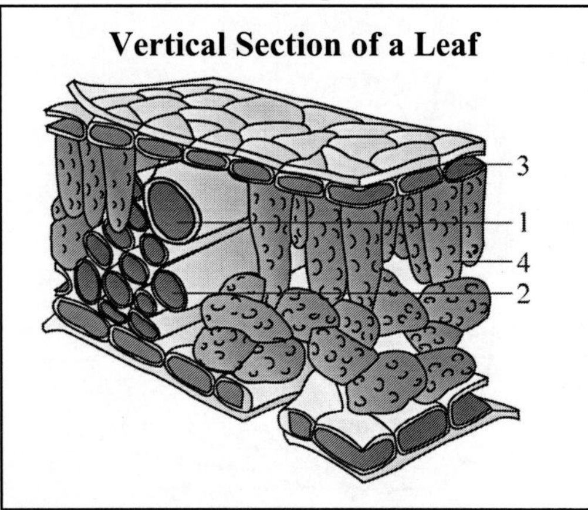

Numerical Response

14. In the given vertical section of a leaf, the two labels corresponding to the structures that comprise the vascular bundle are _________ and _________. (Record your answer as a two-digit number in order from lowest-to-highest numerical order).

15. Which of the following processes is **not** a type of artificial vegetative propagation?

A. Cutting

B. Grafting

C. Perennation

D. Micropropagation

ANSWERS AND SOLUTIONS — UNIT TEST

1. C	5. OR	9. B	13. A
2. C	6. OR	10. OR	14. 12
3. D	7. A	11. OR	15. C
4. D	8. OR	12. 2134	

1. C

Food is produced in photosynthetic tissue and then transported to the roots, where it may be stored.

2. C

A cuticle is a waxy substance produced by the epidermal cells of the leaves. Tracheids are elongated cells found within the xylem, which is a vascular tissue. The phloem is also a vascular tissue.

3. D

Vascular tissue is labelled IV in the given figure. There are two main types of vascular tissue: xylem and phloem. Xylem passes water and dissolved ions from the roots to the photosynthetic tissues. Phloem passes glucose and other photosynthetic products from the photosynthetic cells to the rest of the plant. These vascular tissues also provide support to the stem.

Label I represents the epidermis. The epidermis is a single layer of cuticle-covered cells that protect the inner cells from damage and water loss while allowing light to reach photosynthetic cells. Label II represents the hypodermis. The hypodermis functions to prevent water loss from the plant through the stem. Label III represents the endodermis. The endodermis stores starch and passes nutrients from the vascular tissue to the cortex.

4. D

Vascular bundles are arranged in loose rings in monocot roots, and as branching arms in the dicot root. Therefore, D is the correct answer. Root hairs are present in both monocot and dicot roots.

5. OR

1. Number of cotyledons—A monocot seed has a single cotyledon, and a dicot seed has two cotyledons.
2. Embryonic position within the seed—In dicot seeds, the embryo occupies the entire interior of the seed; in monocot seeds, the embryo occupies only one side of the interior.
3. Presence or absence of embryonic sheath—In monocot seeds, the tip of the plumule (shoot) bears a sheath called a coleoptile, while the tip of the radicle (root) bears a sheath called a coleorhiza. These are not present in dicot seeds.

6. OR

Grafting is the transfer of the **scion** (shoot with buds and/or leaves) from a plant with desirable characteristics onto the **stock** (lower part) of another plant with an established and hardy root system. Grafting is a method of plant propagation widely used in horticulture where the tissues of one plant are encouraged to fuse with those of another. It is most commonly used for the propagation of commercially grown trees and shrubs.

7. A

In this experiment, roots grow in a downward direction toward the force of gravity. Therefore, they are positively geotropic. On the other hand, the stems grow in an upward direction, showing negative geotropism.

8. OR

Auxins are plant growth regulators. 2,4-D is a synthetic auxin, so it will have a mode of action similar to natural auxins. Auxins usually regulate plant growth, so excess amounts of hormone (such as the application of 2,4-D) will most likely lead to excessive and uncontrolled plant growth.
The uncontrolled growth will kill the plant.
The selectivity of the herbicide for weeds is most likely dependent on the difference in absorbance of the herbicide by broadleaf weeds compared to other plants.

9. B

Primary succession refers to the changes in a community of organisms that begins on a site where there is no community at all. The land released from a retreating glacier would qualify (1).

A pioneer community is a group of species that would be the first to populate the area (2).

Since the community begins with the first species to invade an area, after 20 years, the number of species is sure to have increased (3).

10. OR

There are several possible answers.

Yes, the community remains relatively unchanged as the dominant plant and animal species remain constant over the years with minor cyclical changes (dynamic equilibrium) occurring as seasons change or as small natural disasters occur, such as floods. This will cause secondary succession to occur until the climax community is reached again.

No, the community does not remain unchanged as large scale natural disasters (landslides, floods, fires) or man-made changes (land cultivation, logging, industry) create major changes to the biotic elements of the community. A climax community will return, but it may not be the same as the previous one because pollution, soil amounts, or changing nutrient levels alter the abiotic factors, which in turn, are reflected in the type of biotic factors that are able to now grow in the area.

11. OR

1. National Parks bolster local and provincial economies by providing a setting that is ideal for ecotourism, which is a billion dollar industry.
2. National Parks inherently protect natural resources by protecting the natural diversity of an area and the ecological interactions that occur there.
3. National Parks promote sustainable land use practices for future generations.
4. Any other reasonable answer regarding the benefits of a National Park system to the Canadian economy and people.

12. 2134

The following table correctly matches the numerical labels with their corresponding morphological terms:

Morphological Term	Numerical Label
Carpel	2
Sepal	1
Stamen	3
Petal	4

Structure 1 represents the sepal—a modified leaf that encloses the flower before it opens. Structure 2 represents the carpel (or pistil) —the female reproductive structure in the flower. Structure 3 represents the stamen—the male reproductive structure in the flower. Structure 4 represents the petal—a different set of modified leaves that are usually bright in colour to attract pollinators. The correct numerical response is therefore 2134.

13. A

Parenchyma, collenchyma, and sclerenchyma are constituent cells of the **ground tissue** in plants. Parenchyma cells are the most common and versatile, forming everything from the cortex of roots and stems to the endosperm of seeds, the pulp of fruit, and the mesophyll of leaves. Collenchyma cells are elongated and thickened and primarily designed to provide structural support to the growing shoots and leaves of a plant. Sclerenchyma cells are another type of support cell with thickened cell walls designed to provide the majority of the strength to plant tissues that have ceased elongation.

Parenchyma, collenchyma, and sclerenchyma are components of plant tissue, not muscle tissue. Vascular tissue is a type of complex tissue present in vascular plants. The primary components of vascular tissue are xylem and phloem. Connective tissue is present in animals and absent in plants.

14. 12

Label 1 represents the xylem tissue. The xylem provides the mesophyll tissues with water and dissolved ions for use in photosynthesis. Label 2 represents the phloem tissue. The phloem conducts the glucose and other products of photosynthesis from the palisade parenchyma to the rest of the plant. The two tissues together comprise the vascular bundle. The corresponding numerical response is 12.

Label 3 represents the epidermis. The epidermis functions in protection and regulation of gas exchange.

Label 4 represents the palisade parenchyma. The palisade parenchyma functions mainly in photosynthesis and has a high concentration of chloroplasts in order to perform this function.

15. C

Perennation is a type of natural, not artificial, vegetative propagation. A perennial plant that dies after completing its season has surviving underground parts that will produce new plants during the next season. Examples of perennial plants include potatoes, onions, tulips, and crocuses.

NOTES

Key Strategies for Success on Tests

KEY STRATEGIES FOR SUCCESS ON TESTS

THINGS TO CONSIDER WHEN TAKING A TEST

It is normal to feel anxious before you write a test. You can manage this anxiety by using the following strategies:

- Think positive thoughts. Imagine yourself doing well on the test.
- Make a conscious effort to relax by taking several slow, deep, controlled breaths. Concentrate on the air going in and out of your body.
- Before you begin the test, ask questions if you are unsure of anything.
- Jot down key words or phrases from any instructions your teacher gives you.
- Look over the entire test to find out the number and kinds of questions on the test.
- Read each question closely, and reread if necessary.
- Pay close attention to key vocabulary words. Sometimes, these words are **bolded** or *italicized*, and they are usually important words in the question.
- If you are putting your answers on an answer sheet, mark your answers carefully. Always print clearly. If you wish to change an answer, erase the mark completely, and ensure that your final answer is darker than the one you have erased.
- Use highlighting to note directions, key words, and vocabulary that you find confusing or that are important to answering the question.
- Double-check to make sure you have answered everything before handing in your test.
- When taking tests, students often overlook the easy words. Failure to pay close attention to these words can result in an incorrect answer. One way to avoid this is to be aware of these words and to underline, circle, or highlight them while you are taking the test.
- Even though some words are easy to understand, they can change the meaning of the entire question, so it is important that you pay attention to them. Here are some examples.

all	always	most likely	probably	best	not
difference	usually	except	most	unlikely	likely

Example

1. Which of the following expressions is **incorrect**?

A. $3 + 2 \geq 5$

B. $4 - 3 < 2$

C. $5 \times 4 < 15$

D. $6 \times 3 \geq 18$

Test Preparation and Test-Taking Skills

Helpful Strategies for Answering Multiple-Choice Questions

A multiple-choice question gives you some information and then asks you to select an answer from four choices. Each question has one correct answer. The other choices are distractors, which are incorrect.

The following strategies can help you when answering multiple-choice questions:

- Quickly skim through the entire test. Find out how many questions there are, and plan your time accordingly.
- Read and reread questions carefully. Underline key words, and try to think of an answer before looking at the choices.
- If there is a graphic, look at the graphic, read the question, and go back to the graphic. Then, you may want to underline the important information from the question.
- Carefully read the choices. Read the question first and then each choice that goes with it.
- When choosing an answer, try to eliminate those choices that are clearly wrong or do not make sense.
- Some questions may ask you to select the best answer. These questions will always include words like *best*, *most appropriate*, or *most likely*. All of the choices will be correct to some degree, but one of the choices will be better than the others in some way. Carefully read all four choices before choosing the answer you think is the best.
- If you do not know the answer, or if the question does not make sense to you, it is better to guess than to leave it blank.
- Do not spend too much time on any one question. Make a mark (*) beside a difficult question, and come back to it later. If you are leaving a question to come back to later, make sure you also leave the space on the answer sheet, if you are using one.
- Remember to go back to the difficult questions at the end of the test; sometimes, clues are given throughout the test that will provide you with answers.
- Note any negative words like *no* or *not*, and be sure your answer fits the question.
- Before changing an answer, be sure you have a very good reason to do so.
- Do not look for patterns on your answer sheet, if you are using one.

HELPFUL STRATEGIES FOR ANSWERING WRITTEN-RESPONSE QUESTIONS

A written response requires you to respond to a question or directive indicated by words such as explain, predict, list, describe, show your work, solve, or calculate. The following strategies can help you when answering written-response questions:

- Read and reread the question carefully.
- Recognize and pay close attention to directing words such as *explain*, *show your work*, and *describe.*
- Underline key words and phrases that indicate what is required in your answer, such as *explain*, *estimate*, *answer*, *calculate*, or *show your work.*
- Write down rough, point-form notes regarding the information you want to include in your answer.
- Think about what you want to say, and organize information and ideas in a coherent and concise manner within the time limit you have for the question.
- Be sure to answer every part of the question that is asked.
- Include as much information as you can when you are asked to explain your thinking.
- Include a picture or diagram if it will help to explain your thinking.
- Try to put your final answer to a problem in a complete sentence to be sure it is reasonable.
- Reread your response to ensure you have answered the question.
- Ask yourself if your answer makes sense.
- Ask yourself if your answer sounds right.
- Use appropriate subject vocabulary and terms in your response.

What You Need to Know about Science Tests

To do well on a science test, you need to understand and apply your knowledge of scientific concepts. Reading skills can also make a difference in how well you perform. Reading skills can help you follow instructions and find key words, as well as read graphs, diagrams, and tables.

Science tests usually have two types of questions: knowledge questions and skill questions. Knowledge questions test for your understanding of science ideas. Skill questions test how you would use your science knowledge.

How You Can Prepare for Science Tests

The following strategies are particular to preparing for and writing science tests:

- Note taking is a good way to review and study important information from your class notes and textbook.
- Sketch a picture of the process or idea being described in a question. Drawing is helpful for learning and remembering concepts.
- Check your answer to practice questions the require formulas by working backward to the beginning. You can find the beginning by going step by step in reverse order.
- Use the following steps when answering questions with graphics (pictures, diagrams, tables, or graphs):
  1. Read the title of the graphic and any key words.
  2. Read the test question carefully to figure out what information you need to find in the graphic.
  3. Go back to the graphic to find the information you need.
- Always pay close attention when pressing the keys on your calculator. Repeat the procedure a second time to be sure you pressed the correct keys.

Test Preparation Countdown

If you develop a plan for studying and test preparation, you will perform well on tests.

Here is a general plan to follow seven days before you write a test.

Countdown: 7 Days before the Test

1. Use "Finding Out about the Test" to help you make your own personal test preparation plan.
2. Review the following information:
   - Areas to be included on the test
   - Types of test items
   - General and specific test tips
3. Start preparing for the test at least seven days before the test. Develop your test preparation plan, and set time aside to prepare and study.

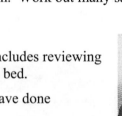

Countdown: 6, 5, 4, 3, 2 Days before the Test

1. Review old homework assignments, quizzes, and tests.
2. Rework problems on quizzes and tests to make sure you still know how to solve them.
3. Correct any errors made on quizzes and tests.
4. Review key concepts, processes, formulas, and vocabulary.
5. Create practice test questions for yourself, and answer them. Work out many sample problems.

Countdown: The Night before the Test

1. Use the night before the test for final preparation, which includes reviewing and gathering materials needed for the test before going to bed.
2. Most importantly, get a good night's rest, and know you have done everything possible to do well on the test.

Test Day

1. Eat a healthy and nutritious breakfast.
2. Ensure you have all the necessary materials.
3. Think positive thoughts, such as "I can do this," "I am ready," and "I know I can do well."
4. Arrive at your school early, so you are not rushing, which can cause you anxiety and stress.

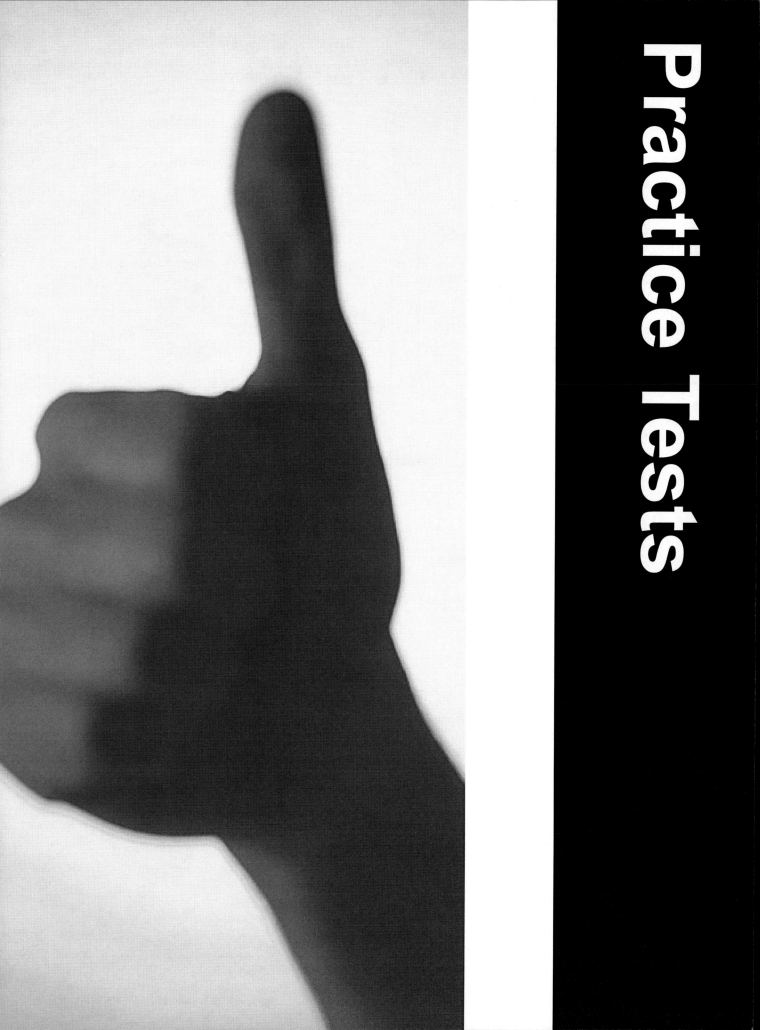

Practice Tests

PRACTICE TEST 1

Use the following information to answer the next question.

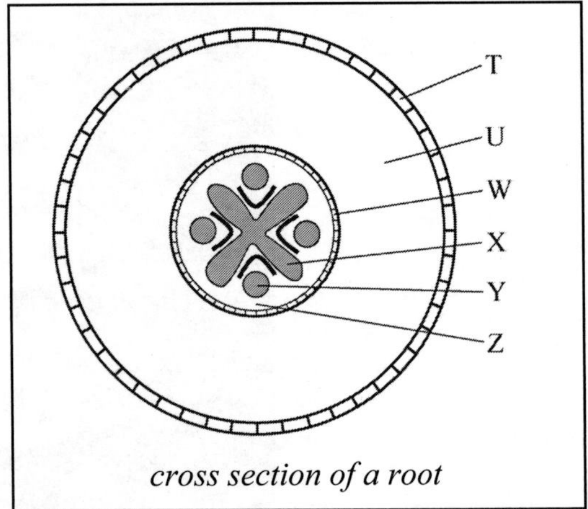

cross section of a root

1. Which of the labelled structures in this cross section of a root is immediately adjacent to the vascular bundle?
   A. W
   B. X
   C. Y
   D. Z

Use the following information to answer the next question.

The given figure shows the cross section of a leaf.

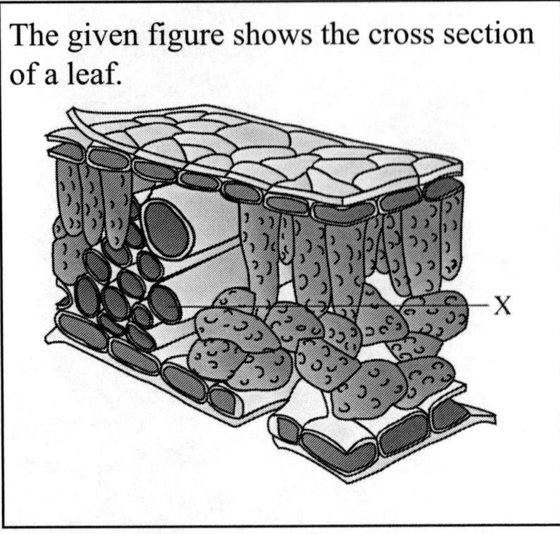

2. In the given figure, structure X represents the
   A. palisade parenchyma
   B. upper epidermis
   C. phloem
   D. xylem

Use the following information to answer the next question.

Tissues found in plants:

1. pith
2. cork
3. xylem
4. phloem

Numerical Response

3. When the given tissues are arranged in order as they would occur in a poplar tree starting from the outside and moving in to the center of the trunk, the order is ______, __________, __________ and __________. (Record your answer as a four-digit number.)

4. Which of these statement regarding monocots and dicots is **true**?
   A. Vascular bundles have a ring arrangement in monocots and a complex arrangement in dicots.
   B. One cotyledon is present in monocots and two cotyledons are present in dicots.
   C. Veins are netlike in monocots and parallel to one another in dicots.
   D. Root system is a taproot in monocots and fibrous in dicots.

5. Asexual reproduction occurs in flowering plants and is called vegetative propagation. Which of the following vegetatively reproducing structures is **not** a stem modification?
   A. Rhizomes
   B. Stolons
   C. Bulbils
   D. Bulbs

6. Which of the following hormones is a type of auxin?
   A. Ethylene
   B. Gibberellins
   C. Abscisic acid
   D. Indole acetic acid

7. Auxins induce apical dominance in plants by suppressing the development of
   A. floral buds
   B. nodal buds
   C. apical buds
   D. lateral buds

Use the following information to answer the next multipart question.

8. Plants all over the world produce on average nine times as much oxygen as they consume.

Open Response

a) **Explain** why plants require oxygen.

____
____
____
____
____

b) How is the balance of oxygen and carbon dioxide maintained over Earth as a whole?

____
____
____
____
____
____
____

9. Migration, which is the second step in the process of succession, involves the movement of
   A. seeds and spores of organisms into a bare area
   B. seeds and spores of organisms out of an area
   C. animals into a bare area
   D. animals out of an area

Open Response

10. Explain how a wildfire can increase the biodiversity in an area.

____
____
____
____
____
____
____

11. One of the impacts of global climate change is rising sea levels. Which of the following outcomes is the **most likely** impact of coastal flooding caused by rising sea levels on the biodiversity of a **terrestrial** coastal community?
   A. Habitat loss, promoting a decrease in biodiversity
   B. Habitat loss, promoting an increase in biodiversity
   C. Habitat expansion, promoting a decrease in biodiversity
   D. Habitat expansion, promoting an increase in biodiversity

Use the following information to answer the next question.

> Bacteria are extremely diverse and are found in virtually every environment on Earth. Some bacteria live endosymbiotically within fungi, plants, and animals. Some of these bacteria live mutalistically with these organisms and are essential to their survival.
> Bacteria are also crucial in the recycling of nutrients, such as fixing nitrogen in soil to be absorbed by plants and ingested by animals.
>
> Bacteria can also be pathogenic and capable of causing a variety of diseases, such as tuberculosis, cholera, leprosy, and the bubonic plague.

12. Which of the following inferences can be made based on the above statements?
   A. Bacteria are harmful
   B. Bacteria are beneficial
   C. Bacteria are both harmful and beneficial
   D. Bacteria are neither harmful nor beneficial

Use the following information to answer the next question.

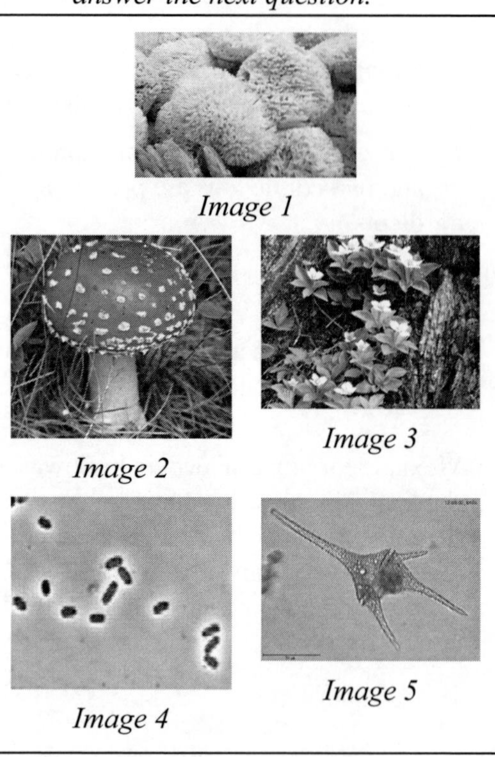

Image 1 *Image 2* *Image 3* *Image 4* *Image 5*

Numerical Response

13. **Match** each of the representative organisms pictured above to their respective kingdom. (Record your answer as a five-digit number.)

Kingdom	Representative Image Number
Monera	________
Protista	________
Fungi	________
Animalia	________
Plantae	________

14. The vast majority of organisms in the kingdom Animalia are
   A. invertebrates
   B. vertebrates
   C. bacteria
   D. protists

Use the following information to answer the next question.

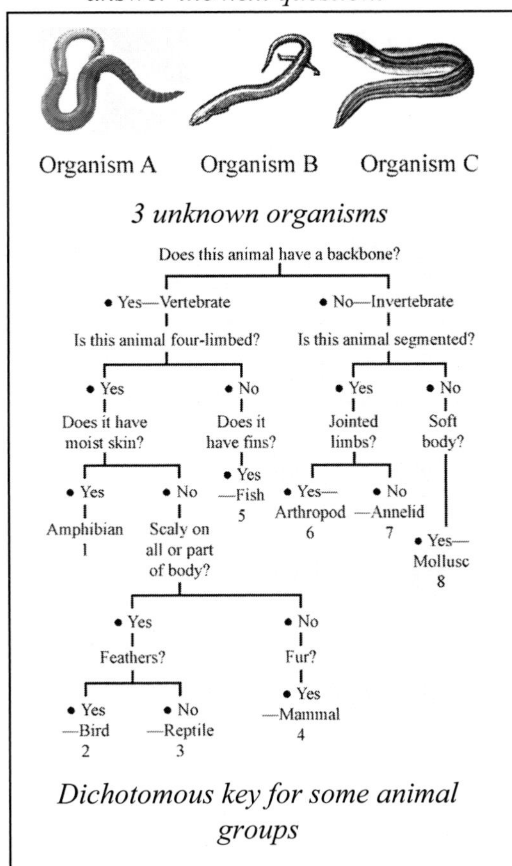

Dichotomous key for some animal groups

Numerical Response

15. Use the dichotomous key to match each unknown organism A, B, and C to the classification number that applies to it. (Record your answer as a three-digit number).

Unknown Organism	Classification Number
A	________
B	________
C	________

16. The taxonomic or binomial name of the tiger is *Panthera tigris*. The terms *Panthera* and *tigris*, **respectively**, are the

A. species and genus

B. genus and species

C. order and class

D. class and order

17. Which of the following appendages is common to both protists and monerans?

A. Cilia

B. Fimbria

C. Flagella

D. Pseudopodia

Use the following information to answer the next question.

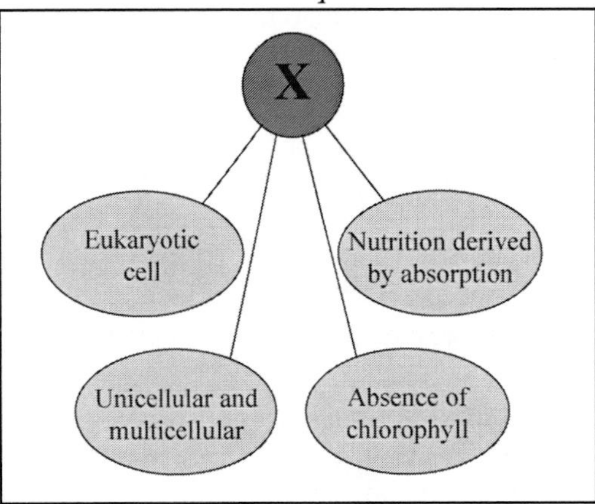

Open Response

18. Which of the following groups of organisms is **most appropriately** represented by *X* in the given figure? Explain.

- Fungi
- Bacteria
- Protists
- Viruses

19. How do single-celled organisms in the kingdom Monera differ from other single-celled organisms?

A. They have a cell wall consisting of cellulose

B. They do not have membrane-bound organelles

C. They are the only single-celled organisms that contain flagella

D. Their chromosomes are found within a circular structure called a plasmid

Use the following information to answer the next question.

Organism *X* is isolated from an aquatic ecosystem. The following facts are known about organism *X*:

- It does not posses a cell wall.
- It has a well-defined nucleus.
- It has the ability to locomote.
- It does not develop from an embryo.

20. To what kingdom does organism *X* belong?

A. Fungi

B. Monera

C. Protista

D. Animalia

Use the following information to answer the next question.

Scientists have discovered that mitochondria are remarkably similar to bacteria. Like bacteria, mitochondria have their own DNA. Also, when cells divide, mitochondria divide in a process that is similar to bacterial reproduction. In light of this evidence, scientists have suggested that hundreds of millions of years ago, one primitive cell engulfed another cell. Instead of digesting it, the primitive cell offered the engulfed cell protection from other cells. In exchange, the trapped cells continued service to the host cell.

21. The process by which a cell engulfs a smaller cell is called

A. osmosis

B. diffusion

C. endocytosis

D. active transport

Open Response

22. How does biodiversity improve the resiliency of some bacteria species, enabling them to become resistant to antibiotics?

____

____

____

____

____

____

____

23. Egg producers depend on reproductive technologies to increase egg production from their laying hens. The technology that they **most commonly** use is

A. natural selection

B. artificial selection

C. embryonic cloning

D. genetic engineering

Use the following information to answer the next question.

An isolated island is populated with rabbits. The rabbits on the island hop and run much more slowly than populations of rabbits on the mainland. Several fast-running wolves are suddenly introduced onto the island from the mainland.

Open Response

24. **Describe** the process of natural selection on the island after the introduction of the new predator and **explain** how the rabbit population on the island might change over time

____
____
____
____
____

25. The phrase "survival of the fittest" is **most closely** associated with the concept of

A. natural selection

B. artificial selection

C. genetic engineering

D. asexual reproduction

26. Which of the following situations describes an example of natural selection?

A. Farmers selectively breeding cattle

B. Genetic engineering of transgenic animals

C. Survival of the most adapted members of a population

D. Inability of members of different species to breed and produce hybrids

Use the following information to answer the next question.

Observations About Rabbits

1. The best fed rabbits are the healthiest.
2. Crowded rabbits tend to get a disease and are more likely to die.
3. Rabbits produce a very large number of offspring.
4. The size of the rabbit population remains roughly the same from year to year.
5. The slowest moving rabbits are most likely to get caught by predators.
6. Some rabbits can run faster than others.
7. Fossil evidence suggests that rabbits have always been fast.
8. Some rabbits live in burrows and some do not

Numerical Response

27. Four observations that provide the **best** evidence for natural selection are _______, _________, _________, and _________. (Record your answer as a four-digit number in lowest-to-highest numerical order.)

Open Response

28. **Describe** a common research process used to evaluate the resistance levels of different strains of bacteria to a particular antibiotic treatment. What is the source of resistance in the strains that survive the antibiotic treatment?

____
____
____
____
____
____
____

29. According to the theory of punctuated equilibria, which of the following statements is **true**?

A. Small changes accumulate in a species over millions of years, making them different from their ancestors.

B. Speciation occurs as a rapid burst, altering with long periods of no change.

C. Gene frequencies of small populations change by chance.

D. Evolution favours homozygous organisms.

Open Response

30. What is the difference between artificial selection and natural selection?

____
____
____
____
____
____
____

Use the following information to answer the next question.

In the 1850s, Charles Darwin introduced the theory of natural selection, which eventually came to be seen as the primary explanation for the process of evolution.

31. In his theory of natural selection, Darwin addressed all of the following phenomena **except** the

A. survival of the fittest

B. origin of new species

C. occurrence of spontaneous mutations

D. struggle for existence among organisms

Use the following information to answer the next multipart question.

32. Adelie penguins live in groups or colonies along the Antarctic coast and islands. The penguins tend to live and breed in the same colonies in which they were born. New Zealand scientist Dr. David Lambert examined microevolution in the Adelie penguin by collecting DNA from the bones of 6 000 year old penguins from different colonies and compared it to the DNA of present-day penguins in the colonies.

Hypothetical data comparing 6 000 year old penguin DNA from two different colonies to identify differences between the two colonies is shown below.

	6 000 Year Old DNA
Colony 1	ATC GAC CGT CAG CGC
Colony 2	TGC GAG CGT GTC CGA

Hypothetical data comparing present-day penguin DNA from the two colonies is shown below.

	Present-Day DNA
Colony 1	CTC GAG CCT GTC ATT
Colony 2	CAC GTG TCT CTC ATT

The same data as above is shown in the next two charts to compare the evolution of the DNA sequence in each of the two colonies.

	Colony 1
6 000 year old DNA	ATC GAC CGT CAG CGC
Present-day DNA	CTC GAG CCT GTC ATT

	Colony 2
6 000 year old DNA	TGC GAG CGT GTC CGA
Present-day DNA	CAC GTG TCT CTC ATT

Open Response

a) What would be expected about the similarities when the DNA sequence of 6 000-year-old penguins is compared to modern day penguins?

b) What would be expected about the similarities when the DNA sequence of colony 1 is compared to colony 2 (past and present)?

How does this compare to what is observed?

c) Propose a hypothesis to account for the results obtained for the DNA comparison between colony 1 and 2 in the present-day penguins.

Use the following information to answer the next question.

> *Macroevolution* can be defined as the formation of a new species. *Microevolution* can be defined as the evolution of a species as the environment changes.

33. There is evidence for macroevolution because

A. a large and diverse number of organisms exist

B. many insects have become resistant to pesticides

C. species today are more complex than in prehistoric times

D. every organism is made up of many unique characteristics

Use the following information to answer the next question.

> If the females of the *Drosophila melanogaster* species prefer to mate only with red-eyed males, then its future generations will consist of mostly red-eyed fruit flies.

34. The given situation is an example of

A. genetic variation

B. natural selection

C. sexual selection

D. genetic drift

Use the following information to answer the next question.

Some examples of different types of selection resulting in phenotypic variability among species:

1. high milk-yielding cows
2. elaborate display of the male peacock
3. a pet chihuahua
4. corn on the cob
5. an elephant's trunk
6. pest-resistant crops

Numerical Response

35. Four examples of phenotypic variability resulting from artificial selection in the given list are _________, _________, _________ and _________. (Record your answer as a four-digit number in lowest-to-highest numerical order.)

Use the following information to answer the next question.

Male peacocks and female peahens exhibit sexual dimorphism. They vary dramatically in the colour patterns of their plumage with males displaying vibrant hues of blue and green, while females are a muted green, brown, and grey pattern.

Open Response

36. Explain how sexual selection promotes sexual dimorphism in a species using the example of the male peacock, and explain why this type of selection does **not** necessarily function to promote adaptation.

____

____

____

____

____

____

____

37. Down syndrome is the result of
   A. linkage
   B. crossing over
   C. sex-linked inheritance
   D. chromosomal non-disjunction

38. Which of the following statements about sexual reproduction is **false**?
   A. Specialized cells in the adult body undergo meiosis to produce gametes.
   B. A zygote undergoes meiosis to form the adult body.
   C. Gametes are hapolid and zygotes are diploid.
   D. Gametes fuse to form a zygote.

39. When plants with the genetic combinations *Tt* and *tt* cross-pollinate, what percentage of offspring will have the genotype *Tt*?
   A. 20%
   B. 50%
   C. 80%
   D. 90%

Use the following information to answer the next question.

A white-eyed female and a red-eyed male fruit fly are crossed. The normal red eye colour is dominant to the white eye colour.

Open Response

40. Use the Punnett method to explain why 50% of the offspring are red-eyed and 50% of the offspring are white-eyed in the F_1 generation.

____

____

____

____

____

Use the following information to answer the next question.

Coat color in mice is controlled by the interaction of two genes.
Three phenotypes result: black, brown, and white.

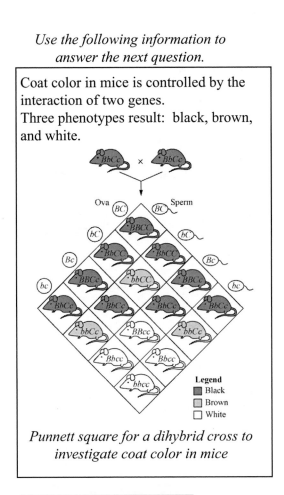

Punnett square for a dihybrid cross to investigate coat color in mice

Numerical Response

41. Given the genotype to phenotype correlation illustrated by the cross in the illustration, what is the expected **phenotypic ratio** resulting from a cross between a *bbCc* female mouse and a *BbCc* male mouse? (Record you answer as a simplified three-digit number.)

Phenotypic ratio	______	______	______
Coat color	Black	Brown	White

Open Response

42. **Name** and **describe** a process that can be used to determine whether an organism that is displaying a dominant trait is homozygous or heterozygous.

____

____

____

____

____

____

____

43. Which of the following processes does **not** occur during meiosis II?

A. Formation of four daughter cells

B. Production of a nucleolus in each cell

C. Disjunction of homologous chromosomes

D. Separation of the two chromatids in a chromosome

Use the following information to answer the next question.

Three Stages in Meiosis II

1. Prophase II
2. Metaphase II
3. Anaphase II

Numerical Response

44. Match each of the numbered stages of meiosis II to the descriptor that applies to it. (Record your answer as a three-digit number.)

Chromosomes align at the equator of the cell.	______
Sister chromatids separate from each other.	______
Chromatin begins to coil and condense.	______

45. Chromosomes are important parts of a cell because they

A. store energy

B. contain genes

C. destroy other cell organelles

D. separate the nucleoplasm from the cytoplasm

Open Response

46. **Compare** and **contrast** meiosis with mitosis in at least **four** ways.

____
____
____
____
____
____
____

47. Mendel put forth the law of segregation based on his observations of the theory of dominance. Which of the following hypotheses is **not** asserted by the law of segregation?

A. After fertilization, alleles show co-dominance.

B. A gamete is always pure for a particular character.

C. Two separated alleles unite in pairs during fertilization.

D. Two alleles of a gamete separate during gamete formation.

Open Response

48. Describe one piece of evidence obtained from the analysis of a pedigree chart that could be used to determine whether the mode of inheritance of a human genetic disorder is X-linked or autosomal and one piece of evidence that could be used to determine whether it is recessive or dominant.

____
____
____
____
____
____
____

Open Response

49. **Describe** the possible nondisjunctions for the sex chromosomes of sperm and eggs and **name** the different syndrome for each of the sex chromosome abnormalities. **Explain** how each abnormality occurs.

____
____
____
____
____
____
____

50. Modern artificial insemination techniques were first developed for the dairy cattle industry to allow

A. one cow to be impregnated with the sperm of a bully carrying traits for increased body mass

B. many cows to be impregnated with the sperm of a bull carrying traits for increased body mass

C. one cow to be impregnated with the sperm of a bull carrying traits for improved milk production

D. many cows to be impregnated with the sperm of a bull carrying traits for improved milk production

Open Response

51. What is the name of the minimally invasive technique that utilizes a small camera attached to a long slender tube to visualize internal body structures? Name three diagnostic or treatment procedures accomplished by this particular technique.

____

____

____

____

____

____

____

52. Which of the following processes facilitates the exchange of oxygen between the blood and the different cells in the body?

A. Osmosis

B. Active transport

C. Passive diffusion

D. Facilitated diffusion

53. Fruits and vegetables typically have large amounts of cellulose. Eating fruits and vegetables that have a high cellulose content is **most** helpful in preventing

A. scurvy

B. anemia

C. diarrhea

D. constipation

Open Response

54. Describe the events that lead to inhalation after stimulation by the respiratory centre.

____

____

____

____

____

____

____

Use the following information to answer the next question.

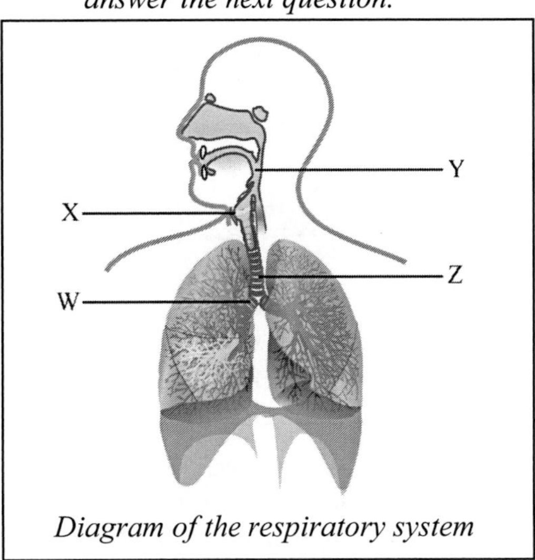

Diagram of the respiratory system

55. Which structure in the given diagram is the passageway for both food and air intake?

A. Structure W

B. Structure X

C. Structure Y

D. Structure Z

Use the following information to answer the next question.

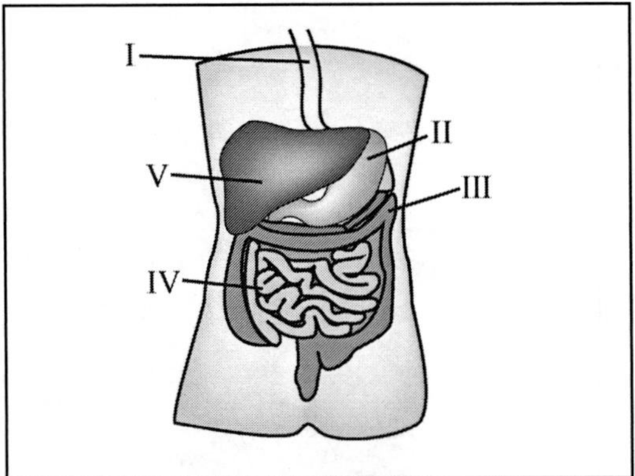

56. Blood low in oxygen but high in nutrients passes through which of the labeled structures before returning to the pulmonary circulation, by way of the inferior vena cava and heart, for oxygenation?

A. II

B. III

C. IV

D. V

57. Respiratory gases are found dissolved within the plasma of the blood. During strenuous exercise which of the following acts as the **main** signal to the body to increase the breathing rate?

A. Higher concentrations of carbon dioxide than oxygen in the blood.

B. Higher concentrations of oxygen than carbon dioxide in the blood.

C. Lower concentrations of carbon dioxide in the blood.

D. Lower concentrations of oxygen in the blood.

58. The human respiratory system can be best described as a

A. network of hollow, muscular tubes that permits diffusion of nutrients from the external environment to the internal system

B. network of moist, tube-like passageways that allow oxygen to flow from the external environment to the lungs

C. series of tiny passages that allows nutrients to be absorbed directly into the cell

D. series of hollow vessels that transports oxygen to cells in the body

59. Which of the following substrates are digested by the pancreatic enzymes trypsin, lipase, and amylase?

A. proteins, fats, and starches

B. vitamins, fats, and starches

C. proteins, lipids, and cellulose

D. polypeptides, lipids, and vitamins

Use the following information to answer the next multipart question.

60.

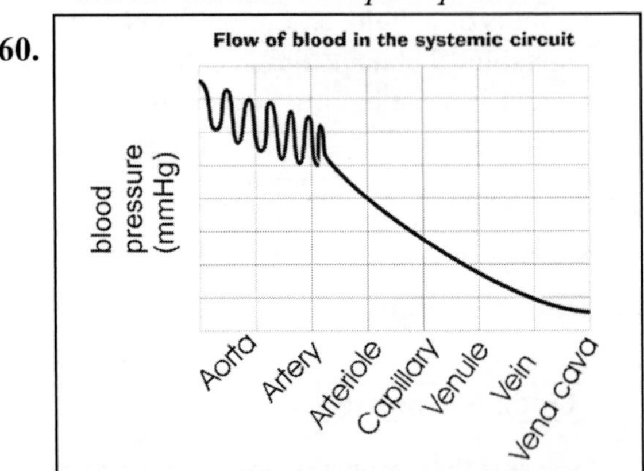

a) The part of the graph that represents the section of the circulatory system with the greatest surface area is the

A. aorta

B. arteries

C. vena cava

D. capillaries

b) The pulsing nature of the blood pressure in the aorta, arteries, and arterioles is due to the contraction of

A. skeletal muscles and the action of the valves

B. the left ventricle

C. both ventricles

D. the atria

61. The red blood cells leave the right side of the heart through the

A. superior vena cava

B. pulmonary artery

C. pulmonary vein

D. aorta

Use the following information to answer the next question.

By the time a person reaches the age of 70, his or her heart has contracted an average of more than 2.5 billion times. The four chambers of the heart contract in a highly regulated sequence to pump blood through the heart in the proper direction.

Four Heart Structures

1. Right atrium
2. Right semilunar valve
3. Right ventricle
4. Right atrioventricular valve

Numerical Response

62. The order in which these structures would be travelled through by a **deoxygenated** red blood cell entering the heart is ______, _________, _________, and _________. (Record your answer as a four-digit number.)

Use the following information to answer the next question.

The following symptoms were identified in a group of women suffering from valvular disease and hypertension related to past or present use of weight loss drugs:

I. Abnormally functioning weak heart valves that caused mixing of blood between the atria and the ventricles

II. Thickening of the heart valves

III. In a few cases, high blood pressure in the vessels carrying blood from the heart to the lungs

Open Response

63. In the diagram provided, name the four heart valves (numbered 1 to 4) that may be affected in this group of women.

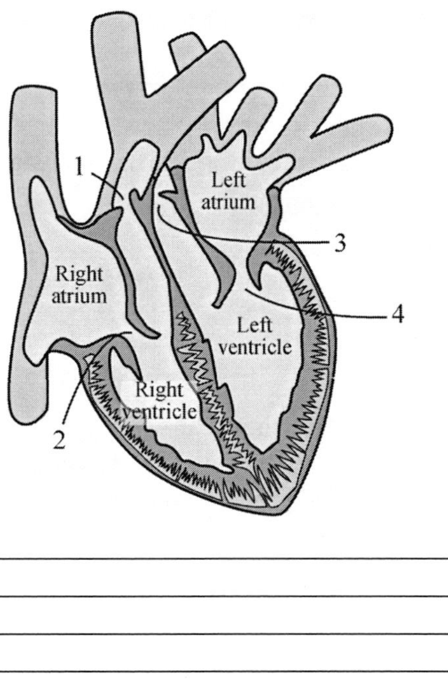

____

____

____

____

____

____

____

64. Sometimes, as a result of colon cancer, a section of large intestine is surgically removed. An outcome of this surgery is that a person experiences

A. less water reabsorption, resulting in watery feces

B. more water reabsorption, resulting in watery feces

C. less water reabsorption, resulting in dry feces

D. more water reabsorption, resulting in dry feces

Use the following information to answer the next question.

Stomata are referred to as "the gateways of transpiration" because their behaviour influences the rate of transpiration. This rate is generally very low at night and increases rapidly from early morning until midday.

65. Which of the following plant cells regulate the opening and closing of the stomata?

A. Parenchyma cells

B. Epidermal cells

C. Root hair cells

D. Guard cells

66. Herbicides are chemical substances that are used for controlling the growth of weeds around crops. Which synthetic hormone is used as a herbicide?

A. Auxin

B. Ethylene

C. Gibberellin

D. Abscisic acid

Use the following information to answer the next question.

1. Xylem
2. Stomata
3. Root hairs
4. Spongy tissue

Numerical Response

67. When the given plant structures are listed in the order in which water moves through them, the order is _________, _________, _________, and _________. (Record your answer as a four-digit number).

Use the following information to answer the next question.

Cutting is a method of vegetative propagation in which plant organs, such as stems, roots, or leaves, are cut from the parent plant and are used to grow new plants.

68. Stem cuttings are used in the large-scale propagation of

A. oranges

B. grapes

C. guavas

D. lemons

PRACTICE TEST 2

1. If the sieve tubes that make up phloem are clogged, the plant will not be able to transport
   A. water
   B. mineral nutrients
   C. organic nutrients
   D. oxygen and carbon dioxide

Use the following information to answer the next question.

> Guard cells are a pair of dumbbell-shaped cells present in leaves and young stems. They regulate the rate of transpiration by opening and closing the stomata.

2. Guard cells are composed of
   A. xylem
   B. phloem
   C. parenchyma
   D. collenchyma

Open Response

3. List two features that can be observed in a fully grown plant to determine whether it is a dicot or a monocot.

   ____
   ____
   ____
   ____
   ____

4. Which of the following plants exhibits hypogeal germination?
   A. Pea
   B. Gourd
   C. Cotton
   D. Castor bean

5. Plant macronutrients are essential nutrients that plants require in large amounts for their growth and development. Which of the following nutrients is **not** a plant macronutrient?
   A. Copper
   B. Oxygen
   C. Nitrogen
   D. Phosphorous

6. When water is scarce, the roots of plants bend toward the water source, even against the force of gravity. This tropic movement is called
   A. heliotropism
   B. hydrotropism
   C. chemotropism
   D. thigmotropism

Use the following information to answer the next question.

Some plant growth regulators are as follows:

1. Gibberellins
2. Auxins
3. Cytokinins
4. Abscisic acid

Numerical Response

7. Match the given plant growth regulators to the general effect it has on plant tissues. (Record your answer as a four-digit number.)

Effect on Plant Tissues	Plant Growth Regulator Number
Inhibits growth and promotes dormancy	________
When functioning together with other plant hormones promotes flower and fruit development	________
When functioning together with other plant hormones promotes shoot, leaf, and root growth	________
Influences seed germination and releases buds from dormancy	________

Use the following information to answer the next question.

Types of succession:

1. Primary succession
2. Secondary succession

Numerical Response

8. Match each type of habitat to the type of succession that will **most likely** occur. (Record your answer as a four-digit number.)

Habitat Type	Type of Succession
Desert sand dune	________
Clear-cut forest	________
Rocky valley exposed by glacial retreat	________
Forest damaged by recent fire	________

Open Response

9. Monoculture is a type of agriculture in which only one type of crop plant is grown on the same piece of land over a number of years. Describe the impacts long-term monocultural practices are **most likely** to have on the biodiversity of the natural environment.

____

____

____

____

____

____

____

Use the following information to answer the next question.

British Columbia is home to five different species of salmon, all with similar life cycles. Salmon are born in freshwater streams and rivers. They follow these river systems to the ocean, where they mature into adults. When they are ready to reproduce, salmon return to the freshwater systems, swimming upstream to the area where they were born.
After they spawn, they die, and their carcasses return valuable nutrients to the ecosystem.

Open Response

10. How might the lowered precipitation associated with climate change affect salmon populations?

____
____
____
____
____

11. Individuals within a population of the same species often exhibit diversity in their physical characteristics.
For example, humans exhibit extreme diversity in hair, eye, and skin colours.
This type of diversity is an example of

A. species diversity

B. genetic diversity

C. structural diversity

D. compositional diversity

Use the following information to answer the next question.

In order to organize and keep track of Earth's biodiversity, living organisms are categorized and named according to a system of classification that uses two Latin name categories, genus and species, to designate each type of organism. This is known as binomial nomenclature.

Open Response

12. **Identify** the person who developed the system of binomial nomenclature, and list **two benefits** to using this system.

____
____
____
____
____
____
____

13. Organisms within the kingdom Plantae are classified as either vascular or non-vascular, depending on the presence or absence of specialized conducting tissues. Which of the following plants is an example of a non-vascular plant?

A. 

B. 

C. 

D. 

Use the following information to answer the next question.

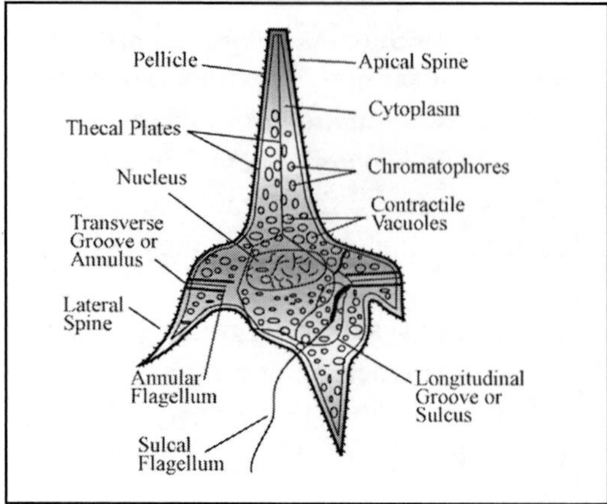

14. The given diagram depicts a representative organism from which of the following kingdoms?
   A. Monera
   B. Protista
   C. Plantae
   D. Fungi

15. A plankton, or dip, net is typically used to collect all of the following pond-ecosystem organisms for closer examination **except**
   A. algae
   B. protozoans
   C. large vertebrates
   D. small invertebrates

16. Taxonomy is a branch of biology that classifies organisms at various levels. What is the **highest** taxonomic level?
   A. Kingdom
   B. Phylum
   C. Species
   D. Order

17. Viruses store their genetic information as
   A. either RNA or proteins
   B. either DNA or RNA
   C. proteins
   D. DNA

Use the following information to answer the next question.

The following are some cell structures and characteristics:

1. Nucleoid
2. Membrane-enclosed organelles
3. Nucleus
4. Cell wall
5. Plasmids
6. Meiotic division
7. Binary fission

Numerical Response

18. Four structures or characteristics that are commonly found in prokaryotic cells are __________, __________, __________, and __________. (Record your answer as a four-digit number from lowest-to-highest numerical order.)

19. In which of the following tables is the kingdom correctly matched with an organism that belongs to it?

A.

Kingdom	Organism
Monera	Pine tree

B.

Kingdom	Organism
Protista	Mushroom

C.

Kingdom	Organism
Animalia	Sea sponge

D.

Kingdom	Organism
Plantae	Seaweed

Use the following information to answer the next question.

Some Characteristics of Different Organisms

1. Unicellular
2. Multicellular
3. Eukaryotic
4. Prokaryotic
5. Heterotrophic
6. Autotrophic
7. Nervous tissue
8. Cell walls

Numerical Response

20. Four characteristics that are associated with organisms in the kingdom Animalia are ______, ______________, __________, and __________. (Record your answer as a four-digit number in lowest-to-highest numerical order.)

21. Mosses are considered to be pioneer plants among land plants. Due to their close evolutionary relatedness, pioneer plants are hypothesized to be directly descendant from which of the following organisms?

A. Red algae

B. Green algae

C. Brown algae

D. Blue-green algae

Open Response

22. Why is the Cambrian period that took place 545 to 505 million years ago often referred to as the Cambrian explosion?

____

____

____

____

____

23. When the biodiversity of a population increases, its resiliency is

A. increased to pests but not to disease

B. decreased to pests but not to disease

C. increased to both pests and disease

D. decreased to both pests and disease

24. Which of the following provides an example of a **disadvantage** of artificial selection technologies?

A. Higher crop yields

B. Disease resistant crops

C. Increased livestock biomass

D. Decreased genetic variability

Use the following information to answer the next question.

The giant panda's primary food source is bamboo.

25. Which of the following conditions makes the giant panda vulnerable to extinction if bamboo becomes scarce?

A. Limited range

B. Habitat renewal

C. Over-specialization

D. Disease resistance

26. Which of the following phenomena acts upon the genetic variability of individuals in a population, resulting in changes in the frequency of certain traits within that population?

A. Migration

B. Extirpation

C. Natural selection

D. Population bottleneck

27. Phyletic speciation is a type of speciation in which a species is transformed into another species over a long period of time through slow and steady changes. Phyletic speciation occurs as a result of

A. seasonal isolation

B. geographic isolation

C. chromosomal mutations

D. environmental adaptations

Open Response

28. Species become extinct when they cannot survive changing conditions.
Describe some human activities that have changed conditions, resulting in high rates of extinction around the planet.

____

____

____

____

____

____

____

Use the following information to answer the next question.

A lab rat was exposed to radiation to induce mutations. Mutation changes were also studied in the next generation of rats.

29. Which body organ of the rat must be affected by radiation in order to observe changes in the next generation?

A. Skin

B. Liver

C. Brain

D. Testes

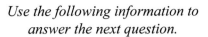

Use the following information to answer the next question.

Jean-Baptiste Lamarck was a French naturalist who developed the law of inheritance of acquired characteristics to explain evolution.

30. According to this law, characteristics acquired by individuals during their lifetime can be passed on to their progeny. Lamarck's theory does **not** address the

A. phenomenon of natural selection

B. effects of use and disuse of organs

C. transmission of acquired characteristics

D. effects of the environment on an organism

Use the following information to answer the next question.

It was observed during an experiment that some bacteria of a specific pathogenic strain grown in small quantities of antibiotic were able to survive by feeding on the antibiotic medium. These bacteria had developed an antibiotic resistance through the process of natural selection. The bacteria that survived the first experiment were then grown in a medium with a different type of antibiotic drug in which the bacteria were unable to survive.

31. Which of the following statements about an organism's ability to adapt can **best** be inferred from the experimental results?

A. Antibiotic resistance is specific to a particular type of antibiotic drug.

B. Resistance to antibiotics is an adaptation that is not heritable by subsequent generations.

C. Adaptations in general only occur to obtain food resources, not against environmental pressures such as antibiotic treatments.

D. Antibiotic resistance adaptations are temporary and can be lost within the same generation, preventing passage of the trait to subsequent generations.

Use the following information to answer the next question.

Today, it is known that radiation and certain chemicals alter the structure of DNA, thus mutating genes.
Mutations also occur because of errors in the replication of DNA or RNA.

32. Knowing that genes can mutate would have helped Darwin explain the

A. inheritance of acquired characteristics

B. theory of the survival of the fittest

C. theory of natural selection

D. source of variation

Open Response

33. Despite Darwin's methodical approach, his theories were initially met with protest. **Explain** why a critic may have rightfully doubted Darwin's theory of natural selection, and explain how this criticism was subsequently addressed.

____
____
____
____
____
____
____

Open Response

34. **Describe** the process of adaptation in terms of natural selection and **explain** how a population of bacteria becomes adapted to the changing environmental conditions associated with an antibiotic treatment.

____
____
____
____
____
____
____

Use the following information to answer the next question.

> A small group of mice are separated from their original population on land and reach an island by floating on a wooden log. Their numbers in the new habitat increase because of an abundant food supply. Over a period of time, these mice become so different from their parent population that they are characterized as a different species.

35. The given speciation is known as

A. sympatric speciation

B. allopatric speciation

C. quantum speciation

D. phyletic speciation

36. The evolution of a giraffe's elongated neck is **best** explained by the concept of

A. artificial selection

B. natural selection

C. mutation

D. mimicry

37. Biotechnology is the application and manipulation of naturally occurring biological processes to aid in the creation of products or processes for specific human use. Which of the following statements about biotechnology is true?

A. Recombinant DNA technology has successfully introduced the genes of one species into the genome of a different species.

B. Genetic engineering is a non-controversial biotechnology used to create genetically modified organisms.

C. Artificial selection crosses different species to create new species beneficial to humans.

D. Pest-resistant crops would not occur if not for biotechnological methods.

Open Response

38. **Distinguish** between gene migration and genetic drift.

____
____
____
____
____

39. Which of the following genotypes corresponds to an organism that is **heterozygous** for two genes?

A. *RrYy*

B. *RrYY*

C. *RRYy*

D. *RRYY*

40. The gene that confers antibiotic resistance in bacteria is located on the

A. plasmid

B. cell wall

C. nucleoid

D. cell membrane

Use the following information to answer the next question.

In humans, the allele for curly hair (C) is dominant over the allele for straight hair (c).

41. If a man that is heterozygous for curly hair marries a woman with straight hair, what is the expected phenotypic ratio of curly hair to straight hair for their offspring?

A. 1:3

B. 2:2

C. 3:1

D. 4:0

Use the following information to answer the next question.

A man with blood group A marries a woman with blood group AB.

Open Response

42. Which blood group in their progeny would indicate that the father is heterozygous? Using the Punnett Method explain why.

Use the following information to answer the next question.

Phenylketonuria is an autosomal recessive disorder caused by a recessive allele, p. A man who is a carrier of the recessive allele, p, marries a woman, and they have four children. Two of the children are carriers, and two of the children are affected by phenylketonuria.

Open Response

43. Explain if the children's mother is normal, affected by phenylketonuria, or a carrier of the recessive p allele.

Open Response

44. In mice, brown hair colour is dominant over black hair colour. If 50% of the mice in a litter have brown hair, what is the **most probable** genetic makeup of the parents?

45. During meiosis I, the uncoiling of the chromosomes occurs during

A. metaphase I

B. telophase I

C. anaphase I

D. prophase I

46. The chromosomes of a somatic cell are arranged on the equatorial plate and attached to the spindle fibres during which stage of cell division?

A. Prophase

B. Anaphase

C. Telophase

D. Metaphase

Use the following information to answer the next question.

Mitosis is the type of cell division that maintains the original number of chromosomes in daughter cells. It starts with prophase and ends with telophase. Prophase is preceded by interphase, while telophase is succeeded by interphase.

47. Which of the following statements is **true** about interphase?

A. The nuclear membrane breaks down during interphase.

B. Sister chromatids are separated during interphase.

C. The replication of DNA occurs during interphase.

D. Chromatin condenses during interphase.

Use the following information to answer the next question.

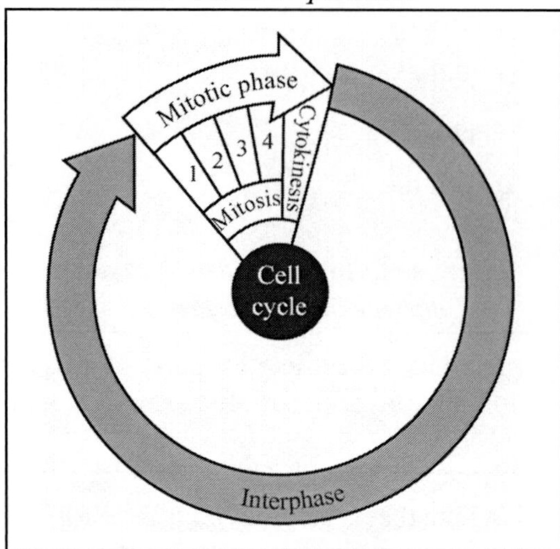

Numerical Response

48. Match the numbered mitotic phases in the given illustration with the appropriate stage of mitosis. (Record your answer as a four-digit number.)

Stage of Mitosis	Numbered Mitotic Phase
Anaphase	________
Metaphase	________
Prophase	________
Telophase	________

49. Incomplete dominance is a phenomenon in which the dominant allele fails to express itself completely and the progeny exhibit intermediate characteristics of the parents. Which of the following traits illustrates incomplete dominance?

A. Plant height in pea plants

B. ABO blood type in humans

C. MN-antigen type in humans

D. Flower colour in snapdragons

Use the following information to answer the next question.

Cystic fibrosis is the most common genetic disorder among Caucasians, affecting one in 2 000 Caucasian children. The cystic fibrosis allele results in the production of sticky mucus in several structures, including the lungs and exocrine glands.
Two parents who are carriers of the allele but are unaffected by the disorder themselves can have a child with the disorder.

A girl and both her parents are unaffected by the disease. However, her sister is affected by cystic fibrosis.

Open Response

50. Which of the following terms **best** describes the allele for cystic fibrosis? Explain why.

- dominant
- co-dominant
- recessive
- X-linked

____
____
____
____
____
____
____

Open Response

51. Huntington's disease is an autosomal dominant disorder that causes progressive degeneration of cells in the brain and will result in death. As with other autosomal dominant disorders, many people decide not to have children, since they have a fifty-fifty chance of having a child with the disease; yet in the past, Huntington's still was passed on. Explain why.

____
____
____
____
____

52. Which of the following is a possible use for recombinant DNA?

A. Producing steroid hormones

B. Producing insulin using bacteria

C. Cloning tissue cells for transplant

D. Encouraging nerve cells to regenerate

Use the following information to answer the next multipart question.

53. Technology and scientific developments have led to the progression of society. Modern day technology has allowed humans to view their internal system and devise mechanisms to correct dysfunctions that may be afflicting individuals. However, despite these advancements, people continue to suffer from ailments such as heart attacks and obesity. In fact, there are often not enough doctors or rooms in the hospital to keep up with demand.

Open Response

a) Describe three things an individual can do to reduce the risk of illness and poor health.

____
____
____
____
____

b) Explain a technological advancement that has allowed individuals to lead more active lives.

____
____
____
____
____
____
____

54. The pressure that the blood exerts on the walls of the arteries when the ventricles are maximally relaxed is the

A. average pulse pressure

B. systolic blood pressure

C. diastolic blood pressure

D. mean arterial blood pressure

55. Which of the following events occurs during inhalation?

A. Oxygen diffuses from the alveoli to the capillary blood.

B. Oxygen diffuses to tissue cells from the capillary blood.

C. Carbon dioxide diffuses from the alveoli to the capillary blood.

D. Carbon dioxide diffuses to tissue cells from the capillary blood.

Open Response

56. Explain how nutrients and oxygen in the blood move first into the tissue fluids, and then into the cells.

____
____
____
____
____
____
____

Use the following information to answer the next question.

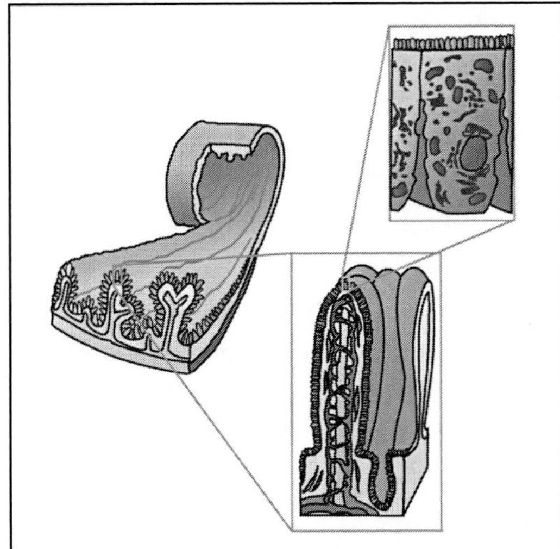

57. Which of the following tables correctly matches the two internal systems illustrated in the given diagram with their respective functions?

A.

Circulatory	Digestive
absorption of materials	transport of materials

B.

Respiratory	Circulatory
exchange of gases	transport of materials

C.

Digestive	Respiratory
absorption of materials	exchange of gases

D.

Digestive	Circulatory
absorption of materials	transport of materials

Use the following information to answer the next question.

During exhalation, the diaphragm becomes ___*i*___, while the internal intercostal muscles ___*ii*___.

58. The given statement is completed by the information in row

A.

i	*ii*
dome-shaped	contract

B.

i	*ii*
dome-shaped	relax

C.

i	*ii*
flattened	contract

D.

i	*ii*
flattened	relax

Use the following information to answer the next question.

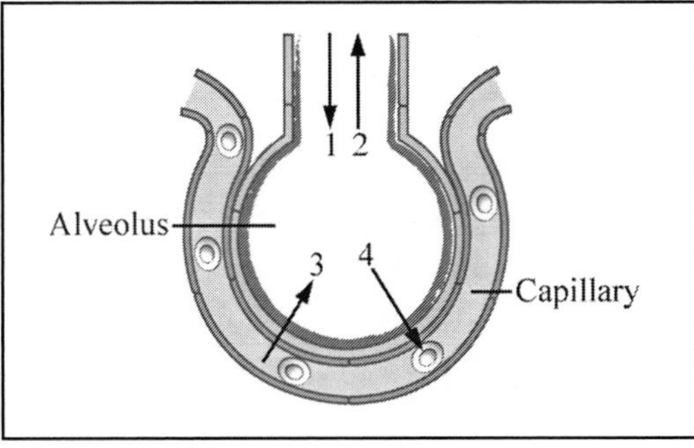

Numerical Response

59. The two numbers that represent carbon dioxide are ________ and ________. (Record your answer as a two-digit number in lowest-to-highest numerical order.)

Use the following information to answer the next question.

The rate of breathing is usually controlled subconsciously by the nervous system in response to the amount of CO_2 present in the blood. As the level of CO_2 rises, the rate of breathing increases in an attempt to bring in more O_2 and remove the CO_2 from the blood. However, humans do have some conscious control over their breathing rate.

Open Response

60. Provide two examples explaining why someone would want to control his or her rate of breathing.

____

____

____

____

____

Use the following information to answer the next question.

The passage of food from the stomach to the small intestine is tightly controlled by a circular muscle at the junction point between these two organs. This muscle is very strong because it plays a crucial role in preventing food from passing from the stomach to the small intestine unchecked.

61. The circular muscle located at the junction between the stomach and the small intestine is the

A. cardiac sphincter

B. pyloric sphincter

C. ileocecal valve

D. tricuspid valve

62. Blood moves through veins due to the

A. force of gravity

B. squeezing of venous valves

C. contraction of heart ventricles

D. contraction of skeletal muscles

63. Beginning from blood returning to the heart from the body, which of the following sequences shows the correct flow of blood through the cardiopulmonary system?

A. aorta → left ventricle → left atrium → pulmonary vein → pulmonary artery → right ventricle → right atrium → vena cava

B. aorta → right atrium → right ventricle → pulmonary vein → pulmonary artery → left atrium → left ventricle → vena cava

C. vena cava → right atrium → right ventricle → pulmonary artery → pulmonary vein → left atrium → left ventricle → aorta

D. vena cava → right atrium → left atrium → pulmonary artery → pulmonary vein → right ventricle → left ventricle → aorta

Use the following information to answer the next question.

Four Events in the Process of Inflammation

1. Swelling of cells
2. Exudation of large quantities of fluid
3. Increased permeability of capillaries
4. Vasodilatation of blood vessels

Numerical Response

64. The order in which these events occur during the process of inflammation is _________, _________, _________, and _________. (Record your answer as a four-digit number.)

Use the following information to answer the next question.

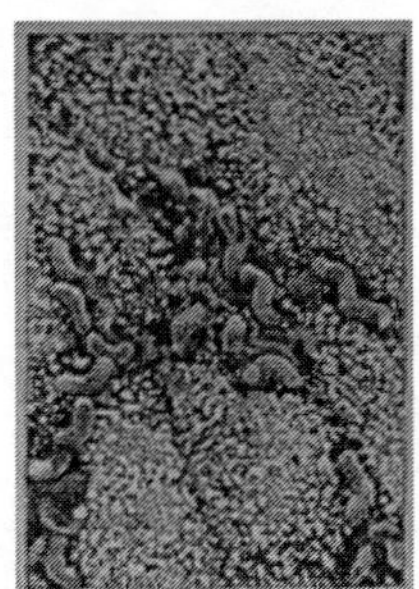

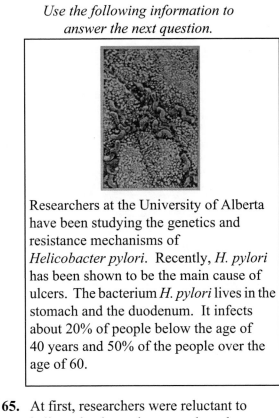

Researchers at the University of Alberta have been studying the genetics and resistance mechanisms of *Helicobacter pylori*. Recently, *H. pylori* has been shown to be the main cause of ulcers. The bacterium *H. pylori* lives in the stomach and the duodenum. It infects about 20% of people below the age of 40 years and 50% of the people over the age of 60.

65. At first, researchers were reluctant to believe that bacteria cause ulcers because

A. the contraction of stomach muscles during digestion should flush out all bacteria

B. there is an inadequate supply of oxygen in the stomach to support bacteria

C. the pH of the stomach should kill most bacteria

D. bacteria have difficulty entering the stomach

Use the following information to answer the next question.

1. coffee
2. tea
3. wine
4. hot chocolate

Numerical Response

66. Match each beverage with the plants from which they are obtained. (Record your answer as a four-digit number.)

Plant Genus and species	Beverage
Camellia sinensis	________
Theobroma cacao	________
Coffea arabica	________
Vitis vinifera	________

Open Response

67. Briefly describe the practice of crop rotation and explain how it is an effective technique for improving crop quality and supporting environmental sustainability.

Use the following information to answer the next question.

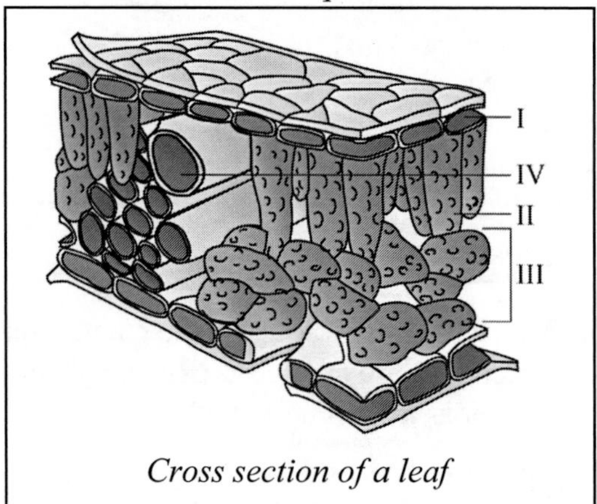

Cross section of a leaf

68. In the given figure, spongy parenchyma is labelled

A. I

B. II

C. III

D. IV

69. Which of the following terms describes the arrangement of flowers on the floral axis?

A. Venation

B. Phyllotaxy

C. Placentation

D. Inflorescence

Use the following information to answer the next question.

Cross section of a woody dicot stem

Numerical Response

70. Identify the part of the tree cross section that corresponds to each of the following morphological terms. (Record your answer as a four-digit number)

Morphological Term	Numerical Label
Phloem	________
Xylem	________
Pith	________
Epidermis	________

71. Ginger root propagates using which of the following reproductive structures?

A. Rhizomes

B. Stolons

C. Tubers

D. Corms

ANSWERS AND SOLUTIONS — PRACTICE TEST 1

1. D	15. 735	30. OR	43. C	58. B
2. C	16. B	31. C	44. 231	59. A
3. 2431	17. C	32. a) OR	45. B	60. a) D
4. B	18. OR	b) OR	46. OR	b) B
5. C	19. B	c) OR	47. A	61. B
6. D	20. C	33. A	48. OR	62. 1432
7. D	21. C	34. C	49. OR	63. OR
8. a) OR	22. OR	35. 1346	50. D	64. A
b) OR	23. B	36. OR	51. OR	65. D
9. A	24. OR	37. D	52. C	66. A
10. OR	25. A	38. B	53. D	67. 3142
11. A	26. C	39. B	54. OR	68. B
12. C	27. 3456	40. OR	55. C	
13. 45213	28. OR	41. 332	56. D	
14. A	29. B	42. OR	57. A	

1. D

The given illustration is a cross section of **dicot** root as is evident by the spoke-like arrangement of the vascular tissues within the stele (vascular cylinder). The vascular bundle is represented by the labels *X* and *Y*, indicating the xylem and phloem respectively. The vascular bundle is **immediately** adjacent to the **pericycle** (*Z*) located just inside the endodermis (*W*) which is the inner most region of the cortex (*U*) delineating the outer boundary of the stele. The outermost layer of the cortex is the epidermis (*T*).

2. C

Structure X in the given figure is the phloem tissue. The phloem provides the plant tissues with the food products formed during photosynthesis.

3. 2431

The outermost layer of a stem is called the epidermis. In a woody tree like a poplar tree, it is called the cork (2). The next layer is the vascular tissue called the phloem (4), followed by the vascular tissue called the xylem (3). The innermost layer is called the pith (1).

4. B

Monocots contain one cotyledon and dicots contain two cotyledons.

Monocots have veins that run in parallel, vascular bundles with complex arrangement and a fibrous root system. Dicots have netlike veins, vascular bundles arranged in a ring, and a taproot.

5. C

Bulbils are fleshy buds that arise from leaves and, therefore, they are not modified stems. When bulbils fall on the ground, they give rise to a new plant.

Rhizomes, stolons, and bulbs are all modified stems that are produced by plants during asexual reproduction.

6. D

Auxins are acidic growth hormones capable of promoting cell elongation in plants. Auxins are synthesized in shoot apices, leaf primordial, and developing seeds. Indole acetic acid (IAA) is the principal natural auxin.

7. D

Auxins induce apical dominance in plants by suppressing the development of lateral, or auxiliary, buds.

8. a) OR

Plant cells must supply their own energy needs, and they do this like most other cells via cell respiration. The plant cells do produce oxygen in photosynthesis, but they also consume it since the oxygen molecule is the final electron acceptor during the electron transport chain.

b) OR

The balance of certain gases in the atmosphere is largely a function of living things. The cycling of carbon and oxygen through living things is in an equilibrium based on the relationship of photosynthesis and cell respiration. Photosynthesis produces oxygen and consumes carbon dioxide, whereas cell respiration does the opposite. Cell respiration produces carbon dioxide and consumes oxygen. Even though plant cells perform both functions, the fact that on balance they produce more oxygen than they consume provides the oxygen needed to support animal life on Earth.

9. A

Migration is the process during which the seeds and spores of organisms reach a bare area and form the pioneer community.

The movement of seeds and spores of organisms out of an area is not a process that occurs during succession. Since a bare area has no vegetation, it cannot support animals. The movement of animals out of an area is not a process of succession.

10. OR

Certain plant seeds only germinate when they are heated to a certain temperature. Fires provide the heat needed to stimulate the growth and development of these plant species. Additionally, a forest fire clears an area of old and diseased wood, providing the setting for new growth. New growth equates to an increase in the diversity of plants and animals in an ecosystem.

11. A

The most likely impact of rising sea levels on a terrestrial coastal community would be a decrease in biodiversity. As coastal flooding destroys terrestrial habitats, the flora and fauna of the community either drown or relocate to a more suitable terrestrial habitat.

12. C

An inference that can be made based on the statements is that bacteria are both harmful and beneficial. They are essential to the survival of some organisms, but they can also be pathogenic, causing diseases and death in some organisms.

13. 45213

Kingdom	Representative Image Number
Monera	4
Protista	5
Fungi	2
Animalia	1
Plantae	3

The kingdom Monera encompasses all bacteria and is properly matched with Image 4 depicting the bacillus bacteria *Escherichia coli*.

The kingdom Protista encompasses the protozoans and algae and is properly matched with Image 5 depicting a common dinoflagellate.

The kingdom Fungi includes: mushrooms, yeasts, moulds, and mildew and is properly matched with Image 2 depicting a small mushroom.

The kingdom Animalia includes: mammals, birds, fish, sponges, worms, insects, amphibians, reptiles and is properly matched with Image 1 depicting a sea sponge.

The kingdom Plantae includes: mosses, ferns, gymnosperms, and angiosperms and is properly matched with Image 3 depicting a small flowering plant growing on the trunk of a larger tree.

14. A

The vast majority of organisms in the kingdom Animalia are invertebrates: animals without a backbone.

15. 735

Unknown organism A does not have a backbone, is segmented, and does not have jointed limbs, which classifies it as an annelid (classification number 7).
Unknown organism B has a backbone, has four limbs, and is scaly all over its body, which classifies it as a reptile (classification number 3).
Unknown organism C has a backbone and is not four-limbed but does have fins, which classifies it as a fish (classification number 5).

16. B

Binomial nomenclature names an organism first according to its genus name, then according to its species name, therefore, *Panthera* is the genus name, and *tigris* is the species name.

17. C

Protists (eukaryotes) and monerans (prokaryotes) both have flagella that can be used in locomotion. Flagella are single-stranded, tail-like structures projecting from the cell bodies of certain prokaryotic and eukaryotic cells. A prokaryotic flagellum consists of a hollow, rigid cylinder made from the protein flagellin. Eukaryotic flagella are made-up of the protein tubulin arranged in microtubules.

Cilia are hair-like appendages found only in eukaryotes. Pseudopodia are cytoplasmic extensions found only in eukaryotes, and fimbria are hair-like extensions found only in prokaryotes.

18. OR

The label **X** most appropriately represents **Fungi**. Fungi are eukaryotes. They can be unicellular or multicellular, and they do not contain chlorophyll. Their nutrition is derived from absorption.

Bacteria are prokaryotic.

Protista is a kingdom consisting primarily of unicellular eukaryotic organisms with multiple modes of nutrient acquisition.

Viruses do not possess a cellular structure. They are neither eukaryotic or prokaryotic.

19. B

Single-celled organisms in the kingdom Monera are bacteria. They differ from other single-celled organisms in that they do not have membrane-bound organelles, which means that they lack a nucleus, mitochondria, chloroplasts, golgi apparatus, and endoplasmic reticulum. These organelles are all found in eukaryotes, including the single-celled protists.

Bacteria have a cell wall consisting of peptidoglycan, not cellulose. Cellulose is found in the cell walls of plants.

Bacteria are not the only single-celled organisms that contain flagella. The single-cell eukaryotic protist *Euglena* has a flagellum.

Chromosomes in bacteria are also found within the nucleoid region, not only the plasmid region. Additionally, some single-celled yeasts (eukaryotes) have plasmids present.

20. C

Protistans are eukaryotic organisms. They are capable of locomotion. They lack a cell wall and do not develop from an embryo. Therefore, organism *X* belongs to the kingdom Protista.

Fungi have a cell wall made of chitin. Monerans lack a well-defined nucleus. Animals develop from embryos.

21. C

Endocytosis is the process by which a cell ingests material from its surroundings. It can sometimes involve the ingestion of one whole cell by another cell. Diffusion involves the movement of very small molecules across a membrane. Osmosis is the diffusion of water across a membrane. Active transport allows larger molecules to move across a membrane.

22. OR

Biodiversity ensures that some bacterial infections become resistant to antibiotic treatment when mutations in their genetic material provide them with antibiotic-resistant genes that allow them to survive in the environment of the antibiotic.
Those organisms with the adaptive mutation will be the ones to survive and reproduce, passing on the antibiotic resistance trait and ensuring the survival of the species and the maintenance of bacterial biodiversity (i.e., increased resiliency). If the mutation did not occur, all of the bacteria would be wiped out in response to the treatment, and the species could ultimately become extinct.

23. B

Human scientists select the best traits of several breeds to produce one breed with a combination of all the desired traits; this is artificial selection.

24. OR

The slowest rabbits on the island would be killed by the predators. Only the fastest rabbits or the rabbits best able to hide from the predators (camouflage) would be the ones to survive to pass on their genes. Over time, the population of rabbits would become faster and/or more camouflaged. This evolution would be in response to the natural selection by the wolf predators.

25. A

Environmental conditions (nature) "select" certain individuals that have the traits necessary to survive in that environment—these individuals are the "fittest." These organisms live long enough to reproduce, passing on their genes to the next generation.

26. C

Natural selection leads to the survival of the individuals of a population that are best adapted to their environment.

27. 3456

Rabbits produce a large number of offspring (3), some of which will be able to run faster than others (6) due to genetic variability. The population of rabbits remains roughly uniform from year to year (4) because some rabbits, usually the slowest moving ones, are caught (5) by predators. Nature selection is "selecting" the faster rabbits for survival.
The correct response in lowest-to-highest numerical order is therefore 3, 4, 5, and 6.

28. OR

A common research process that investigates the resistance levels of different strains of bacteria to a particular antibiotic treatment involves growth of the microorganism of concern on an agar plate that houses small, absorbent discs soaked with different concentrations of the antibiotic treatment.
As growth of the bacteria ensues, antibiotic will diffuse out of each of the discs into the surrounding agar medium and then, depending on the relative concentration of the antibiotic on the disc, different-sized zones of inhibited bacterial growth will appear in circular patterns surrounding each of the discs.

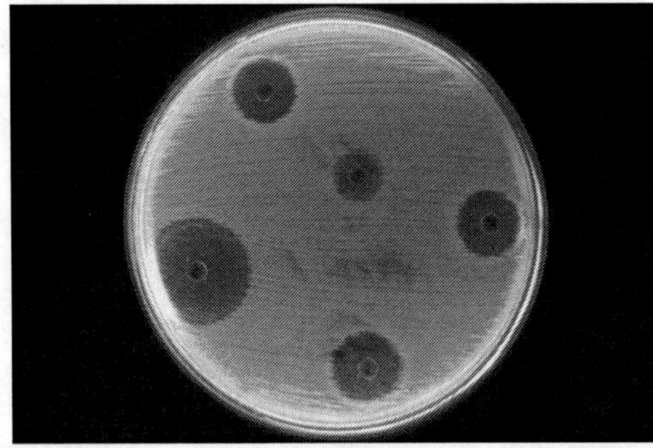

Antibiotic resistance testing

The diameter of the inhibition ring can be compared with a known antibiotic resistance standard to determine whether or not the bacteria have developed a resistance to the particular antibiotic treatment being investigated. Random genetic mutation supplies the source of resistance in those strains that survive.

29. B

According to the theory of punctuated equilibria, evolutionary changes are rapid bursts of speciation called punctuations. Changes in a species occur with long periods of no change. These are known as the periods of equilibria.

30. OR

Natural selection is a process by which the environment selects which individuals will survive and reproduce.

Artificial selection is the process by which humans select the most desirable traits in order to produce offspring with these traits.

31. C

Darwin did not address the occurrence of spontaneous mutations in his theory of natural selection. Hugo de Vries explained the phenomenon of spontaneous mutations in the mutation theory of evolution.

32. a) OR

Through evolution, it would be expected that the DNA sequence will change, but remain similar, from 6 000 years ago to the present. This should be seen in both colonies examined, as evolution (through natural selection) should be acting on both colonies. In colony 1, nine out of fifteen nucleotides have changed over the time period, which is the same as colony 2.

b) OR

Because the penguins tend to live and breed in the same colonies in which they were born, the two colonies should have separate populations. Colonies 1 and 2 should show differences in DNA sequence both in the past and in the present. The DNA sequence comparison between colonies 1 and 2 from the population from 6 000 years ago shows a difference of seven nucleotides. However, the present-day colonies 1 and 2 only show a difference in four nucleotides, which is unexpected.

c) OR

It is possible that there has been a disruption to the penguins' practice of living and breeding in the colony they were born in. One hypothesis may be that when the icebergs break, it disrupts the colonies or prevents penguins from returning to their home colony. The isolated penguins may then have integrated into other colonies. Interbreeding over time between the colonies would have resulted in increased similarities between the DNA sequences of the different colonies (microevolution). In fact, this is the hypothesis that was tested and verified by Dr. David Lambert and his team.

33. A

The fossil record seems to indicate that there are many more species today than there has ever been. In fact, there seems to have been a gradual increase in the number of species over time. Only macroevolution, evolution involving the formation of new species, could explain this.

There is no reason to suggest that species today are more complex than in the past. Regardless, there is evidence for evolution from one species to another in the fossil record. Just because organisms have unique characteristics does not mean there has been macroevolution; it simply indicates genetic variability. Becoming resistant to pesticides represents change within one type of organism in response to environmental changes, as is characteristic of microevolution.

34. C

This is an example of sexual selection. In sexual selection, one sex of a species chooses its mate. This affects the genetic variation of the entire population of the species.

35. 1346

High milk-yielding cows (1), a pet chihuahua (3), corn on the cob (4), and pest-resistant crops (6) all provide examples of artificial selection as they are plant varieties and animal breeds that were selected by humans for their desirable or beneficial traits. Therefore the examples of artificial selection from the list in lowest-to-highest numerical order are 1, 3, 4, and 6.

The elaborate display of the male peacock (2) provides an example of sexual selection, and an elephant's trunk (5) provides an example of natural selection.

36. OR

The elaborate, showy plumage of the male peacock relative to the plain, brown colouration of the female peahen is an example of sexual dimorphism in a species. Sexual selection resulted in the development of this difference because over successive generations, males with the most colourful and elaborate displays were more successful in gaining the attention of the females and, therefore, more likely to reproduce as the females favoured them over males with less colourful and elaborate displays. Because the females permitted the more colourful males to mate with them, it was their traits that were successfully passed on to the next generation, resulting in the gradual accumulation of these colourful plumage characteristics in the offspring. Sexual selection does not necessarily function to promote adaptability because it does not favour those traits that better enable an organism to survive under given environmental pressures, but instead it favours those specific traits that increase the individual's chance of mating and reproduction.

37. D

In 96% of cases, the cause of Down syndrome is non-disjunction of chromosome 21 during anaphase of meiosis. This can take place during sperm production but is more common during the production of eggs. About 70% of non-disjunctions occur in meiosis I and 30% in meiosis II.
In meiosis I, it is caused by the failure of the homologous chromosome pairs to separate; whereas in meiosis II, the sister chromatids fail to separate. The final effect is the same: two chromosomes or two chromatids entering one daughter cell and none entering the other, instead of one entering each. This leads to an equal number of cases of monosomy 21 (only one chromosome 21).

38. B

A zygote undergoes mitosis, not meiosis, to form the adult body.

39. B

As a result of cross-pollination, the gametes from each parent plant are separated. Of the offspring produced, 50% will be of the genotype *Tt*, and 50% will be of the genotype *tt*.

40. OR

F_1 generation: white-eyed female $X^W X^W$ crossed with a red-eyed male $X^R Y$

Parental Gametes	X^W	X^W
X^R	$X^W X^R$	$X^W X^R$
Y	$X^W Y$	$X^W Y$

In the F_1 generation, 50% of the offspring have red eyes because all the females have the genotype $X^W X^R$ and 50% of the offspring have white eyes because all the males have the genotype $X^W Y$.

41. 332

Draw a Punnett square.
bbCc × *BbCc*

PG	*BC*	*Bc*	*bC*	*bc*
bC	*BbCC*	*BbCc*	*bbCC*	*bbCc*
bc	*BbCc*	*Bbcc*	*bbCc*	*bbcc*
bC	*BbCC*	*BbCc*	*bbCC*	*bbCc*
bc	*BbCc*	*Bbcc*	*bbCc*	*bbcc*

According to the genotype to phenotype correlation illustrated by the Punnett square in the question, if a dominant *B* allele is present in any combination (that is the allele combination is either *BB* or *Bb*) and the dominant *C* allele is present in any combination (that is the allele combination is either *CC* or *Cc*) then the mouse will have a black coat. If the dominant *B* allele is present in any combination but the dominant *C* allele is not present at all (that is the allele combination is *cc*) then the mouse will have a white coat. If the dominant *C* allele is present in any combination but the dominant *B* allele is not present at all (that is the allele combination is *bb*) then the mouse will have a brown coat. If neither the dominant *B* allele nor the dominant *C* allele are present the mouse will once again exhibit a white coat.

Therefore, from the Punnett square illustrating the *bbCc* × *BbCc* cross:

Phenotypic ratio	6	6	4
Coat color	Black	Brown	White

Or more simplified:

Phenotypic ratio	3	3	2
Coat color	Black	Brown	White

42. OR

A **test cross** could be used to determine whether the organism is homozygous or heterozygous.
To perform a test cross, you would breed the individual in question with another individual that is homozygous for the recessive trait. If all of the offspring display the dominant trait, you know the individual in question is homozygous dominant.
If some of the offspring display the recessive trait, you know the individual in question is heterozygous.

43. C

The disjunction of homologous chromosomes occurs during anaphase in meiosis I, not meiosis II.

44. 231

Chromosomes align at the equator of the cell.	2
Sister chromatids separate from each other.	3
Chromatin begins to coil and condense.	1

Metaphase II is the stage of meiosis II that comes after prophase II. During this phase, chromosomes align at the equator of the cell (2).

Anaphase II is the stage of meiosis II that comes after metaphase II. During this phase, sister chromatids separate from each other and move to the opposite poles (3).

Prophase II is the first phase of meiosis II. During this phase, chromatin begins to coil and condense to form chromosomes, while the nuclear membrane and nucleolus disappear (1).

45. B

Chromosomes contain genes, which are responsible for the transmission of hereditary characteristics from one generation to the next.

46. OR

Similarities:

- Both are part of cell division with the four different phases.
- Both have cytokinesis occur after the chromosomes have divided.
- Both have an interphase where the chromosomes duplicate.

Differences:

Factor	Mitosis	Meiosis
Number of daughter cells	2	4
Number of chromosomes	diploid $2n$	haploid n
Is there genetic variation?	no	yes
Type of cell	somatic (body) cells	gametic cells
Number of divisions	1	2

47. A

Mendel did not propose a theory on co-dominance. After the process of fertilization, the dominant allele expresses itself, whereas the recessive allele does not express itself. Therefore, this assertion is not a component of the law of segregation.

48. OR

Determining Form of Inheritance

Evidence of X-linked Inheritance vs. Evidence of Autosomal Inheritance	
X-linked Evidence	**Autosomal Evidence**
Greater number of males than females have the disorder	Number of males and females with the disorder is roughly equal
Disorder appears to be inherited from the maternal side of the family	Disorder appears to be inherited from either parent equally

Evidence of Recessive Inheritance vs. Evidence of Dominant Inheritance	
Evidence of Recessive Inheritance	**Evidence of Dominant Inheritance**
Two parents without the disorder have a child with the disorder	Two parents with the disorder have a child without the disorder
The disorder skips generations	The disorder is present in each generation or disappears completely from successive generations

49. OR

If an egg's sex chromosomes does not split, then the egg could have an extra X chromosome or have no sex chromosomes altogether.

If a sperm's sex chromosomes do not separate properly, the resulting sperm could contain both X and Y or no sex chromosomes at all.

If an egg with an extra X chromosome (XX) fuses with a normal sperm with one sex chromosome (Y), it results in a triploid zygote having an XXY genotype. This is called Klinefelter syndrome. If the same egg (XX) fuses with a normal sperm containing an X chromosome, it results in a XXX called triple X or a superfemale. A superfemale could also result from a sperm with two X chromosomes and a normal egg.

If an egg that contains no X chromosome fuses with a normal sperm with a single X chromosome, the result is Turner's syndrome (X). If an egg that contains no X fuses with a normal sperm with a single Y chromosome, the zygote will not survive.

If a sperm contains two Y chromosomes (YY) and fuses with a normal egg (X), the result is XYY, called supermale syndrome.

50. D

Artificial placement of bull's sperm into a cow's uterus (intrauterine), or cervix (intracervical), was done to improve the amount and quality of milk production on a large scale by impregnating many cows at a single time.

51. OR

The technique referred to is **endoscopy** and the tool referred to in the question is called an endoscope.

Endoscopy can be used to:

1. visualize internal structures, such as organ surfaces or tissues, for abnormalities
2. biopsy for internal tissue samples
3. surgically remove tumours or abnormal growths

52. C

Gases (such as oxygen) and certain liquids readily diffuse across the cell membrane from an area of high concentration to an area of low concentration along their concentration gradient, this is referred to as passive diffusion. The concentration of oxygen in cells is very low compared to that in blood. Therefore, oxygen readily diffuses from the blood into the cells.

53. D

Cellulose fibres do not undergo digestion but help to maintain the peristaltic movement of the intestine. Hence, they are helpful in preventing constipation. Scurvy is a disease that is prevented by eating fruits and vegetables containing vitamin C. Anemia is a blood disorder with multiple underlying causes and is not influenced by a diet high in cellulose. Diarrhea is the rapid movement of feces through the bowels resulting in frequent loose and high-liquid content bowel movements. A high cellulose diet does not typically help prevent the underlying causes of the different types of diarrhea.

54. OR

Describe the events that lead to inhalation after stimulation by the respiratory centre.

- rib muscles (intercostals) contract / ribs move up and out
- diaphragm contracts / flattens
- this increases the thoracic volume
- negative pressure is created
- air pulled into negative pressure (or into larger unoccupied volume)

55. C

Structure Y is the pharynx, which serves as the passageway for both food and air intake.
The pharynx branches into the esophagus, dorsally, and the trachea, ventrally.

The trachea (structure Z) passes air to the bronchi (structure W), bronchioles, alveolar ducts, and finally to the alveoli for gas exchange. Between the trachea and the pharynx lies the larynx (structure X). The larynx is responsible for voice production, so it is also called the voice box.

56. D

Blood traveling to the digestive organs delivers oxygen to the tissues and collects nutrients from the absorptive surfaces of the digestive tract. It then travels through the hepatic portal vein to the liver (structure labelled V) which is responsible for regulating circulating levels of sugars, fats, and proteins. This permits for the liver to remove, store, convert, or excrete nutrients and toxins from the blood before it returns to the systemic circulation.

57. A

During strenuous exercise the body is not able to provide enough oxygen through ventilation to balance the amount of carbon dioxide produced by the muscles. The higher concentration of carbon dioxide relative to oxygen will be detected by chemoreceptors in the medulla oblongata. There are also oxygen receptors that detect lower concentrations of oxygen in the blood, however the carbon dioxide receptors are more sensitive and are the main regulators of the breathing rate.

58. B

Ventilation requires oxygen in the air to be inhaled and exhaled via the respiratory system. This system is composed of various passageways that allow oxygen to travel to the lungs. This passageway is lined with cilia and moist, mucus-producing cells, which trap foreign particles and expel them through the nose and mouth.

59. A

Pancreatic juice contains components that digest the three major food groups: carbohydrates, fats, and protein. The functions of the three pancreatic enzymes are listed as follows:

Trypsin—digests small peptides/proteins into shorter peptide chains. The pancreas secretes the inactive form of this enzyme, trypsinogen, which is activated in the small intestine by enterokinase. Protein digestion begins in the stomach with pepsin that breaks down long polypeptides into short peptides.

Lipase—breaks down lipids/fats. There are 3 types of lipases: (*i*) Pancreatic lipase hydrolyzes triglycerides into glycerol and 3 fatty acids. (*ii*) Cholesterol lipase breaks down steroid cholesterol molecules. (*iii*) Phospholipase breaks down phospholipids (components of membranes) into glycerol and phosphorylated fatty acids.

Amylase—hydrolyzes starch (a complex sugar/carbohydrate) into maltose, a disaccharide. Disaccharides are broken down into monosaccharides by disaccharidases present on the inner cell membranes of cells lining the lumen of the small intestine. Vitamins are usually absorbed directly either in the stomach or the small or large intestine. Cellulose cannot be broken down by any enzymes of the human body. Cows and other ruminants are able to digest cellulose (plant fibre) with the aid of microbes present in their stomachs.

60. a) D

A large surface area is required in the circulatory system to facilitate gas exchange, and to transport nutrients and wastes into and out of tissues. These functions occur in the capillaries.

Moreover, capillary walls are composed of a single cell layer and have a diameter just wide enough for red blood cells to travel in single file. Each cell in the body is no more than two cells away from a capillary. Capillaries are therefore designed for efficient exchange of material across membranes. The aorta and vena cava (superior and inferior) are the largest arteries and veins, respectively. The aorta conducts blood directly from the powerful left ventricle of the heart and, like all arteries, is built to withstand high fluid pressure and volume. The vena cavae conduct deoxygenated venous blood back to the heart (right atrium).

b) B

Blood is pumped throughout the body by the muscular heart. Venous blood enters the heart at the left and right atria. The right atrium collects deoxygenated blood from the systemic circuit and passes it to the right ventricle, which pumps blood to the lungs (the pulmonary circuit).

At the lungs, blood becomes oxygenated. Oxygenated blood returns to the heart through the pulmonary vein, which carries blood to the left atrium. From the left atrium, blood travels to the left ventricle. The left ventricle is the largest and most muscular heart chamber because it pumps blood to the entire body (the systemic circuit). The top of each peak from the aorta to the arterioles in the given graph represents ventricular systole (the contraction of the ventricles, specifically the left ventricle).

Because the left ventricle pumps with great force, the aorta (the first artery to conduct blood from the heart) has a very thick, muscular wall to withstand high blood pressure. As the aorta is divided into numerous smaller arteries and then arterioles, the overall blood pressure drops, as represented in the graph by the gradual downward slope.

The atria pump blood to the ventricles, not to the arteries. Valves and skeletal muscle contraction are relevant only to veins. Both valve (to prevent backflow of blood) and skeletal muscle contraction are necessary to pump blood through the veins because of the relatively low blood pressure in the venous system.

61. B

The deoxygenated red blood cell leaves the right ventricle through the pulmonary artery. Recall that arteries carry blood *away* from the heart and veins carry blood to the heart. In systemic circulation, arteries carry oxygenated blood, whereas veins carry deoxygenated blood. The opposite is true for pulmonary circulation. The pulmonary arteries carry deoxygenated blood from the heart to the lungs. The pulmonary veins carry blood from the lungs to the left side of the heart. From the left side of the heart, blood is pumped to the rest of the body (systemic circulation) via the aorta, which branches off the left ventricle. The superior vena cava empties deoxygenated blood from the head into the right atrium.

62. 1432

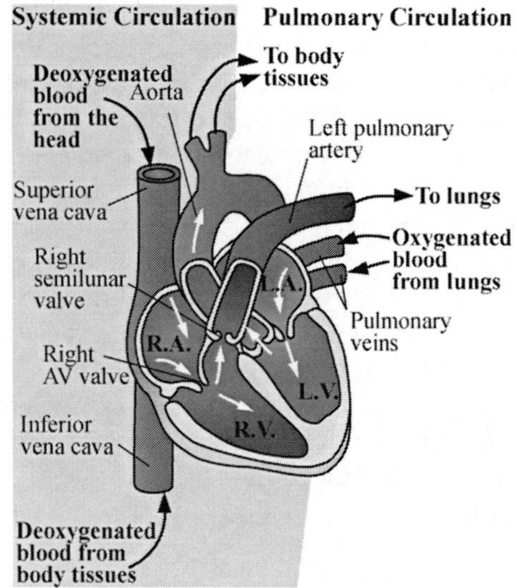

RA—right atrium; RV—right ventricle; LA—left atrium; LV—left ventricle.

Deoxygenated blood travels in veins from body tissues to the right side of the heart. Deoxygenated blood enters the heart at the right atrium (1). Contraction of the RA forces blood through the right atrioventricular valve (4) and into the right ventricle (3). The AV valves on both sides of the heart function to prevent blood from flowing the wrong way—from the ventricles back into the atria. AV valves are supported by strong connective tissue bands called chordae tendinae. Contraction of the right ventricle forces blood out of the heart and into the pulmonary arteries that carry blood to the lungs, where blood becomes oxygenated. A second set of valves, the semilunar (half-moon shaped) valves (2), are present at the junction between the right ventricle and the pulmonary artery (which subsequently branches into left and right pulmonary arteries). The correct path of a deoxygenated red blood cell is 1, 4, 3, 2.

63. OR

1. Pulmonary (semilunar) valve—passes oxygen-poor blood travelling from the body through right atrium and ventricle to the pulmonary artery for transport to the lungs.
2. Tricuspid (atrioventricular) valve—passes oxygen poor blood travelling from the body that entered the right atrium from the superior vena cava and inferior vena cava into the right ventricle.
3. Aortic (semilunar) valve—passes oxygen rich blood travelling from the lungs through the left atrium and ventricle to the aorta for transport to the rest of the body.
4. Mitral or Bicuspid (atrioventricular) valve—passes oxygen-rich blood travelling from the pulmonary veins (coming from the lungs) that entered the left atrium into the left ventricle.

64. A

The main function of the large intestine is water reabsorption. Water is reabsorbed from fecal matter and passed back into blood. Shortening the length of the large intestine by surgically removing a portion of it would decrease the amount of time and surface area available for water reabsorption. Therefore, the patient would experience less water reabsorption, resulting in more watery feces.

Watery feces result from insufficient water reabsorption by the large intestine and can result when fecal matter moves too quickly through the digestive system, or possibly because of ingestion of food contaminated with some strains of bacteria. The extreme case of watery feces is called diarrhea. Long-term diarrhea can lead to severe dehydration.

65. D

Each stomata is surrounded by two guard cells that control its opening and closing by changing the turgidity. The guard cells become turgid when they absorb water from the surrounding cells. When the guard cells become turgid, the outer elastic walls become convex in shape. As the guard cells take this shape, they draw the inner walls apart, resulting in a larger opening or aperture. When the turgor pressure decreases, the reverse situation occurs and the stomata opening becomes smaller.

66. A

Synthetic auxins, such as 2,4-D (dichlorophenoxy acetic acid), are used as herbicides to control the growth of weeds around crops.

Ethylene functions as a hormone in plants to stimulate ripening of fruit and shedding of leaves. Gibberellin helps promote stem elongation and the expansion of leaves. Abscisic acid functions in abscission, which occurs in response to environmental stresses, such as pathogens or changing weather, resulting in the shedding of leaves, flowers, or other structures.

67. 3142

Water enters the plant from the soil through the large surface area of the root hairs (3). Then, water travels through the roots, up the stem, and into the leaves via the xylem (1). When the water is in the leaf, it can move into the spaces of the spongy tissue (4). From the spongy tissue, the water molecules can diffuse out of the leaf through the stomata (2).

68. B

Stem cuttings are used for propagation during the cultivation of grapes.

ANSWERS AND SOLUTIONS — PRACTICE TEST 2

1. C	16. A	31. A	46. D	60. OR
2. C	17. B	32. D	47. C	61. B
3. OR	18. 1457	33. OR	48. 3214	62. D
4. A	19. C	34. OR	49. D	63. C
5. A	20. 2357	35. B	50. OR	64. 4321
6. B	21. B	36. B	51. OR	65. C
7. 4231	22. OR	37. A	52. B	66. 2413
8. 1212	23. C	38. OR	53. a) OR	67. OR
9. OR	24. D	39. A	b) OR	68. C
10. OR	25. C	40. A	54. C	69. D
11. B	26. C	41. B	55. A	70. 4317
12. OR	27. D	42. OR	56. OR	71. A
13. D	28. OR	43. OR	57. D	
14. B	29. D	44. OR	58. A	
15. C	30. A	45. B	59. 23	

1. C

Phloem is responsible for transporting the organic nutrients formed during photosynthesis to the rest of the plant. If a sieve tube were clogged the plant would not be able to transport organic nutrients such as glucose.

Xylem transports water and mineral nutrients. Oxygen and carbon dioxide move through the cells of the plant by diffusion, entering and exiting by way of the lenticels and stomata.

2. C

Guard cells are modified parenchyma cells. The pores of the stomata close when turgor pressure in guard cells is low and open when turgor pressure is high. This mechanism controls the process of transpiration.

Xylem and phloem are vascular tissues. Collenchyma is a part of the ground tissue and binds other cells together.

3. OR

Monocots will have parallel leaf veins, a fibrous root system, and dispersed vascular bundles in the stem. Dicots will have a net-like leaf vein structure, a large taproot, and vascular bundles in the stems arranged in a ring.

4. A

Hypogeal germination, in which the seed leaves, or cotyledons, remain below the surface of the soil, occurs in the pea plant. In hypogeal germination, the seed coat softens and facilitates the quick absorption of water and the exchange of gases. The embryo becomes animate, and the radicle is the first to grow. It breaks the seed coat, bending downward to form the primary root. The cotyledons separate and remain in the soil. The epicotyl increases in size, curves, and forms the plumule above the soil, ultimately straightening to form the shoot system.

5. A

Copper is a plant micronutrient that is required by plants in small amounts.

6. B

Growth movement in plants in response to the external stimulus of water is called hydrotropism.

Heliotropism is plant growth movement in response to a light stimulus. Chemotropism is plant growth movement in response to a chemical stimulus. Thigmotropism is plant movement in response to the stimulus of contact.

7. 4231

Effect on Plant Tissues	Plant Growth Regulator Number
Inhibits growth and promotes dormancy	4
When functioning together with other plant hormones promotes flower and fruit development	2
When functioning together with other plant hormones promotes shoot, leaf, and root growth	3
Influences seed germination and releases buds from dorman-cy	1

Abscisic acid (4) promotes inhibition of plant tissues. Generally, it inhibits plant growth and promotes bud and leaf dormancy. Auxins (2), when functioning together with cytokinins, stimulate cell division and promote the growth of fruits and the development of flowers from stems. Cytokinins (3), when functioning together with auxins, stimulate cell division promoting the elongation and growth of cells in roots, shoots, and leaves. Gibberlins (1) function to promote seed germination by inducing enzyme activity required for food production. They also function to release buds from dormancy.

8. 1212

Desert sand dune: there is no soil present, and the area is fundamentally deserted. If succession were to occur, it would be primary (1). Clear cut forest: there is soil still present, but the trees and vegetation have been removed. The type of succession that will occur is secondary (2). Rocky valley exposed by glacial retreat: there is no soil present, only rocky substrate. The type of succession that will occur is primary (1). Forest damaged by recent fire: there is still soil present, but the trees and vegetation have been destroyed. The type of succession that will occur is secondary (2).

Habitat Type	Type of Succession
Desert sand dune	1
Clear-cut forest	2
Rocky valley exposed by glacial retreat	1
Forest damaged by recent fire	2

9. OR

Monoculture cultivation of one type of crop for many years will tend to **decrease** the **diversity** of the flora and fauna in the area. This is because most plants and animals are not equipped to adapt to the extreme environmental changes or shifts in community dynamics that take place when a native land area is cleared and utilized for single-crop production.

Also, monocultures, although useful in the short term, will ultimately **decrease crop yields** as soil fertility in the area is depleted of the same nutrients year after year and local pest resistance to pesticides begins to increase. This usually leads to an **increase** in the use of **pesticides** and **fertilizer**, which in turn damages the environment and decreases the local biodiversity even further as native organisms become increasingly subjected to pollution and habitat degradation.

10. OR

Salmon depend on healthy streams and rivers to make their long journeys. Lower precipitation might dry up some bodies of water, making them impassible. If droughts interrupt spawning routes, salmon populations are likely to **decline**.

11. B

Genetic diversity refers to variations in physical characteristics among individuals within the same species. Differences in hair, eye, and skin colours among humans provide an example of the genetic diversity of a population within a species.

Species diversity refers to the number of different species within a given area and their relative distribution and proportions. Structural diversity considers biodiversity based on the variation in patterns and organization of species genetics and morphology, specific habitats, populations, and communities within the system. Compositional diversity considers biodiversity based on the different number of elements within the given system, such as the total number of genes within species, species within communities, and communities within ecosystems.

12. OR

Carl Linnaeus, known as the father of modern taxonomy, was responsible for developing the system of binomial nomenclature.

Any two of the following advantages are examples of benefits to using the binomial nomenclature system:

1. Promotes consistency and stability in naming
2. Standardizes the naming process
3. Name stays the same regardless of language
4. Decreases the probability of misnomers
5. Eliminates confusion associated with common names

13. D

Moss is an example of a non-vascular plant. Mosses lack specialized conducting tissues and instead directly absorb nutrients and water from the environment through their stem and leaf-like appendages. They usually grow as a thick mat in the shady moist areas at the base of trees.

This image depicts a vascular flowering cactus

This image depicts a fern, which is a seedless vascular plant

This image depicts a type of vascular flowering grass

14. B

The diagram depicts a dinoflagellate, which is a common representative from the kingdom Protista.

15. C

Plankton, or dip, nets are typically used to collect samples of small and microscopic organisms found within a pond ecosystem. Larger vertebrates common to pond ecosystems, such as fish, waterfowl, and small mammals, would require different tools that would be safer for both the animal and the researcher.

16. A

In biological classification, kingdom is the highest taxonomic category, with all of the individuals of related phyla grouped together. While classifying organisms, taxonomic categories follow this order from lowest to highest:
Species → Genus → Family → Order → Class → Phylum → Kingdom

Phylum is the taxonomic category below kingdom. Species is the lowest taxonomic category, and order is the taxonomic category that includes related families of organisms.

17. B

Viruses can use either DNA or RNA to store their genetic information. They are classified as DNA viruses or RNA viruses, depending on the type of genetic material they use.

18. 1457

Nucleoid (1), cell wall (4), plasmids (5), and binary fission (7) are characteristics that are commonly found in prokaryotes.

1. Nucleoid—dense region of DNA located within the cytoplasm of prokaryotic cells only.
2. Membrane-enclosed organelles—structures specialized for certain functions located in the cytoplasm of eukaryotes only.
3. Nucleus—membrane-enclosed organelle containing the DNA of eukaryotes.
4. Cell wall—provides cells with structural support; found in prokaryotes, plants and fungi.
5. Plasmids—a tiny piece of circular bacterial DNA that carries accessory genes not located on the bacterial chromosome.
6. Meiotic division—cellular division of sexually reproducing organisms that results in the production of gametes—eukaryotes only.
7. Binary fission—prokaryotic cellular division in which each daughter cell receives an identical copy of the single parent chromosome.

19. C

A sea sponge belongs in the kingdom Animalia. Pine trees belong in the kingdom Plantae, mushrooms belong in the kingdom Fungi, and seaweed is a multicellular algae in the kingdom Protista.

20. 2357

The correct numerical response in lowest-to-highest numerical order is: 2, 3, 5, 7.

Organisms within the kingdom Animalia are multicellular (2), eukaryotic (3), heterotrophic (5) organisms that commonly have cells arranged into nervous tissue (7) responsible for integrating sensory information from the environment with appropriate motor actions.

Members of this kingdom are not unicellular, prokaryotic, or autotrophic, nor do they possess cell walls. These characteristics are associated with some or all of the other four kingdoms: Monera, Plantae, Protista, and Fungi.

21. B

Green algae played an important role in the evolution of land plants. Green algae are photosynthetic protists that are similar to land plants in chloroplast structure (that is, they both have chloroplasts with thylakoid membranes arranged as grana), chloroplast pigmentation (that is, they both have chlorophyll b and beta-carotene), and in the structure of the cell wall (that is, they both have cell walls comprised primarily of cellulose). Specifically, through comparison of cell ultra-structure and biochemistry, it is believed that a group of green algae called charophytes is the most likely direct ancestor to all land plants.

The blue-green algae are actually prokaryotic organisms known as cyanobacteria, from which it is hypothesized that chloroplasts evolved early on through endosymbiosis. However, these organisms are not hypothesized to be the direct descendants of land plants. Due to the presence of fucoxanthin pigments and a phycocolloid cell wall composition, red and brown algae are considered primitive forms of plants, but not the evolutionary ancestors of land plants.

22. OR

The Cambrian period is often referred to as the Cambrian explosion because it was during this time that all known animal phyla diversified from a common protistan ancestor. This extreme diversification occurred relatively quickly in geological terms. Because so many different animal forms evolved so rapidly during this period, it is referred to as an explosion.

23. C

An increase in the biodiversity of a population will increase the resiliency of that population to both pests and disease because it provides the population with the genetic variability necessary to adapt to the changing environmental conditions presented by the pests or disease.

24. D

Artificial selection technologies tend to inadvertently decrease the genetic variability of the organisms being selected for their desirable traits. This decrease in genetic variability limits the adaptability of the artificially selected population in the face of unpredictable environmental change.

Higher crop yields, disease resistant crops, and increased livestock biomass all provide examples of the advantages of artificial selection as they all equate to economic benefit to the farmer.

25. C

Due to natural selection, the giant panda has evolved to specialize on bamboo as its food source. If due to deforestation or some other aspect of environmental change, bamboo becomes scares, the giant panda would become vulnerable to extinction because it would no longer be able obtain it's primary food resource in high enough quantities to ensure survival and adequate reproduction.

26. C

Natural selection acts upon the genetic makeup of either an organism or a group of organisms.
Any genetic adaptation will either increase or decrease the ability of an organism to survive, depending on the environment. If the organism does not survive, the frequency of the genes that the organism possesses will decrease in the population because the organism will not reproduce. If the organism survives and reproduces, the organism's gene frequency will increase in the population.

Migration, extirpation, and population bottleneck will all alter the frequency of certain traits in a population, but these phenomena do not act directly upon the genetic variability of individuals present in the population.

27. D

Phyletic speciation occurs when organisms adapt to a shifting environment.

28. OR

There are many human activities that can cause extinction.

- Loss of habitat is a major cause of extinction. Humans have been clearing land for building communities and growing food. A population may be unable to move to a new habitat when their original habitat is destroyed.
- Over-hunting/over-harvesting of species—some species have been hunted to extinction or to the brink of extinction.
- Introduction of new species—humans have introduced new species to habitats, resulting in some organisms being unable to compete against the introduced species.
- Pollution—releasing wastes can destroy habitats and make organisms sick.

29. D

Genetic mutations are passed from one generation to the other only if the mutations occur in the sex cells. Sex cells, or gametes, are produced by the reproductive system. Testes produce sperm that carry the paternal genetic material into the next generation.

30. A

Lamarck did not explain natural selection in his theory. Charles Darwin introduced the idea of natural selection in his theory of evolution.

31. A

The resistant bacteria adapted to a specific type of antibiotic. They died once the type of antibiotic was changed. Antibiotic resistance is due to genetic variability and is therefore heritable by subsequent generations. Adaptation is due to inherent genetic variability and is therefore not temporary; it cannot be lost within a generation. Adaptation occurs not only to obtain food resources but also against environmental factors.

32. D

Individuals within a population have variable characteristics. According to Darwin, those individuals that are best suited to survive in a particular environment will survive to produce future generations. However, Darwin could not explain why all organisms of a species are not born with all the same characteristics. It is now known that differences in the outward appearance (called the phenotype of an organism) and other traits (e.g., biochemical enzymes) are due to differences in the genetic material (DNA) between individuals. These genetic differences can arise by mutation.

33. OR

Darwin developed the concept of evolution as an explanation for the diversity of life on Earth and derived the principle of natural selection as the mechanism by which it occurred. Darwin provided a reasonable explanation on how variations were selected, but not why variations existed. This was the basis for the criticism of the theory of natural selection. This criticism was subsequently addressed by the findings of Mendel, which described the transmission of heritable traits through genes and the occurrence of alleles and mutations as a source of genetic variation.

34. OR

Natural selection promotes adaptation of an organism to its environment by acting on inherent genetic variations and favouring those individuals with characteristics that best able them to compete under particular environmental conditions making them more likely to survive, reproduce, and pass the favourable trait onto the next generation.
The gradual accumulation of favoured traits over successive generations promotes adaptation of the organism to its environment. A population of bacteria becomes adapted to the changing environmental conditions associated with an antibiotic treatment by developing an antibiotic resistance. A given population of bacteria will display genetic variation among its individuals with the potential for one or more to possess a gene conferring antibiotic resistance. Under the changing environmental conditions of the antibiotic treatment only those individuals that possesses the antibiotic resistance gene will survive and reproduce, subsequently passing the gene to their offspring and creating a generation that is entirely antibiotic resistant.

35. B

Allopatric speciation occurs when two populations of a species are separated by a geographical barrier.

36. B

Natural selection proposes that giraffes evolved elongated necks because longer-necked giraffes were more successful in feeding on leaves on tall trees. Mutation may have given rise to the long neck in giraffes but it was natural selection that led to this trait becoming a characteristic of the species.

37. A

- True – There are many successful examples of recombinant DNA biotechnology introducing the genes of one species into the genome of a different species. Some examples include human insulin-producing bacteria and fluorescent aquarium fish.
- False – Genetic engineering is a biotechnology used to create genetically modified organisms; however, it is highly controversial because the ramifications of its impacts on natural biodiversity are poorly understood, unforeseeable, and potentially irreversible.
- False – Artificial selection does not cross different species to create new species, but rather it crosses individuals of the same species with desirable traits in the attempt to produce offspring possessing both beneficial traits.
- False – Pest resistance is a characteristic that occurs naturally in the inherent genetic variation of many plants. Although frequently favoured by artificial selection techniques, pest-resistant crops could potentially result simply through the process of natural selection.

38. OR

Gene migration refers to the migration of animals and the genes that they carry. Genetic drift refers to the random fluctuations in allele frequency that can occur if a population is small.

39. A

In a dihybrid cross in which two pairs of characters are involved, heterozygous or hybrid organisms are produced in the F_1 generation that possess all four alleles. These organisms therefore have the genotype *RrYy*.

40. A

The gene that confers antibiotic resistance is located on the plasmid. Plasmids are hereditary determinants that are not found on the chromosome (extrachromosomal) and contain resistance factors that can help bacteria resist the effects of common antibiotics.

41. B

A man that is heterozygous for curly hair will have the genotype *Cc*.

Since straight hair is a recessive characteristic, a woman that has straight hair will be homozygous recessive and will have the genotype *cc*.

Use a Punnett square to carry out the genetic cross to obtain the phenotypic ratio.

	C	**c**
c	*Cc*	*cc*
c	*Cc*	*cc*

The expected phenotypic ratio of their offspring is 2 curly (*Cc*) to 2 straight (*cc*), or 2:2.

42. OR

Blood **group B** in their progeny would indicate that the father is heterozygous.

The blood group A can result from either the heterozygous $I^A i$ genotype or the homozygous $I^A I^A$ genotype, while the AB blood group results only from the $I^A I^B$ genotype.

Make a Punnett square of the two possible crosses using the blood group of the father, considering that he could be either homozygous or heterozygous.

The following cross depicts the blood group of the progeny when the father is considered **heterozygous** $(I^A i)$.

$I^A i$ × $I^A I^B$

A AB

↓

Gametes	I^A	i
I^A	$I^A I^A$	$I^A i$
I^B	$I^A I^B$	$I^B i$

I^AI^A, I^Ai, I^AI^B, and I^Bi are the four possible genotypes resulting from the given cross.

Thus, the blood groups of progeny in this case will be A, AB, and B.

The following cross depicts the blood group of the progeny when the father is considered **homozygous** (I^AI^A).

I^AI^A × I^AI^B

A ↓ AB

Gametes	I^A	I^A
I^A	I^AI^A	I^AI^A
I^B	I^AI^B	I^AI^B

I^AI^A and I^AI^B are the only possible genotypes resulting from the given cross.

Thus, the blood group of the progeny in this case will be A and AB.

By comparing the results of the two crosses, it is observed that blood group B is obtained only if the father is heterozygous.

Blood group O cannot be present in the offspring of parents that have blood groups A and AB, since it would be impossible to get two *i* alleles.
Blood groups A and AB will be present in the offspring whether the father is heterozygous or homozygous, so they cannot be used to determine the genotype of the father.

43. OR

The mother's genotype is either affected (*pp*), a carrier (*Pp*), or normal (*PP*). The father is a carrier (*Pp*). Use the Punnett method to evaluate the different parental cross possibilities.

Possibility A
The mother is affected (*pp*): parental cross
Pp × *pp*

Gametes	*p*
P	*Pp*
p	*pp*

When the mother is affected, 50% of the children are carriers (*Pp*) of the recessive allele and 50% of the children are affected (*pp*)1 carrier to 1 affected ratio

Possibility B
The mother is normal (*PP*): parental cross
Pp × *PP*

Gametes	*P*
P	*PP*
p	*Pp*

When the mother is normal, 50% of the children are normal (*PP*) and 50% of the children are carriers (*Pp*).1 normal to 1 carrier ratio

Possibility C
The mother is a carrier (*Pp*): parental cross
Pp × *Pp*

Gametes	*P*	*p*
P	*PP*	*Pp*
p	*Pp*	*pp*

When the mother is a carrier, 25% of the children are normal (*PP*), 50% of the children are carriers (*Pp*), and 25% of the children are affected (*pp*). 1normal to 2 carriers to 1 affected ratio

Since two of their four children are carriers (*Pp*) and the other two of their four children are affected (*pp*), the percentage of carriers in their progeny is 50% and the percentage of affected in their progeny is 50%. This is equivalent to a 1 carrier to 1 affected ratio. Evaluation of cross possibilities A, B, and C reveals that the mother is affected (possibility A) since the Punnett square depicting the *Pp* × *pp* cross resulted in a 1 carrier to 1 affected progeny ratio.

44. OR

The traits of parents can be figured out based on the appearance of the offspring.

First, assign the capital letter *B* to the dominant brown allele and the lowercase letter *b* to the recessive black allele.

If one of the parents is homozygous dominant for the brown hair gene, the offspring can only have brown hair. Since only 50% of the offspring have brown hair, the parental crosses cannot be *BB* with *Bb* or *BB* with *bb*. In other words, neither parent can be homozygous dominant.

Similarly, it is known that the parental cross *bb* with *bb* is not possible because 50% of the offspring have brown hair; therefore, at least one of the parents must have the dominant brown allele.

Therefore, the two remaining possible parental crosses are *Bb* with *Bb* and *Bb* with *bb*.

If the cross is *Bb* with *Bb*, the Punnett square is as follows:

	B	***b***
B	*BB* (brown)	*Bb* (brown)
b	*Bb* (brown)	*bb* (black)

The result of this cross is that 75% of the offspring will have brown hair and 25% of the offspring will have black hair. This does not concur with the expected 50% offspring with brown hair, so this is not likely the most probable makeup of the parents.

If the cross is *Bb* with *bb*, the Punnett square is as follows:

	B	***b***
b	*Bb* (brown)	*bb* (black)
b	*Bb* (brown)	*bb* (black)

The result is 50% of the mice have brown hair and 50% of the mice have black hair. Therefore, the most probable genetic makeup of the parents is one heterozygous parent, *Bb*, and one homozygous recessive parent, *bb*.

45. B

The uncoiling and regrouping of the chromosomes at the poles takes place during telophase I.
The chromosomes are condensed during division. They begin to uncoil and form long strands during telophase I. The nuclear membrane also starts appearing around the chromosomes at this stage.

During metaphase I, the chromosomes start to align at the equatorial plane. During anaphase I, the chromosomes start moving toward the poles. During prophase I, the slender and thread-like chromosomes begin to condense and appear as distinct chromosomes.

46. D

During metaphase, chromosomes are drawn toward the equator of a cell. They are aligned along the cell's equator.

47. C

During interphase, the cell prepares itself for division by producing protein and cytoplasmic organelles. This process takes place in three phases. The cell grows in the first phase. In the second phase, the cell continues its growth. The synthesis and replication of DNA also take place during this phase. In the third phase, the cell prepares for division by mitosis.

The sister chromatids of each chromosome are separated during anaphase, not interphase. Chromatin condenses during prophase, not interphase. The nuclear membrane breaks down during metaphase, not interphase.

48. 3214

First, recall the order of the mitotic phases in the diagram: prophase is 1, metaphase is 2, anaphase is 3, and telophase is 4. Next, arrange the numbers to match the names of the stages in the table.
The correct numerical response is 3, 2, 1, 4.

Stage of Mitosis	Numbered Mitotic Phase
Anaphase	3
Metaphase	2
Prophase	1
Telophase	4

49. D

Flower colour in snapdragons is an example of incomplete dominance. Flowers of a snapdragon are red and white. When these varieties are crossed, the F_1 progeny have pink flowers. Therefore, this illustrates incomplete dominance.

50. OR

The term that best describes the allele for cystic fibrosis is **recessive**.

If two normal (non-affected) parents can have a both a non-affected child and an affected child, then the allele must be recessive and both parents must be carriers of the allele that causes cystic fibrosis.

If *CF* = normal, and *c f* = cystic fibrosis allele:

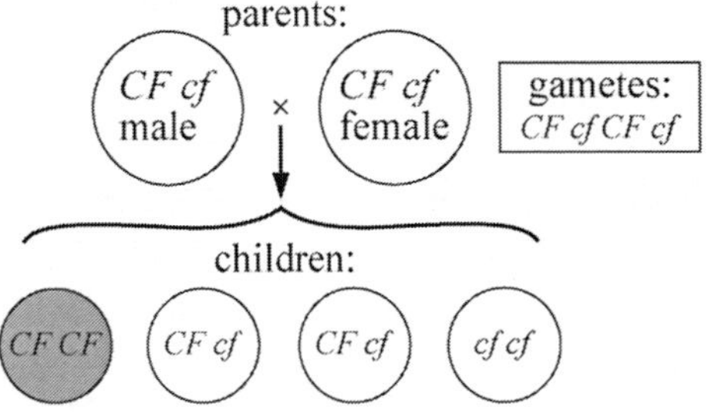

If both parents can be carriers of the cystic fibrosis allele but not have the disease themselves, then the disease allele must be recessive.

The term X-linked is incorrect because if the disease were X-linked (meaning the gene for cystic fibrosis is on the X chromosome), the father would have been affected by the disease, whether the allele was recessive or dominant. This is because, males have only one X chromosome, so the father's genotype would have been $X^{cf}Y$, and he would have had the disease.

The terms co-dominant and dominant are incorrect because we are told that both parents are carriers and therefore would also have been affected with the disease if the allele were either dominant or co-dominant. Recall that dominant alleles are always expressed and co-dominant means that both alleles are expressed. For example, roan cattle have both red and white hairs (giving them the "roan" colour) due to expression of the allele coding for red hair as well as expression of the allele coding for white hair.

51. OR

Huntington's disease does not usually show symptoms until the person is over 30. By the time the symptoms appear, the person has often had a family and may have passed on the gene. Symptoms include impairment of a person's ability to walk, think, talk, and reason.

52. B

Recombinant DNA is the process in which DNA from one organism is inserted into a different organism. Genes can be inserted into crops to give them a desired quality. For example, some crops have been given the ability to withstand frost or resistance to a disease. As well, genes can be inserted into bacteria so the bacteria will produce a desired substance. The gene for insulin has been placed into bacteria so that the bacteria now produce human insulin.

53. a) OR

Some things an individual can do to reduce the risk of illness and poor health are the following:

- Eat nutritious foods.
- Exercise regularly.
- Spend time relaxing with activities such as yoga and meditation.

b) OR

Advancements in technology, such as prosthetics and organ donation, have allowed individuals who suffer from physical disorders to gain mobility and lead more active lifestyles. Prosthetics have allowed individuals that were born with a defect or have lost an arm or a leg a chance to write, walk, and run. Organ donations have given individuals whose organs do not function properly a change to lead more active lifestyles.

54. C

Diastolic blood pressure is measured during maximum ventricular relaxation (diastole).

55. A

During inhalation, a gaseous exchange takes place between atmospheric and alveolar air, and between alveolar air and the blood in lung capillaries. So, during inhalation, oxygen diffuses from the alveoli to the capillary blood of the lungs. Carbon dioxide diffuses out from the capillary blood into the alveolar air to ultimately be expelled during exhalation.

56. OR

Oxygen and nutrients moving from blood into tissue fluids:

- Blood carrying oxygen and nutrients reaches the capillary bed and slows down (blood velocity is lower in the capillary bed)
- Oxygen is released from hemoglobin (red blood cells/blood) at a lower pH and higher temperature
- Blood pressure at the arteriole end of the capillary bed is higher than the osmotic pressure of the tissue fluids
- Blood pressure pushes plasma containing oxygen and nutrients into the tissue fluid

Oxygen and nutrients moving from tissue fluid into the cells:

- Oxygen and nutrients diffuse passively from the tissue fluids into the cells (moving from high to low concentration)
- Nutrients can also be moved by active transport (use ATP), facilitated diffusion (use protein carriers) and endocytosis (pinocytosis) into the cells
- Water moves by osmosis

57. D

Dissection and microscopic examination of the interior surface of the small intestine of the **digestive system** would reveal a unique internal structure of small folds and microscopic projections called villi, illustrated by the given diagram. This unique internal structure is specifically designed to maximize **absorption** of nutrients and other materials that pass through the digestive system. Within each villus is an extensive network of capillaries designed for collection and **transport** of the absorbed materials by the **circulatory system** to the rest of the body.

58. A

During exhalation, the diaphragm becomes dome-shaped, and the internal intercostal muscles contract. This leads to a decrease in the volume of the thoracic cavity and an increase in the pressure inside the lungs. This process results in the expiration of air from the lungs.

59. 23

The correct numerical response in lowest-to-highest numerical order is 2 and 3.

Carbon dioxide is collected from respiring body cells and transported to the lungs by the blood. At the alveolus the carbon dioxide exits the blood and enters the alveolar air space as is depicted by the arrow labelled 3. The carbon dioxide is then expelled from the alveolar air space into the environment via the conducting air passages as is depicted by the arrow labelled 2.

The arrow labelled 1 depicts oxygen entering the alveolar air space from the environment by way of the conducting airways. The arrow labelled 4 depicts oxygen entering the blood from the alveolar air space so that it can be transported to the body tissues.

60. OR

A person might want to control the rate of breathing in order to play a musical instrument or sing because the amount of air expelled creates sound.
Other examples that illustrate a need to control the rate of breathing include diving or swimming under water or avoiding noxious gases.

61. B

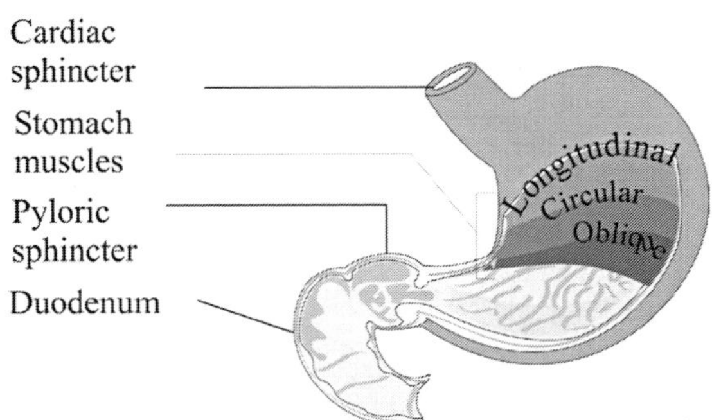

Circular muscles are called sphincters. There are two sphincters in the stomach.

The pyloric sphincter is located at the junction between the stomach and the small intestine (duodenum) and helps to regulate the passage of chyme (digested food) from the stomach to the small intestine. The pyloric sphincter is a stronger muscle than the cardiac sphincter because when closed, it must hold the chyme in the stomach against gravity.

The cardiac or esophageal sphincter is located at the junction between the esophagus and the stomach. The cardiac sphincter regulates the amount of food entering the stomach and prevents food from travelling backward from the stomach to the esophagus. The ileocecal valve (also a sphincter) regulates the passage of food from the small intestine (ileum) to the large intestine. The tricuspid (atrioventricular) valve is located in the heart between the right atrium and ventricle.

62. D

Blood moves through the veins due to the contraction of skeletal muscles.

63. C

The correct sequence of the flow of blood through the cardiopulmonary system is as follows:
vena cava → right atrium → right ventricle → pulmonary artery → pulmonary vein → left atrium → left ventricle → aorta

64. 4321

The process of inflammation starts with vasodilatation of the local blood vessels with consequent excess local blood flow (4). This leads to increased permeability of the capillaries (3) and results in the outflow of large quantities of fluid (plasma) into the interstitial spaces (2). Clotting of this fluid takes place because of the presence of excessive amounts of fibrinogen and other proteins and results in swelling of the cells (1).

65. C

Normally, the lining of the stomach is protected from the corrosive acid (pH ~ 2–3) and proteases in gastric juice by a layer of mucus. When the layer of mucus disappears, cells lining the stomach are destroyed, creating a lesion in the stomach wall called an ulcer. The corrosive nature of gastric juice also was believed to prevent survival of bacterial cells in the stomach.

Multiple additional factors also cause ulcers. For example, ulcers can also be caused by frequent use of aspirin and anti-inflammatory drugs. All bacteria will never be flushed out by contraction (peristalsis). Bacteria are small, allowing them to become trapped in small folds in the lining of the digestive tract. They also multiply very quickly and may even have special structures that allow them to attach themselves to the digestive tract. Bacteria do enter the stomach frequently as part of ingested material or through oral contact with non-sterile surfaces. Bacteria that are pathogenic in the human digestive tract are mostly anaerobic (survive in the absence of oxygen). For example, *E. coli* bacteria that normally live in the intestines are anaerobic.

66. 2413

Plant Genus and species	Beverage
Camellia sinensis	2
Theobroma cacao	4
Coffea arabica	1
Vitis vinifera	3

Tea (2) is obtained from *Camellia sinensis*.

Hot chocolate (4) is made using cocoa obtained from *Theobroma cacao*.

Coffee (1) is obtained from *Coffea arabica*.

Wine (3) is made from the grape of *Vitis vinifera*.

67. OR

Crop rotation is the sequence of cropping in which two dissimilar types of crops, such as cereals and legumes, are grown one after the other. Crop rotation increases soil fertility because those plants (such as cereals) that remove essential nutrients like nitrogen from the soil are replaced with plants (such as legumes) that add nutrients like nitrogen back into the soil. In this manner, crop rotation ensures that soil quality is always ideal for the crop being grown. It improves crop yields and prevents the formation of barren fields, and the subsequent need for relocation to an undisturbed land area.

68. C

In the given figure, spongy parenchyma is labelled III. The spongy parenchyma functions in photosynthesis and gas exchange.

- In the given figure, label I represents the epidermis. The epidermis is a single layer of cuticle-covered cells that protect the inner cells from damage and water loss, while allowing light to reach photosynthetic cells.
- In the given figure, label II represents the palisade parenchyma. The palisade parenchyma functions mainly in photosynthesis, and they have a high concentration of chloroplasts in order to perform this function.
- In the given figure, label IV represents xylem tissue. The xylem conducts water and minerals absorbed from the soil to the rest of the plant.

69. D

The term *inflorescence* describes the arrangement of flowers on the floral axis. Venation refers to the vein pattern within the leaf. Phyllotaxy refers to the leaf arrangement along the length of the stem. Placentation refers to the type and structure, or arrangement, of placentas within mammals.

70. 4317

Morphological Term	Numerical Label
Phloem	4
Xylem	3
Pith	1
Epidermis	7

In the woody stems of vascular dicot plants, the pith is located in the centre of the stem; in the diagram it is labelled as 1. The pith is surrounded by woody tissue called the xylem; the xylem is labelled as 3. The xylem is surrounded by a bark tissue called the phloem; the phloem is labelled as 4. The outermost, single cell layer that covers the stem is called the epidermis; the epidermis is labelled as 7.

71. A

Rhizomes are horizontal underground stems capable of forming new plants. Ginger root propagates through rhizomes.

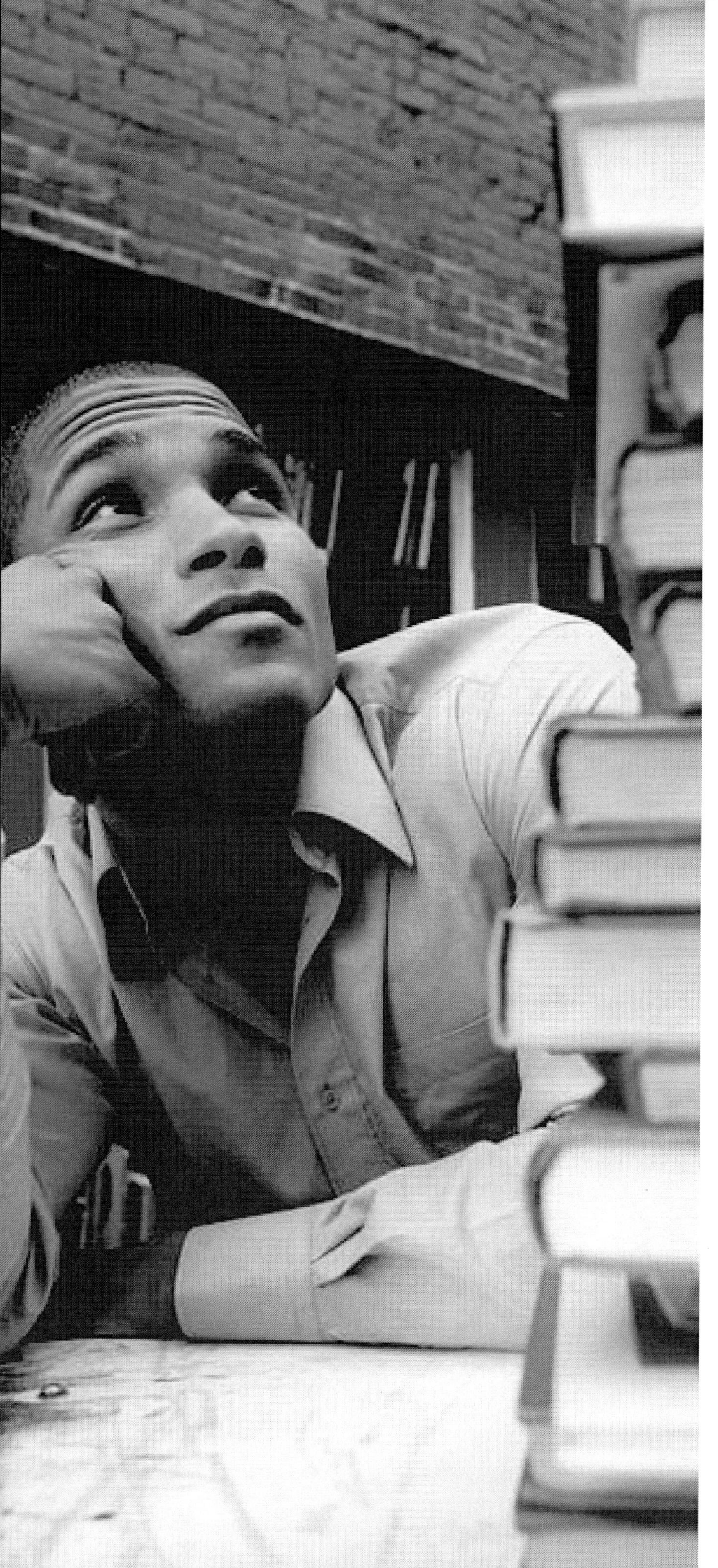

Appendices

Massenger RNA Codons and their Corresponding Amino Acids

First Base	Second Base				Third Base
	U	C	A	G	
U	UUU phenylalanine UUC phenylalanine UUA leucine UUG leucine	UCU serine UCC serine UCA serine UCG serine	UAU tyrosine UAC tyrosine UAA stop** UAG stop**	UGU cysteine UGC cysteine UGA stop** UGG tryptophan	U C A G
C	CUU leucine CUC leucine CUA leucine CUG leucine	CCU proline CCC proline CCA proline CCG proline	CAU histidine CAC histidine CAA glutamine CAG glutamine	CGU arginine CGC arginine CGA arginine CGG arginine	U C A G
A	AUU isoleucine AUC isoleucine AUA isoleucine AUG methionine*	ACU threonine ACC threonine ACA threonine ACG threonine	AAU asparagine AAC asparagine AAA lysine AAG lysine	AGU serine AGC serine AGA arginine AGG arginine	U C A G
G	GUU valine GUC valine GUA valine GUG valine	GCU alanine GCC alanine GCA alanine GCG alanine	GAU aspartate GAC aspartate GAA glutamate GAG glutamate	GGU glycine GGC glycine GGA glycine GGG glycine	U C A G

* Note: AUG is an initiator codon and also codes for the amino acid methionine.

**Note: UAA, UAG, and UGA are terminator codons.

Information About Nitrogen Bases

Nitrogen Base	Classification	Abberviation
Adenine	Purine	A
Guanine	Purine	G
Cytosine	Pyrimidine	C
Thymine	Pyrimidine	T
Uracil	Pyrimidine	U

NOTES

NOTES

NOTES

NOTES

ONTARIO • CANADA

BOOK ORDERING INFORMATION

HIGH SCHOOL TITLES

Castle Rock Research offers the following resources to support Ontario students. You can order any of these materials online at:

www.solaro.ca/ontario

SOLARO.ca - Online Learning	
$29.95 ea.*	
Biology 12	**Math 12**, Advanced Functions
Biology 11	**Math 11**, Functions and Apps
Chemistry 12	**Mathematics 10**, Academic
Chemistry 11	**Physics 12**
English 12, U Prep	**Physics 11**
English 11, U Prep	**Science 10**, Academic
English 10, Academic	**Science 10**, Applied

*Prices do not include taxes or shipping.

SOLARO Study Guide		
$29.95 ea.*		
Biology 12	**Math 12**, Advanced Functions	**Cdn & World Politics 12**
Biology 11	**Math 12**, Calculus & Vectors	**Cdn History 10**, Academic
Chemistry 12	**Math 12**, Data Management	**Cdn History 10**, Applied
Chemistry 11	**Math 11**, Functions	**OSSLT**, Secondary Lit Test
Civics 10	**Math 11**, Functions and Apps	**Science 10**, Academic
English 12, U Prep	**Math 11**, Found'ns for College	**Science 10**, Applied
English 12, Coll Prep	**Math 10**, Academic	**World History 12**, U Prep
English 11, U Prep	**Math 10**, Applied	**World History 11**, U/C Prep
English 10, Academic	**Physics 12**	

SNAP
$29.95 ea.*
Physics 12
Physics 11
Math 10, Academic

Study online using **SOLARO,** with access to multiple courses available by either a monthly or an annual subscription.

The **SOLARO Study Guide** is specifically designed to assist students in preparing for unit tests, final exams, and provincial examinations.

The **Student Notes and Problems (SNAP) Workbook** contains complete explanations of curriculum concepts, examples, and exercise questions.

If you would like to order Castle Rock resources for your school, please visit our school ordering page:

www.castlerockresearch.com/school-orders/